Edited by Marie Corbin The Couple

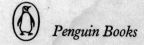 Penguin Books

Penguin Books Ltd, Harmondsworth,
Middlesex, England
Penguin Books, 625 Madison Avenue,
New York, New York 10022, U.S.A.
Penguin Books Australia Ltd, Ringwood,
Victoria, Australia
Penguin Books Canada Limited, 2801 John Street,
Markham, Ontario, Canada L3R 1B4
Penguin Books (N.Z.) Ltd, 182-190 Wairau Road,
Auckland 10, New Zealand

First published 1978

Printed in the United States of America by
Offset Paperback Mfrs., Inc., Dallas, Pennsylvania
Set in Linotype Plantin

Everyman as sociologist is concerned only with his own society and his own segment of it, and not with a general science of man or with an understanding of the exotic forms of social life. The two types of inquiry overlap, however, in that both are concerned with an observation of the chaos of the human condition and a reduction of its seeming randomness to modality and order . . . Both the folk and the professional sociologist generalize as a means of understanding the particular. It should surprise nobody that their results are frequently similar and that sociology, especially, appears to be the science of the obvious.

It is indeed possible for a sociologist to survey the courting behaviour of several hundred students and arrive at the conclusion that there is direct covariation between the number of times that a couple dates and the chances of occurrence of sexual intercourse. The wisdom of the street corner also tells us that if one tries hard enough and long enough he can't go wrong . . . The very fact that people have always speculated on these matters requires that scientific study be couched in terms unsullied by past usages and unclouded by the multiplicity of meanings that characterizes vernacular speech. But the latent function of social science terminology, as has long been understood, is a bit different. The true professional derives order, to be sure, but he then renders it unintelligible to all but the initiated. Language functions to provide communication, but the existence of thousands of mutually incomprehensible languages suggests that it serves also to block communication – a form of anticommunication, one might say. So also do professional sublanguages provide a means to establish the limits of the discipline and a measure of professional competence.

ROBERT F. MURPHY, *The Dialectics of Social Life*

Contents

1. Introduction

This book is about couples; about mundane, ordinary relationships which nearly all adults experience and in which many are involved for most of their lives. Despite, or perhaps because of, their mundaneness, couples are and have been of interest to many different people, among them novelists, playrights, historians, demographers, statisticians, social workers, family planners, sociologists, anthropologists, psychiatrists. Few of us do not wonder about the kinds of relationships our friends have with their spouses or lovers, and the popularity of journalistic accounts of 'My Life with X' bears witness to the fascination of the personal and sexual lives of famous strangers.

The vast literature relating to couples demonstrates many concerns and analytic approaches. Social scientists have asked numerous questions about sex and marriage in societies varying from the primitive to the highly complex, and investigated everything from the legal obligations of marriage to individual personality and how this affects sexual relationships. In some respects at least, novelists, poets and playwrights have captured the essence of personal interaction more completely than social scientists, who often feel they should not rely on insight and therefore attempt to base their understanding on objective accounts of what a carefully selected sample of people say and do and on systematic observations of behaviour.

To understand such relations for even a small number of people is difficult: many aspects of such relations are not open to observation by outsiders; the two people involved in a social relation may perceive it quite differently and give different accounts of it, if they are prepared to discuss it at all; relations are not static but change over time; they involve emotions which neither the natural nor the social sciences fully understand and which those experiencing them can often describe only in the most general terms. Social scientists share with those they observe some difficulty in being analytic about the personal, and to generalize about relations of this kind, even within one society, presents formidable problems.[1]

The authors of this book are all social scientists. Most of the chapters are based on small-scale studies, and all address a particular theme arising from the author's own research on couples in a particular country – Britain, U.S.A., Sweden, Japan, Italy. Although the term 'couple' may suggest 'a man and a woman' or, indeed, 'a husband and wife', our concern with couples is more generally with those relations which are sexual and long term, irrespective of whether they are between two people of the same or different gender, married or unmarried.

The focus of the book as a whole is on differences among sexual relations, constraints upon them and choices people make about them. The chapters reflect the differing interpretations and interests of sociologists, anthropologists and psychologists. We have not written as academics for other academics but for anyone who has ever asked 'What is it like to be a husband or wife in a society very different from the one in which I live?', 'Why do some people get married and others not?', 'Why do so many people in Britain still get married in church?', 'What problems face men who fall in love with men?'. The more academic elaborations, qualifications and references are, however, provided in the Notes for those readers who wish to pursue them.

My specific task as editor has been to frame the discussions with a more general consideration of differences in and limitations on sexual relations. Out of many possible ways of distinguishing among these relations I have found that three aspects may usefully be isolated. The first is the extent to which the relation is personal, the second is the degree to which the two people involved conceive of themselves as a unit and act accordingly, and the third is whether or not they are married.

PERSONAL RELATIONS AND SEXUAL FRIENDSHIP

To label all social relations involving sexual behaviour 'personal' is tempting, given the physical intimacy of such behaviour and our tendency to associate sex with emotional attachment. But a moment's thought is sufficient to suggest that a relation between a prostitute and her client which involves a straight exchange of sex for money is qualitatively different from that of a man and woman who have been married for years. To designate all relations between people who are married 'personal' is similarly tempting, but to do so reflects an ethnocentric bias and ignores the fact that in many complex societies like Britain we accept that some marriages are more personal than others.

In other words, the notion of personal relation is deceptively simple. It is used to suggest, among other things, intimacy, emotional involvement, 'private' as opposed to public inter-action, particularity. For the purposes of this discussion I have attempted to give a more technical meaning to the term, though undoubtedly one with which not everybody would agree. Basic-ally, a personal relation is a relation structured primarily by two individuals' personal experience of each other rather than, for example, by the social positions or statuses the two individuals occupy.

The notion of personal relations emphasizes that although people in all societies have ideas about proper behaviour, what occurs between any two people is not always simply and only a product of these ideas. Interaction in which two people do deal with each other primarily or exclusively in terms of these norms is impersonal. For example, the interaction between a doctor in a hospital and a patient brought in as an emergency case may be determined entirely by the respective ideas of the two people about how doctors should treat patients and how patients should deal with doctors – the doctor treating the patient as a bundle of medical conditions, for example, and the patient the doctor as someone qualified to cure him.[2] The limits of their interaction are set initially by their statuses, and these allow each to deal with the other even if they are strangers. Over time the doctor and patient may come to know each other better, even if their interaction remains confined to the hospital. To the extent that each starts to take into account the characteristics and idiosyncrasies of the other, the relation becomes more personal. The statuses they occupy still structure the relation, but the behaviour associated with them is increasingly affected by their personal experience of each other.

The doctor may have another patient who is also a golf partner or with whom he goes drinking. In such a case the two people may feel that, at least in the hospital, they should treat each other strictly as doctor and patient, discounting their personal experience of each other.[3] Or their experience of each other as golfing or drinking companions may greatly affect the way they treat each other in the hospital, so they deal with each other in terms of their total experience of each other. In the former instance, the relation may be said to be more impersonal than in the latter.[4]

Among the most personal relations are those between friends. Friendship depends almost exclusively on the experience individuals have of each other. Though 'friendship' may involve ideas about what is expected of friends – loyalty, sharing, help in difficult circumstances – a person does not become a friend until he has acted in this way and given good grounds for the belief that he will continue to do so. In this sense 'friend' is a very different kind of concept to 'doctor', being primarily a label for a particular kind of experience. The expectations any one individual has of his different friends will vary with his past experience of them.

In summary, behaviour of two individuals in a social relation may, at particular times, be more or less structured by social positions or by personal experience; to designate a social relation as personal or impersonal is to characterize it in terms of the way in which it is primarily structured throughout its duration, for obviously the mix and balance may change over time.[5] Impersonal relations often focus on behaviour associated with social position, and the behaviour proper to it, to the exclusion of everything else. Such relations may be of limited duration, presuppose no personal experience (often occurring between strangers), and involve very specific and well-defined areas of interaction. Other relations which may be considered impersonal to some degree are those where on many occasions such personal expereince as does exist is excluded from particular times or fields of interaction. In contrast, personal relations always involve personal experience with or without formally defined statuses or social positions. But the relation is not limited to and focused on the expected behaviour associated with these and what occurs between the two people usually takes account of the *totality* of their experience of each other.[6]

Personal relations are more 'open' than impersonal ones in that people's experience of each other grows and changes over time, but this experience still structures, still patterns and limits what happens between two people. The past experience and future expectations particular individuals have of each other may, in other words, constrain their behaviour as forcibly as notions about status.

Sexual relations which endure without becoming constrained by notions of status, of obligation, of exclusivity, which remain almost entirely personal, acquire the characteristics of ordinary non-sexual acquaintance and friendships. Such relations are what they are because of the unique experience the two people involved have of each other, and not because of what the two people think the relation ought to be. Interaction is a matter of fact, not of definition.

COUPLES

Many people involved in sexual relations come to think of themselves as a unit, a couple. Their relation is marked off from others, acquiring some degree of exclusivity. Because they define themselves as 'a couple' they may feel that they *ought* to behave in certain ways – to meet, to do things together – and that their relation should have some precedence over others. To this extent at least some of their interaction is more impersonal. These notions do not preclude friendship, but they do constrain it.

The unit may also be recognized, even insisted upon, by other people. Invitations may be issued to the couple; couples may be bracketed in people's minds as 'nice' or 'odd' and so on; one person may be treated as a representative of the other or they may be regarded as interchangeable.[7]

This conceptual bounding is made easier if the couple may be neatly and simply labelled. In our society this seldom happens unless they are married – 'the Joneses', 'the Smiths', etc. But the fact remains that two people may be a couple without being married and an individual may be married without being part of a couple.

MARRIAGE

Marriage minimally refers to a 'contract' between a woman and/or her kin and a man and/or his kin, such that any children the woman bears will have the right to the full social identity determined by kinship classifications in that society.[8] Such a 'contract' is always the result of deliberate intent and its existence always implies that children born outside such a 'contract' will have either no social identity at all or one that is incomplete. The 'contract' endows the woman and her kin with particular statuses in relation to the man and his kin and endows the children with particular status in respect of both.

These statuses do not necessarily imply rights, duties and obligations or sustained and ongoing interaction between the woman and the children, the man and the children, or indeed between the man and woman themselves.[9] In other words, marriage refers basically to 'a state of being' – the placement of people in a system of classification is its defining feature. To say that two people are married does not necessarily tell us anything about the nature of the social relation between them.

However, in most cases to achieve the statuses of husband and wife also means to incur some rights and duties. The contract may give the two people claims, for example, on each other's property and oblige them to behave towards each other and each other's kin in specific ways – to live together, to mourn for each other at death, to act as father and mother to their children. Obviously one of the most common rights of marriage

concerns sex, for whatever other peculiar sexual restraints
people in different societies have devised, 'no society', in the
words of one anthropologist, '... is bloody-minded enough to
ban sex from marriage'.[10] A husband usually has the right to
control his wife's sexuality, the wife the duty to be sexually
available to her husband.[11] More generally, husband and wife
may have claims on each other simply as 'man' and 'woman',
social categories which in all places include far more than reference to biological differences. Men as hunters, as public
speakers, as protectors of women may, for example, be obligated
to provide meat for their wives, to 'represent' them in public
affairs, to protect them; women as cooks and as subjects of
general male authority may have the duty of cooking for their
husbands and bowing to their specific authority.

Obviously, the rights and duties vary from society to society.
But two further points may be made about variation in marital
relations. Firstly, the extent to which the interaction of husband
and wife is focused on and limited to these rights and duties
may be similarly varied: if the relation is focused and limited
in this way and the married people act primarily out of duty,
obligation or propriety because they are husband and wife,
father and mother, man and woman, it is impersonal – husband
and wife are behaving in ways analogous to those of doctor and
patient. Secondly, the nature of marital obligation and interaction may mean that some spouses cannot be thought of as
couples in any meaningful sense. However, although 'couples'
and 'personal sexual relations' are separate analytic concepts it is,
perhaps, true to say that where few couples are found, personal
sexual relations will be minimal.

These points may seem somewhat academic and obscure. But
I think they are significant. Perhaps the argument may be
clarified by considering some specific examples.

SOME EXAMPLES

To generalize about all human societies would, to say the least,
over-simplify a complex reality, and my intention here is to
indicate only some of the possible combinations of couples,

personal relations and marriage, bearing in mind that whatever the ideal in any society there will always be people who circumvent or ignore the rules.

Legitimate sexual relations are, obviously, a feature of all societies, and personal relations develop over time among people everywhere, but many social factors act to prevent or inhibit the development of couples and of relations which are both sexual and personal. Societies in which the sexual division of labour is extensive and rigid, in which marriages are arranged without reference to the preferences of those being married, in which husbands and wives do not live together or in which they form part of much larger households, in which the duties and obligations of marital status are strongly felt, and in which sex outside marriage is prohibited, are societies in which couples are unlikely to exist. Typically in such societies people who marry are complete strangers to each other; sexual distinctions are hedged around with ritual and punctilious observance of the differences; men do men's work, women women's, the tasks often being done at different times and in different places either alone or with members of their own sex; men spend their free time with men, women with women from whom their primary satisfactions are expected to come and with whom they are expected to share interests; sex is thought of as a duty or even as unclean and polluting, to be avoided when possible, and may take place when husband and wife are surrounded by sleeping kin who must not be disturbed.[12]

Nevertheless, even when relations between the sexes are stringently controlled, few societies manage to entirely suppress personal sexual relations. Illicit love affairs do occur, and over time even the impersonal relations of married strangers may become personal, for as children grow up the obligations of parenthood decrease, and as the husband and wife themselves grow old the socially defined sexual differences become less significant. Some people may even institutionalize a period of time for a man and woman to get to know each other before they actually get married, though only after they are committed to marriage. Such 'courtships' represent a time when the two are brought into relation with each other without the strong and often divisive obligations and duties which marriage itself will bring. The relation during this period is seldom free and easy, however, and the time allowed may be short. In parts of rural Greece, for example, marriages are negotiated by parents and kin with the aid of intermediaries, account being taken of the dowry the prospective bride will bring to the marriage, the property the prospective husband will inherit and the relative honour and status of their respective families. Often the wide net cast by kin in their search for a suitable bride or groom results in arrangements involving a man and woman who have not met or even seen each other. When negotiations are complete they are allowed to meet together under the close supervision of their kin before the marriage takes place.[13] Depending on the time elapsing between the end of the negotiations and the actual wedding, and the wishes of their kin, the two have some opportunity for getting to know one another. But only if either expresses the most dire antipathy or repugnance is the marriage likely to be called off.

The idea that commitment to marriage should follow from a developing personal relation rather than precede it is one found in conjunction with both personal and more impersonal marital relations and with both premarital chastity and sexual licence. But in some societies where sexuality is highly controlled, the development of a couple may in itself be taken as a commitment to marriage. In parts of rural southern Spain, for example, boys and girls tend to congregate in the streets in separate groups between which a great deal of teasing and flirtation occurs.[14] At about the age of fifteen or sixteen, a boy and girl single each other out for special attention on the basis of sexual attraction and general manner and deportment. Unless their parents intervene, they meet regularly and spend an increasing amount of time together.[15] But this behaviour may be tantamount to a declaration of intent to marry; once the relationship is embarked upon publicly, it cannot easily be broken off. Often couples who later discover they do not really like each other very much still marry, for a broken relation damages reputations and damaged reputations may prevent subsequent marriage – a highly undesirable state of affairs in a society with little place for the unmarried. Youthful infatuation frequently commits young people to being together for the rest of their lives.[16] In this respect, the development of couples and of personal sexual relations is almost as firmly associated with getting married as it is in rural Greece, even though the means of establishing the relations are considerably different.

Although couples in southern Spain have a certain amount of freedom during their courtship and are allowed to go out alone together, their relations develop under the watchful eyes of an interested community, and are highly structured by the fact that they are unmarried men and women and 'a couple'. Gallantry and coquetry (both impersonal forms of behaviour associated with 'man' and 'woman') play a major part; the sexes are assumed to have little in common to talk about, and meetings are often confined to situations in which they do not have to rely on talking to each other – going to the cinema or to dances, or meetings with other couples when the boys can happily talk to the boys and the girls to the girls. The main interests the couple have in common are the future setting up of their home together and the consummation of their sexual relation. Neither are permitted before marriage. Were the girl to succumb to her boyfriend's advances he would conclude that she lacked shame and moral fibre, could therefore equally be tempted by others and was consequently undesirable as a wife. Frequently both the couple and their kin are concerned that behaviour which would either threaten the marriage, or detract from the couple's social standing once they are husband and wife, should be avoided. In their concern for the effect of their individual behaviour on the reputation of them both, the couple already assume some of the responsibility of a husband and a wife to each other.

Despite these limitations, engagements are often lengthy (I knew of one which lasted twenty years), at least in part because some couples recognize that this is a time in their lives when they are least bound by obligation and duty and most free to spend their time together. Many girls, even the more emancipated among them, feel that one or two weeks is sufficient for a commitment to marriage to be made but that engagements should last *at least* one or two years – they are less anxious actually to get married than they are to secure for themselves the certainty that they ultimately will.

Once married, and particularly after the birth of children, most couples cease to go out together and each spouse spends his/her free time with friends and relatives of the same sex. The relation becomes focused on the performance of what each considers to be their respective and separate duties, and often the only time they spend together is at mealtimes and in bed.[17] For most wives sex is seldom a simple pleasure. Their attitudes are coloured by the fear of pregnancy and the belief that sex is something they owe their husbands. Many wives praise their husbands for their lack of sexual appetite, limited demands and considerate restraint. For some at least, however, old age lightens the burdens and old couples are often good companions, their relations intensely personal though often ones in which sex itself is simply a memory, pleasurable or otherwise.

For those married people who have largely lost interest in each other either before marriage or at the time of its consummation, such limited interaction proves a blessing rather than a disappointment. They have achieved their desire for marriage *per se* and fulfilled their social obligation in this respect; as long as they carry out their duties they may ignore each other with impunity.

Among many peoples, however, even though a personal relation almost invariably precedes marriage, couples may be formed quite indepenently of it; sexual friendships are common, and the relations of married people themselves may be generally much more personal than those I have been describing. Modern complex societies like Britain and the U.S.A. spring almost immediately to mind. But in this respect at least some men and women of the Trobriand Islands, a simple, small-scale society of North West Melanesia studied by the anthropologist Malinowski, have more in common with some of their Western counterparts than the immense differences in technology, political and economic behaviour, and kinship organization would tend to suggest.[18]

Among the Trobriand Islanders some marriages are arranged by kin; a few men, usually chiefs, may have more than one wife and may know none of them particularly well; incest taboos are stringent; parents are highly interested in the more utilitarian aspects of their children's marriages as, indeed, may be the children themselves. But most boys and girls from a very early age are allowed both to observe sexual behaviour and to indulge in it themselves. As they get older they form a variety of sexual liaisons, some of a very casual and temporary nature, others more lasting – the amorous meetings of the uncommitted being conducted in the buildings in which the harvest is stored or in the hut of an unmarried relative, those of the more involved in the bachelor houses belonging to groups of young men of a village where the couples may spend their nights together. When one relation becomes much more important than others, sexual affairs with others are gradually abandoned and the couple appear more often in public. People then expect them to marry, but even so the relation does not yet involve formal obligations, their community of interest being limited still to the sexual and personal.

Despite the sexual freedom accorded young Trobriand couples, they, like their Spanish equivalents, are expected to avoid behaviour considered the perogative of married people, though their avoidances may seem strange to Western eyes.

In the Trobriands two people about to be married must never have a meal in common. Such an act would greatly shock the moral susceptibilities of a native, as well as his sense of propriety. To take a girl out to dinner without having previously married her – a thing permitted in Europe – would be to disgrace her in the eyes of the Trobriander. We object to an unmarried girl sharing a man's bed – the Trobriander would object just as strongly to her sharing his meal.[19]

Sharing food in this way has great significance, for one day

the girl instead of returning in the morning to her parents' house, will remain with her husband, take her meals in the house of his parents and accompany him throughout the day ... Such proceedings constitute the act of marriage.[20]

Marriage for the Trobrianders involves duties and obligations of husbands and wives to each other and changes the behaviour of couples. Sexual exclusivity is expected, husband and wife separate on public and festive occasions, each going with members of their own sex, public displays of affection or sexual interest are frowned upon.

> There is an interesting and indeed startling contrast between the free and easy manner which normally obtains between husband and wife and their rigid propriety in matters of sex, their restraint in gesture which might suggest the tender relation between them. When they walk they never take hands or put their arms about each other in the way ... which is permitted to lovers and to friends of the same sex. Ordinarily a married couple walk one behind the other in single file. You will never surprise an exchange of tender looks, loving smiles or amorous banter between a husband and wife in the Trobriands.[21]

Malinowski makes a great deal, however, of the companionable and egalitarian relations of Trobriand husbands and wives.

> The frank and friendly tone of intercourse, the obvious feelings of equality, the father's domestic helpfulness, especially with the children, would at once strike any observant visitor. The wife joins freely in the jokes and conversation; she does her work independently, not with the air of a slave or a servant, but as one who manages her own department. She will order her husband about if she needs his help.[22]

Although a sexual division of labour exists and shame results from doing something which is intrinsically the attribute of the other sex,

> Husband and wife in the Trobriands lead their common life in close companionship, working side by side, sharing certain household duties, and spending a good deal of their leisure time with each other, for the most part in excellent harmony and with mutual appreciation.[23]

Such a picture of married life is one of more personal relations and is reminiscent of that of many married couples in more complex societies, a similarity commented upon by Malinowski when exploring the domestic difficulties which do arise.

> Two married people ... frequently indulged in lengthy quarrels, to such a degree that the matter became a serious nuisance to me and

disturbed my field-work. As their hut was next door to my tent, I could hear all their domestic differences – it almost made me forget I was among savages and imagine myself back among civilised people.[24]

Obviously, despite the similarities between the Trobriand Islands and modern complex societies, there are striking differences, in particular the much greater and more varied number of ways in which men and women interact in complex societies. Unrelated men and women may be interested in each other for many reasons, only some of which involve physical attraction, need for sexual conquest, 'romantic love' or desire for marriage. Many relations result simply from the fact that men and women often work together and share the same leisure activities. Both long-term and more casual relations may be part of a search for a spouse, but though such relations may be necessary to finding one, they often have a validity in their own right quite apart from marriage. Some relations may provide only sexual pleasure or only conversation and companionship. Some may combine both and add to them emotional support and involvement. Others may involve living together, children, domestic services, financial interdependence, and usually, though by no means always, marriage.

In Britain, marriage itself is varied.[25] It is possible to find wives who go out to work and those who do not, husbands who depend on their wives for financial support, husbands who do no domestic chores at all and others who do only those specifically designated 'men's work'; couples who both go out to work and pay others to do the chores;[26] those who divide up the chores but do so to suit their particular skills and interests, irrespective of their gender, or who regard themselves as interchangeable in almost all tasks – who does what depending on who is available, interested or less tired at any time; married people who spend their free time separately with their respective friends and relatives, those who spend it together alone or with mutual friends.

Such variation in the relations of married people implies that many people have far greater scope for choosing the kinds of relations they have with members of the opposite sex than they do in many other societies. However, some people in Britain may have much less scope in this respect than others.

One of the best known and insightful attempts to deal with some differences in and constraints upon marital relations in Britain is that of Elizabeth Bott.[27] She suggests that 'the degree of segregation in the role-relationship of husband and wife varies directly with the connectedness of the family's social network'. In other words, that whether husbands and wives maintain separate domestic tasks and social lives or do most things together may be related to the kinds of relations they have with other people and, even more interestingly, whether their friends and relatives know each other and interact independently of the husband and wife. According to Bott, a segregated conjugal role-relationship implies that

husband and wife have a clear differentiation of tasks and a considerable number of separate interests and activities. In such cases husband and wife have a clearly defined division of labour into male and female tasks. They expect to have different leisure pursuits, the husband has his friends outside the home, and the wife has hers.[28]

A joint conjugal role-relationship is characterized by the fact that

Husband and wife carry out many activities together with a minimum of task differentiation and separation of interests. They not only plan the affairs of the family together, but also exchange many household tasks and spend most of their leisure time together.[29]

Highly segregated conjugal roles correspond in many ways to those I have labelled impersonal. They are largely focused on and limited to obligations and duties of husband and wife, behaviour appropriate to men and women, and a sense of duty may extend even into attitudes to sex itself. Remarks, all highly suggestive of sexual duty, have been reported for married people with these kinds of relationships – 'I was never refused, but it was grudging', 'I've never refused him', 'I'm not really interested, it's something that's got to be done and the quicker the better'.[30] Bott herself interestingly remarks of one of the women she interviewed,

... it seems likely that she felt physical sexuality was an intrusion on a peaceful domestic relationship rather than an expression of such a relationship. It was as if sexuality were felt to be basically violent and disruptive.[31]

Joint relations, in which a great deal of what occurs results from experience, negotiation and individual inclination, are more personal, though if the couple feel they *must* be companions and share things simply because they are married the relation is to this extent more impersonal.

The idea behind Bott's hypothesis is that more segregated relations are associated with situations in which most of the people known by the husband and wife do know each other and meet with one another independently of the husband and wife – they have a 'close-knit' social network, while more joint relationships will be associated with 'loose-knit' networks – those in which the majority of people do not know and interact with each other independently.

Later studies of marital relations, many instigated by Bott's work, suggest that the association between segregated role-relationships and close-knit networks stands up empirically to a much greater extent than that between joint role relationships and loose-knit networks, and that the concept of different kinds of networks needs further elaboration and refinement.[32] But as one sociologist put it, 'Perhaps the really lasting significance of Bott's study is that she made impossible the proliferation of studies of the internal structure of the family which took no account of its social environment.'[33]

For present purposes a simpler approach to social environment will suffice to indicate at least one of the factors which constrain individuals in their marital relations – that is, whether or not they live in established communities all or at least most of their lives.

Talking of the conditions under which close-knit networks and segregated relationships are likely to be found, Bott says:

Close-knit networks are most likely to develop when husband and wife, together with their friends, neighbours and relatives, have grown up in the same local area and have continued to live there after marriage. Many people know one another and have known one another since childhood. Women tend to associate with women and men with men. The only legitimate forms of heterosexual relationships are those between kin and between husband and wife. Friendship between a man and woman who are not kin is suspect.

In such a setting, husband and wife come to marriage each with his own close-knit network. Each partner makes a considerable emotional investment in relationships with the people in his network. Each is engaged in reciprocal exchanges of material and emotional support with them. Each is very sensitive to their opinions and values, not only because the relationships are intimate, but also because the people in the network know one another and share the same norms so that they are to apply consistent informal sanctions on one another. The marriage is superimposed in these pre-existing relationships.[34]

Such a description fits many of the more traditional British working-class communities.[35] In such communities marriage may alter to some degree the relationships husband and wife have with their friends, but their continuing involvement with them, as well as providing a source of companionship, means that people of the appropriate sex are available to step in should husband or wife be unable to do the things they would normally do – if a wife is unable to cook or look after the children, her mother or sister, for example, may want or feel obliged to take over. The connections among the people the husband and wife know make the marital relation a highly 'visible' one, making them in turn subject to pressures to conform. As one of Bott's informants put it, 'A lot of men wouldn't mind helping their wives if the curtains were drawn so people couldn't see.'

Although these communities are working-class communities, the important variable is community rather than class; people moving out of such communities usually remain members of the same class, but such a move may precipitate a shift towards more joint relationships.[36] Similarly, irrespective of class, if husband and wife are born in different places, meet somewhere else, marry and live in yet another place and possibly move several times in the course of their married life, they are unlikely to be living near relatives and old friends. Often the lack of other established relationships may make them more dependent on each other for companionship and the simple satisfaction gained from social intercourse, as well as throwing them on their own resources if domestic difficulties arise, so they may expect at least on some occasions to take over from each other. The people they do know are less likely all to know each other, let alone meet independently of the husband and wife, and are less likely to share a common body of ideas about how husbands and wives should behave. The 'visibility' of the relation between husband and wife is less and the pressures to conform considerably different, if present at all.[37]

Unmarried people living away from kin and old friends in a fairly anonymous situation may similarly have greater freedom of choice about the way they behave towards members of the opposite sex, while those in traditional communities may be under considerable pressure from peer groups, for example, to maintain the accepted norms of masculinity and femininity, and to resist becoming a couple.

When a young man begins 'courting strong', the group reacts with strongly discouraging sanctions to the possible diversion of attention. He is teased and threatened with social isolation. 'Well we'd ask thee to come for a pint,' the others say, 'but we expect tha's off to get they feet under t'table.' To stay with the girl and enjoy her company would be a form of unmanliness. Tenderness is not thought of as part of a man's psychological equipment. The young man has to insist that he is 'getting something out of it'. He will play down his emotional involvement with the girl, justifying to the group the time he spends with her by claiming that she allows him sexual intercourse ... In the group's behaviour and the youth's relation to it at this stage, we see the beginning of what will be a continuing conflict between home ties and peer ties.[38]

The constraints of living in a community are, of course, not the only ones affecting sexual relations. The variety of ways in which such relations are constrained and the extent to which people do have choices to make about them provide the focus for the rest of this volume.

2. Couples in Communities

The 'visibility' of the relations of husbands and wives or of any couples is important not only in the kinds of urban areas of industrial societies to which I have just referred (p. 25) but also in small-scale rural communities. Sometimes the deliberate demonstration to others in a community that the proprieties are being observed, the specifically public nature of social interaction, may also be extremely important. To be out of sight may simply raise suspicions.[1] If a young couple in southern Spain, for example, are known to have been alone together out of the public gaze, the question immediately arises, 'What have they been up to?' The conclusions drawn are unfavourable, for courting couples should limit their behaviour to that appropriate to public places – to the street, the cinema, the doorway of the girl's home. Only those without shame or virtue would allow themselves to be compromised.

More generally, for people to be secretive about their relationships may be not only to invite suspicion but to court disaster. In many societies of the northern Mediterranean region, knowledge of people's social relations with others provides the major way of assessing them as people worthy of one's own association, respect and friendship. For one individual to designate another 'an honourable man' means he considers him worthy of trust, someone with whom he may have dealings. In his conclusion that a man is honourable he will take into account not only whether the man has fulfilled his obligations to him but his total experience of how the man fulfils his obligations and obeys the rules in relation to others. A man of whom nothing has been experienced except the particular contact of the moment – even if the man acts with propriety and sensitivity – cannot truly be assessed as honourable. In assessment of honour and claims to it, a man's relations with his wife and members of his family are often paramount, and not to have such relations means that a whole area of a man's potential basis for a claim to honour is missing. These are the primary people towards whom he should have obligations. Men must control their women – wives and daughters should not flaunt their sexuality. The women themselves should have shame – the fact that they may not acts to their detriment and also reflects mightily on their husbands or fathers. Honour is concerned primarily with the social standing of men and their families as a whole, rather than of women separately, and women are a constant threat both to the honour of their own men and to others who may be tempted by their shamelessness from duty to their own wives and families. Honour is a flexible and often mercurial quality, based on changing experiences, open to claims and counterclaims and only of relevance within the social field of these experiences – the community.

Under such circumstances marriage involves the husband and wife in mutual interests in their children and in the honour of the family – they stand and fall together. They share a home and a sexual relation, but for a man to take undue interest in housekeeping would be unnatural, and for a woman to satisfy anything but her desires for children through her sexuality is often considered shameless. For the pair to devote a disproportionate amount of time to each other would imply not fulfilling other obligations, a lack of interest in being with others. Though women often play an important part in 'passing on' information about other people to their husbands, for a man to be known to be too interested in 'women's gossip' may suggest that the opinions of his wife hold too much sway in the household.

Seldom are husband and wife social units in the sense of doing things alone together, and of being the building blocks of social occasions as they often are in Britain and the U.S.A. Even where they are, such arrangements do not always attest to ease or freedom of social discourse between the sexes, as I had very forcibly demonstrated to me at a party held by a wealthy couple in Spain.[2] Everybody came in pairs, husbands and wives and courting couples, but very shortly after all had arrived, the men and women gradually split into two groups at opposite ends of an L-shaped room and I was left in the middle talking to a man locally famed as a *beato* – a man of religious convictions, a 'do-gooder', a 'proper' man. The conversation was not, however, allowed to continue, the suspicious and hostile glances of the women and the hoots of encouragement and ribald jokes from the men causing us both to retreat in haste and embarrassment.

In the following chapter Barbara Littlewood discusses the significance of couples in a rural community in southern Italy, where she lived for over a year as an anthropologist participating in the everyday life of the people. Her discussion focuses on the concern for public behaviour and family honour.

South Italian Couples

BARBARA LITTLEWOOD

I

THE PLACE

The following discussion of couples is based on fourteen months' field work in Quercio, a town of about 11,000 inhabitants in the Province of Bari in Apulia, the 'heel' of Italy.

The region is predominantly agricultural but most people prefer to live in towns (of between 5,000 and 100,000 inhabitants) rather than on their land. Each day they travel to their scattered smallholdings, sometimes leaving as early as 3 a.m., to return home in mid-afternoon or evening. Compared with the North, South Italy is generally poor and depressed, but Bari is probably the richest province in the South. In Quercio itself, about 75 per vent of the economically active population is engaged in agriculture; they grow olives, grapes, tree-fruits, nuts and some vegetables. Quercio is fortunate in the diversification of its agriculture; there is always employment, except for a short time in winter, because there is always at least one crop to be planted, pruned or harvested.

Those not working the land are engaged in industrial processing of agricultural produce, or in construction or in services.[1] The women have always worked, too, mostly on the land with their husbands, or hiring themselves out as day labourers. But now more stay at home, and of those who do work more are becoming clerks, teachers and garment workers rather than agricultural labourers.[2]

The trend towards replacing the older wine grapes and olives with more profitable table grapes and fruits such as peaches has brought prosperity to a number of families, and the town itself is growing rapidly. New houses and flats have been built around the old town, a jumble of narrow cobbled streets and white-washed houses clustered round the old Marquis's palace, the main church and the town hall. The main shops now sell television sets, clothes and French liqueurs as well as general groceries, pots and pans and agricultural implements.

Most households conform to the Quercio ideal – a married couple and their unmarried children. Dwellings are small and the desire for a home of one's own is no new development. If they are able, parents contribute towards buying a house or flat for their children when they marry, though many are content to live for years in rented accommodation, which is plentiful.[3] Crucial for the newly-weds is not the possession of a house but their separation from parents. Cost and comfort weigh equally in the choice of a home with the nearness of the wife's mother. Other things being equal, the house nearest to her is preferred, though, as many mothers correctly say, their daughters can never live more than ten minutes' walk away, despite the fact that Quercio is growing.

COUPLES IN QUERCIO

Is the couple a significant social unit in this setting? If so, how, if not, why not, and what other units are significant, either in terms of the roles they play or their meanings for the people involved?

Initial impressions, from walking around or living in the town, suggest that couples do not exist there. During the day, the majority of men are away in the fields; one sees only odd individuals and mothers and children out on errands. In the evening when the men have returned, cleaned up and eaten, they go off to the *piazzas*, the bars and the clubs to meet their friends. The women put chairs out in the streets and gossip with their neighbours. On fine Sunday evenings, however, everybody puts on their best clothes and goes for a *passeggiata* (stroll) around the public gardens. But families who start out together break up as women meet their sisters, men meet workmates, children meet friends. Even a young married couple with no children will probably separate or join a larger group of relatives. The only people who appear as couples are boys and girls who are officially engaged and whose watchful parents agree that they may walk together a few paces ahead, though not behind. Some do, of course, 'get lost' in the criss-crossing paths, but rarely for more than a few minutes. From puberty to marriage all girls, except the very few most sophisticated or the 'bad', are chaperoned by friends or relatives and, though accorded more freedom than their parents had when young, boys and girls have no opportunities to go out alone together. (Sometimes, however, a sympathetic friend may arrange for a couple to sit together in the back of a car coming home from a dance.) Young people are generally seen in groups of their own sex or with family and kin.

Privately organized leisure also follows a family pattern – invitations to picnics, days on the beach, and to dinner on feast days are issued to whole families; children are included as a matter of course, except the smallest babies who are likely to be left with a grandmother. In short, a man and a woman together alone is a rare sight.

But although not immediately evident in the streets of Quercio, couples do exist there in as much as people do go courting, get married, grow old together. As isolatable social units with certain functions they have little significance; the relationships are by no means always the major focus of the individual's attention. My concern in the remainder of this chapter is to examine the significance they do have and the limitations upon them.

THE ROAD TO MARRIAGE

Nearly everyone in Quercio does marry, and the route to marriage is more or less the same for all.[4] A man ought to be married by his early thirties, a girl by her mid-twenties. Only four kinds of girl do not marry: the daughters of the old élite whose parents either feel that no suitors in the area are worthy of their daughters or who want to keep their property intact; the girls with tarnished reputations, though a good dowry might tempt a widower or a man from another town if the scandal had not been too serious; crippled or mentally defective girls; those women living with men who are unable, for various reasons, to marry them (these unions are recognized in the town, though frequently the children suffer more than the mother). As yet very few, if any, women or men simply do not want to marry or even consider alternatives.

Women are thought to be incapable of fending for themselves, economically or morally. They must be looked after or controlled by a man. Since fathers die and brothers marry, a husband must be found to take on these responsibilities. Men can look after themselves, but without marriage and children they are not considered really adult. (Indeed, a man remains dependent on his father until the father divides the patrimony on the children's marriages. The dowry brought by a wife helps to establish the independence of the new family.) A man must consider those who are dependent on his efforts and resources when he does anything. These responsibilities, the Quercesi reckon, make a man more stable and thoughtful, less likely to act rashly or try to cheat people. Of course, not all do meet their responsibilities and a man's home life, a fairly accurate barometer of his success, will be carefully monitored by neighbours. Although some families are able to 'put on a show' some of the time (for example, by rattling pots and pans at lunchtime even if there is nothing to put in them), this cannot be kept up for long when neighbours drop in and out all day.

The majority of marriages in Quercio are now love-matches between economic and status equals, though the consent of parents is essential. A few marriages are still arranged either by parents or occasionally by a licensed *mediatori*, who acts as a marriage broker for a fee of about £35.[5]

In spite of strict chaperoning of girls, more opportunities now exist for young people to meet in informal situations, after school, in the public gardens on Sundays, at private parties at *Carnevale*.[6] Many romances blossom at this time, though by no means all survive. As long as very few people know about it, a romance can later be dismissed as 'only a friendship' with no damage to the girl's reputation.

But sometimes these romances do last. The boy begins to

write notes to the girl, but she does not reply until she is sure he is looking for a commitment and not simply a conquest. (He might otherwise show her letters to friends, who would label her 'flighty'.) For a while *l'amore di nascosto* (secret love) is exciting, but if too many people come to suspect, it can prove dangerous. For a girl to find a husband if her name has previously been linked with another boy, regardless of whether he was formal fiancé or simply a boyfriend, is very difficult. If the girl thinks that word is leaking out, which could take a matter of weeks or months depending on their discretion, she presses the boy to declare his intentions to her father. If these are welcomed the boy is permitted to visit and write to the girl. In the meantime, both sets of parents are making discreet inquiries among relatives and friends about the reputation and prospects of the potential son or daughter-in-law. If the parents discover embarrassing episodes in the girl's past or insecurity in the boy's prospects, they quietly advise their child not to see the offender again.

'Feelers' about the girl's dowry are also put out, but this, too, must be done discreetly. One mother nearly made her daughter break her engagement because she felt the boy's mother was too bluntly concerned with what the girl's dowry would be. The boy's mother had mentioned in the course of conversation that a neighbour of hers had remarked, 'I suppose Maria won't bring a dowry with her when she marries Tonio, as her parents have spent so much on putting her through college,' to which she, Tonio's mother, had replied, 'Oh, we're not worried about that at all. Her parents will look after her, and besides, what matters is that Tonio loves her.' Tonio's mother then left a pregnant pause in the conversation for Maria's mother to describe just how her daughter would be looked after. She was not rewarded, and both mothers were angry for several weeks, threatening to break off negotiations.

After a boy and girl have been seeing each other for a short time, the boy suggests that his parents should meet the girl's family formally. Over a dinner provided by his parents, gifts are given to the girl, usually a ring, chain or bracelet. The serious discussions which begin at this point are usually restricted to consideration of when the marriage should take place – allowing the boy time to complete college, find a job, or do his military service. Again, open questions about dowry would be regarded as very bad manners in these discussions, for people not only provide what they can but understand very well what is the least that it would be proper to give.

The dowry has two parts, *la dote*, consisting of immovable wealth, such as land,[7] and *il corredo* consisting of movable wealth, such as linen, furniture and clothing. No particular tradition exists about the exact composition of *la dote*,[8] though the composition of *il corredo* is controlled by very specific norms, which vary directly with the girl's status.[9] Though many girls scorned the custom, none, except those who eloped or married without consent, married without *il corredo*. Though boys claimed that they would marry a girl for herself and not for what she brought with her, mothers still invariably put money and linen aside for their daughters.[10] To calculate the cost to a family of a daughter's marriage is very difficult; certainly it is expensive and means years of saving. The sum spent depends not only on the family's status but on other factors such as the girl's eligibility and the number of younger sisters she has. The less eligible a girl in terms of honour, age or beauty, the greater her *dote* and *corredo* must be for her to make a match consonant with her social status.

Only when the marriage is arranged or when one set of parents is reluctant do open negotiations about dowry take place.

The period of formal engagement, which might be only a few months but is much more likely to be two or more years, should see all the dowry accumulated and the boy *sistemato* (fixed up with a job).

This is the pattern of courtship for almost all Quercesi; with few exceptions, boys and girls start going around in mixed groups at about the age of sixteen; they form individual relationships in their late teens or early twenties; engagement follows on in another year and, if all goes well, marriage in another year or so again. Boys are sometimes able to prolong the time before they enter into official relationships by going around with girls from another town, girls who therefore cannot bring local pressure on the boys to formalize the courtship. Sometimes, too, a couple whose parents have objected to their relationship continue to meet in secret and try to persuade a sympathetic relative to intervene on their behalf. If this fails, they may elope, spending a few nights in another town with a relative. When they return, the families usually agree to marriage because of the shame, though a final reconciliation does not always occur until after the birth of the first child.

Whether the courtship is official or secret, the couple do not really have an opportunity to get to know each other well. Even if engaged they are still never allowed to be left alone together, and their activities are much as they were before engagement – the occasional dance, private party, visit to the cinema, and Sunday *passeggiata*, though they will probably spend more time at each other's houses and with one another's relatives. Both are on their best behaviour all the time, and the girl comes to define the relationship in terms of gift-giving, compliments and deferential behaviour. Though a very worrying time (since the girl has a great deal to lose should the relationship end), it is also the time which many women look back on as the best in their lives![11] Girls need not hide their attachment and can discuss their emotional states with relatives and friends; it is a romantic time – Quercesi fiancés are prolific writers of letters and poetry. At this stage, the relationship is both intensely emotional and quite different from what it will be after marriage. Everybody recognizes courtship to be a time out of the ordinary, when the couple can concentrate just on each other. But any deep exploration of character is prohibited by lack of privacy and formality of meetings. This need, however, make very little difference to the couple when they are married. If roles are stable and well defined, the boy and girl have a good understanding of what they expect from each other when they marry (even if this is unarticulated). But in a marriage where there is room for manoeuvre and for the relationship to be redefined, surprise, disillusionment and anger could, and sometimes do, follow marriage. Young wives resent the amount of time a husband spends with friends; young husbands are horrified that a wife would like to work. (This last complaint is ironic, since a professional qualification and the higher wages it brings raise a girl's position on the marriage market.) Men and women may disagree over the definition of a 'good husband' or a 'good wife', and present restrictions during courtship make it hard for them to discover or resolve this problem before they are actually married.

Though a courting couple may be relatively self-centred, they never forget, nor are allowed to forget, the presence and importance of the wider social context of their relationship, represented by the friends and relatives who chaperone their encounters, intervene in quarrels, and listen to their problems, and by their parents who are almost entirely responsible for providing the economic basis of the young couple's independent life together.[12]

HUSBAND AND WIFE

Once a couple marry, the demands of work and children tend either to keep them apart or to focus their attention on the family as a whole. Changes in agriculture have, perhaps, accentuated the segregation of husband and wife.

Rationalization of agriculture, greater prosperity and higher expectations have meant a decline in the participation of women on the land, so that fewer married couples now work their land together. Agricultural tasks, too, are more specialized. Women sort and pack fruit or clean nuts for commerical sale, leaving the hard work, the pruning and grafting to men. Of course, cooperation continues; the incomes of husband and wife are combined and some processing of produce still goes on at home – tomatoes are made into paste, cherries preserved, figs dried. Nevertheless, direct interaction is reduced, and even when husband and wife do work side by side, other household members or kin are present and the jobs are divided between men and women. Men, for example, climb the trees to pick olives; women and children gather them from the ground. The core family work-force is a man and his sons; the wife and daughters participate when extra hands are needed.

Traditional families were held together primarily by their functions of production and processing (in which all but the smallest children joined), of welfare and training. But these are changing.[13] With a decline in subsistence agriculture, family survival no longer depends on what its members can grow and process. Bread is bought rather than made at home (a task which often required the help of neighbours and sisters as well as daughters); knowledge of new techniques required for cash-crop farming comes from agricultural colleges rather than from father. Sons are no longer automatically expected to work on the land, even if their fathers own substantial amounts, and the more abstract and formal learning provided in local schools has therefore assumed a new importance as a means to alternative employment. As the functions change or are delegated to other institutions, the constituent units within the family, men and women, parents and children, can assume a greater independence.

Traditionally, men and women, young and old, divided tasks and duties, but each person's labour was essential to the whole enterprise, like pieces in a jigsaw. But now it is not so much the content of particular tasks performed by different family members which is essential but the cash income from independent jobs. A clerk with a regular wage is at least as useful as a son who knows how to prune olive trees. For women the situation is somewhat different, since their full-time employment is relatively uncommon. But as they cease to process home-grown crops or sew the family's clothes, they too are likely to look for alternatives in (at least) part-time employment, to provide another source of income. As a result, the relationship between husband and wife is likely to remain or become even more segregated, each spouse having his or her own area of competence and interests, and independently organizing and pursuing their jobs in the home and outside.

Although one dimension of authority and role allocation within the family is that of age, husband and wife do not automatically unite, as parents, *vis à vis* their children; sex is also important and often unites a man and his sons against a woman and her daughters.

The mother is responsible for all small children. After puberty, the father and brothers become publicly responsible for a girl's sexual activities,[14] though her mother is held ultimately responsible for character defects. '*Tale matre, tale figghie*' (like mother, like daughter), the Quercesi say. The tie between mother and daughter remains strong even after marriage and leads to much visiting and mutual aid. Boys, when they start school at around six years old, are more likely to become their father's responsibility and perhaps begin to help him in the fields, gathering firewood or looking for edible wild plants, but as a son matures, feelings of respect are likely to replace those of warmth towards his father.[15] His mother remains a loving and permissive figure, though the tie between mother and son is more likely to be broken by his marriage than that between a mother and daughter by hers. Mother and daughter-in-law are seen as rivals for the son's affection, but the property the wife brings to the marriage which enables the son to establish his independence gives her a greater lever of influence. Thus, parents act individually and have different roles to play in the upbringing of their children who, in turn, perceive and judge them differentially.

Husband and wife do cooperate in decision-making. Women not only bring property to marriage but possibly earn some money and usually hold the family purse. They therefore expect and are expected to have an equal say in crucial decisions affecting the family – the purchase of new clothes, investment in land, assessment of the suitability of a suitor for a daughter. Arbitrary or authoritarian decision-making is condemned, though the husband's opinion carries more weight in business matters and the wife's in domestic ones, the fields of their respective day-to-day competence.

THE SIGNIFICANCE OF COUPLES

However, the couple exists in an observable way and takes on importance during two phases of married life – the beginning and the end.

Children normally follow soon after marriage, but the couple are usually alone for a short period.[16] Even though most have a separate home when they marry, it is common for young couples to eat at the house of one set of parents. Which parents offer this, how often and for how long, is determined by the nearness, prosperity and emotional ties of the three families, which usually means that the wife's parents provide them more often.

People expect the young couple to be happy to be left alone during the honeymoon and the first few months of marriage, while they get to know and adapt to each other. (Honeymoons are increasingly popular, in part as a result of prosperity, but also because of changing conceptions of marriage. Traditionally, the groom's mother would inspect the sheets on the first morning of a marriage, and lack of evidence of the bride's virginity could break a marriage. It still can; but if the first night is spent away from home in a hotel, it is up to the groom alone to decide upon what is now often felt to be a private matter.) The sexual nature of this adjustment is explicitly recognized and blushing brides eagerly relate their nightly encounters, even in mixed company (though not in front of unmarried males).

But in a matter of months the first child is on its way and interaction changes. The husband goes out in the evening and the wife stays at home. Once children are born the same leisure pattern continues, with them included. Leisure is enjoyed individually or as a family. Those couples who cannot have children go out as a couple only because this is the limit of their household, not because there is necessarily any other or stronger tie between them.

Later, when the children are grown and married, husband and wife are alone together again. However, the children's marriages have meant the dissolution of the family patrimony which, though seldom leaving them poor, diminishes their local significance. The remaining land is worked by married sons; the father need no longer cultivate contacts or be cultivated by aspirants for jobs. His role in the political arena declines. In contrast, his wife comes into her own: she fills the honourable role of *nonna* (grandmother), called upon by married daughters for help and advice, and rests content that her main worries –

bringing up and marrying off her children – are over. There is no respected male role corresponding to *nonna*. The man, too, has done his duty by his family but his status, largely dependent on his role as worker, now inevitably declines. He must potter in his remaining fields but his sons do the real work; he can chat to old friends in the market place but his real social significance is over.

Although at both these stages couples exist as residential units, they are not necessarily socially significant. By 'significant' I mean whether the unit performs significant functions and whether the relationship has special significance for the actors. Clearly, the couple has certain tasks, but these are largely segregated in both productive and domestic spheres. Also, other people always enter into what the couple does – neighbours and kin help with domestic chores and child-bearing; friends, employees and kin help with work in the fields; kin help to establish a home and an economic base; leisure is enjoyed with friends, neighbours and kin. These people participate, of course, in more than a physical sense; they have certain expectations about appropriate behaviour in particular situations and apply sanctions to those who deviate from them. This leads us to the meaning a relationship has for the actors, to the information taken for granted by them but which cannot be taken for granted by the observer. As I have suggested, for most of their lives a couple's primary orientation is not towards each other; they cannot adequately perform their basic tasks without taking into account the presence of others and sharing their assumptions and expectations. For them, the middle of the domestic cycle, when men are politically active, consolidating their property, advancing their careers, and women are raising children to make good marriages, is the most important time of their lives.

The family is a more important social unit than the couple in terms of the orientation of individuals. Even for the short time of courtship when the couple can concentrate on themselves, their behaviour is controlled by others, upholding 'correct' behaviour. Their relationship cannot be understood in isolation from this.

This orientation towards the family is due in part to the fact that, until recently, children were the natural and speedy consequence of most marriages. A man cannot ignore the well-being of his dependents if he wishes to maintain his good name. To provide for them he must seek ways to improve the property they will inherit, or find money to keep them at school. Daughters, in particular, mean commitments, and many men with teenage daughters lament '*la donna é una cambiale*' (woman is an IOU).

The father also has moral responsibilities to his family, especially its women. The economic and moral responsibilities are intimately connected: a poor man who fails to provide adequately for his dependents is assumed to be unable to care for them morally, and to be generally unreliable.[17] Economic and moral status have important political consequences:[18] to succeed – and this means at the very least ensuring that his children will have as much as he did – a man must be ready to make alliances, to cooperate.[19] In the absence of swift, cheap and effective legal sanctions, this means being able to trust and be trusted. Trust requires information about people, in particular about how they meet their primary commitments to their families. A man who does not meet these cannot be trusted to meet commitments to anyone else. Women play a vital role in acquiring and disseminating this information.

II

We usually think of the relationships of couples as the most private and intimate of all; those whose form is determined by individual adjustments. But in fact these relationships are patterned in a way which makes sense in relation to other institutions, customs and norms. This patterning is controlled by values upheld and sanctioned by other people. In Quercio, the need for respectability and the concern with reputation are the factors shaping the form of these relationships.[20]

The Quercesi rarely use the term *honore* (honour), but talk of *reputazione* (reputation), which has similar overtones and implications – an honourable person is one of *buona reputazione* (good reputation) and a dishonourable one is of *cattiva repu-*

iazione.[21] Women in particular are sometimes said to be *seria* (serious), in contrast to the disapproving phrase *non é seria* (she's not serious) which has definite sexual implications which *reputazione* does not necessarily have. A woman's honour is most easily lost by sexual misconduct, which not only jeopardizes her marriage chances (though seldom now her life) but also contaminates other household members. A local saying lists the relative gravity of this for a man;

> 'Corne de pariinde, nan so nninde.
> Corne de mamme, corne de canne.
> Corne de sore, corne d'ore.
> Corne de meggiere, corne vere!'

('Horns for a relative, I don't know anything about it.
Horns for my mother, a dog's horns.
Horns for my sister, golden horns.
Horns for my wife, real horns!')

The threat of loss of honour through one's own actions or through contagion is a powerful control. Family members have an interest in keeping one another in line, especially siblings, who still have to make a good marriage. Men do not suffer directly from accusations of unchastity as women do, but indirectly. They are responsible for the sexuality of the women in their households, and a man unable to control them is thought not to make a trustworthy or reliable business partner.

No organized groups control the daily lives of the Quercesi, but networks of social relationships are extremely important.[22] A 'map' of their relationships would look rather like a fishing net – the knots being people, the strings joining them relationships of kinship, friendship and economic contract. Some knots would be joined only tenuously to the main fabric by a few strands, others would be surrounded by a tangle of threads, but everybody would be linked somehow. Taking one person as a starting point, his relationship to, say, A, B and C could be traced out; relationships (if they exist) between A, B and C could also be traced independently of the starting point. Not all links are qualitatively the same – some are stronger and more long-lasting; the net also changes over time as people die or end relationships, are born or embark on new relationships. These networks of personal acquaintances are the key to understanding Quercesi life. When asking why A does something, one must remember that A bears in mind not only what is possible and in his own immediate interests, but also what is in the interests of those to whom he is connected in diverse ways whose reactions will, in turn, affect him. Of course, if people did not do this it would not make sense to talk to them living in a society at all, but societies do vary in the way in which the behaviour of their members is classified as 'public', of general concern, and 'private', which is not.

People in some societies are allowed a great deal of privacy, of freedom to be idiosyncratic or eccentric in certain respects; people in others are subject to a great deal of control over matters we would regard as private. Eccentric or non-criminal deviant behaviour does occur in the latter kind of society, but there is generally less room for manoeuvre and experiment, and fewer areas of life are defined as private. We tend to take privacy very much for granted, resenting the intrusions of both neighbours and state into our lives, feeling that, as long as no damage is done, what families do is their own affair. Not everybody feels this way – in Quercio freedom to regulate 'private' behaviour at home and towards relatives is neither possible nor desirable.

Firstly, the physical environment itself imposes limits on privacy. In the evenings, raised voices can be heard through the walls, making it difficult to keep quarrels private. During the day, doors and windows are left open to air and light the house. When heavy chores are finished, the women put their chairs in the street and here mend clothes, prepare vegetables, comb and plait hair, and discuss news. All comings and goings have an audience eager to note them; what X is cooking for dinner, the new clothes Y has bought, who is coming to see Z while her husband is out. All are pieces of information which help the audience assess and reassess the respectability of X, Y and Z. Are they prospering, getting above themselves, letting things slip? The gossip is passed round the neighbourhood and eventually, if significant, to the husbands.

Relations between neighbours are by no means all hostile, and cooperation is expected and valued. The Quercesi are aware of differences in financial and moral standing of their neighbours but *'la strada dovrebb'essere una famiglia'* (the street should be a family). In the same way as differences among relatives should not mean differential treatment, neither should (small) differences between neighbours. Neighbours continually pop in and out of each other's houses, which further diminishes privacy. But this lack of privacy is the means of maintaining respectability. People depend on the judgement of others who, on the basis of this intimate knowledge, will treat them as inferior, equal or superior. The offer of a glass of liqueur, the request for some tomatoes, or a tight-lipped *'buongiorno'* as someone passes without stopping, are clues to status.

A neighbourhood may impose severe sanctions on a delinquent. Gossip which reaches men's ears can have a significant effect on a family's life chances. The case of Pina, the wife of a spasmodically employed bricklayer and mother of three children under six, illustrates this point. The couple's close relatives are all in Germany and the husband has a bad reputation as a heavy drinker and a spendthrift. Pina starts at a disadvantage. Because of her quick temper, her relationships with her neighbours are poor, and though people will see that her children do not stray when she leaves them to go out shopping, they are reluctant to do more. Her husband shows no understanding of her difficult position and leaves the house when she starts to complain. She made one attempt to improve her position by going to the Town Hall to see if she was eligible for an allowance to pay for the baby's milk. She was told that her own should be sufficient, and was turned out before she had a chance to explain that it had dried up. Perhaps not too inaccurately, she is convinced she was treated badly because she is poor, because of her husband's bad reputation, because no one of importance would speak up for her. Her neighbours, fearing contamination through association, are unwilling to step in and help. She finds no help at an institutional level, because no one is interested in helping the family of a disreputable and unimportant man who can offer nothing in return. But Pina and the children feel the effects of this. They also suffer because she cannot get credit at local shops; debts are allowed only to those who can settle at the end of the week.

Those who try to keep themselves to themselves are condemned. If visitors are not welcomed, whether they have come to borrow oil or to offer cherries, this creates antagonism and animosity. Is the family getting above itself; do they feel themselves too good to talk with their neighbours; do they, perhaps, want to hide a reverse in their fortunes, which visitors would note from seeing a depleted larder? Any of these could have serious consequences for the plans of men associated with the family. Therefore, the news goes round. A family that does experience change, for better or for worse, often finds it easier to move to a new neighbourhood than to try to establish a new footing with old neighbours. On the wife fall two duties : first, to maintain the family's respectability by keeping a clean house (which includes a weekly scrub of the pavement in front of it), by watching the behaviour of her daughters, by not gossiping too much; second, to report to her husband about others, information vital to the system.

Some things in Quercio are changing; some women continue to work after marriage with the full support of their husbands; a few engaged couples do go out alone; young middle-class families who live in new blocks of flats cannot be under such close surveillance by their neighbours. As yet such people are rare, for the most part coming from comfortable, professional homes of doctors and lawyers, a small class of people traditionally somewhat outside the normal pattern of neighbourhood relations. Their claims to status are based less on personal qualities of respectability and more on a combination of wealth, education and influence. Fathers of such families are sometimes given the honorary title of *Don* and, even if not directly involved in local politics, are probably substantial patrons, giving help with legal matters, recommendations for jobs or advice on bureaucratic procedure to those who offered their loyalty, respect and small services.

More recently, a new sort of patron is appearing in Quercio, men in local government or officials in trade unions, men with more effective contacts in the national system, with new information, and sometimes jobs, at their disposal. These men seldom come from the established middle class but have been socially mobile, well known as children and adolescents by those to whom they now act as patrons. Their home lives, unlike those of the traditional middle-class families, are subject to very close scrutiny by the local community.

But because of their status, potential power and, perhaps, the difficulties of knowing in detail what goes on in their homes, more allowances are made for idiosyncrasies in their behaviour. Parties of young wives go to the beach with their children in the summer; teenage daughters wear trousers and short skirts. However, a wife would still not dream of letting a man into the house in her husband's absence and would take such a visit or request as an insult.

Inevitably, some families find themselves in between these groups or classes, and their situation is an unhappy one. Their claims to middle-class status and respectability have not been recognized; people suspect that the new flat or the big car were obtained by going heavily into debt or by dubious, if not exactly criminal, means. In other words, people fear that the seeming prosperity has no secure basis and to be associated therefore carries a high risk. Such families are accepted by neither the respectable middle class nor the working class, and even the most innocent actions of their women are suspect and subject to hostile gossip.

How do the men and women themselves view their relationships? Most older married couples with adult children feel there is only one proper way of conducting a married relationship. They recognize that romantic love may form and bind the union initially but are somewhat sceptical about its long-term importance – '*U prim'anne a core a core, u seconde a cule a cule, u terza a calce ngule*' (The first year, heart to heart, the second, arse to arse, the third, a kick up the backside').

Once children are born the couple settles to the real business of life – working the family holdings, improving their security, bringing up children to good careers and marriages. That men and women should live fairly separate lives is thought right and

proper. If a wife falls ill and daughters are too young to cook
and clean, a sister or neighbour helps out, not a husband. One
young man, now married, often used to recount the story of the
evening he found himself alone in the house, a student, hungry,
without female help. His account of the extraordinary meal he
produced, working on the rational but arbitrary principle that
if something was in the refrigerator it was edible, was always
greeted with howls of horror by the men and delight from the
women at his incompetence. Of course, a great deal is show put
on for spectators – a visit to another home found the husband
cooking spaghetti and opening tins for the sauce while his wife
marked her pupils' homework.

Inevitably, though, years of working for the benefit of the
family breeds a certain affection and intimacy between many
older couples. This is rarely expressed, but occasionally a slap
on a comfortable backside is repaid with a smacking, if tooth-
less, kiss from the wife. Basically, however, their task is seen as
cooperation in a productive enterprise, in economic and in
moral terms.

Younger couples talk more romantically, emphasizing their
love and considering seriously problems of mutual adjustment.
The relationship is valued, entered into and pursued for more
personal motives of emotional satisfaction. To carry out tasks
responsibly is no longer sufficient to qualify as a 'good' husband or wife; a spouse must remain attractive and affection-
ate.

Many influences have helped to change people's conception
of marital relationships, returned emigrants in particular, with
their stories of sophisticated life in Luxembourg, Turin and
Strasbourg. Often these emigrants are younger married couples
without children, in a good position to sample the entertainments of a big city, and less likely than the long-term migrants
to Canada and Australia to settle into expatriate communities
with close resemblances to home.[23] Films on television and at
the cinema, photographs and stories in magazines, widen the
horizons of many, especially of the women, who read more
magazines and watch more television than men. If films and
magazines do not immediately provide alternative models for

behaviour, at least they make clear that there are other, equally respectable, ways of doing things.[24]

Women are perhaps beginning to change their attitudes and hopes to a greater extent than men, but growing prosperity and leisure may make this change easier. Television now keeps a number of husbands at home for at least a few evenings a week; planning (or trying to plan) births reflects a growing interest of parents in their children's development and education. These changes are no guarantee that new shared interests between husband and wife will be generated, but they at least open the way for them. Perhaps, too, an increasingly instrumental attitude to work associated with lack of attachment to the land,[25] rationalization of agriculture and the movement into industry and other sectors of the economy, may increase the chances of companionate marital relationships developing.

Traditionally, physical and emotional affection was reserved for children rather than the spouse. Once a Quercesi child is born, room is made for him and love is wholeheartedly offered him, even if his conception was unwanted. This call on a woman's affections remains for many the supreme one, especially if the child is male. A number of couples are now trying to plan their families, but few people know alternatives to the withdrawal method, which is thought unreliable, and the pill, which is thought to be dangerous.

Thoughts of mortal sin seldom seemed to enter these calculations and women bitterly resented pointed questions of priests at confession. Wealthier women finding themselves pregnant after they had hoped their family was complete did not hesitate to turn to local midwives for abortions. As in most other countries, the cost of abortion put it out of reach of those most in need of it.

Despite these changes, ties with other people are still strong, making it difficult to talk about the couple as a particularly significant unit. Looking out from the household, a woman's 'natural' companions are other women, especially kin, neighbours, and to a lesser extent, affines (in-laws). Unrelated friends retain importance for a woman only if ties with kin are severed. These networks of the women have a more permanent significance than those of the men with their shifting alliances. Looking inwards, the couple's attention encompasses the household as a unit – their work is directed towards maintaining and promoting its welfare. The success of one member reflects on all, as does the failure. In turn, the family is judged as a whole by the community, which discriminates little between the achievements and characters of individual members.

Terms such as 'the family', 'the couple' or 'the individual' have substance only in the context of values, customs, institutions, and perceptions. To try to get at other people's understanding of their world is always difficult and it is even more difficult when the world greatly resembles our own taken-for-granted one. Certainly, these units provide useful and manageable starting points for analysis, but are useful for cross-cultural comparison only when the more general context is examined.

Similarly, to look at a community where the couple exists in a very different way from our own society can lead us to re-evaluate our own conceptions, to see, perhaps, that its importance, even its development and portrayal in romantic literature as the most gratifying relationship, or by commercial interests to sell diverse goods, is the result of a particular process, and reaction to other changes in our society. The break-up of traditional close-knit communities, the spread of birth control techniques, ease of hire purchase, all have an effect (though not an equal one), and facilitate development of particular forms of couple relationships. Similar changes seem to be occurring in Quercio: women are beginning to look for companionate relationship with their husbands; men, to a lesser extent, are responding. This should not, however, lead us to assume that our way is therefore better. Relationships are adapted to certain social contexts and respond to pressures and controls; as these are modified so the relationship changes.

3. Getting Married

Perhaps in most societies, as in Quercio, to talk of the choice to marry or not to marry may be almost as irrelevant as to talk of the choice to grow old or not to grow old. To marry is simply part of the natural progression through life, part of the inevitable unless catastrophe or bad management intervene. Not to marry may deprive people of many things, though the consequences of remaining single may be more strikingly stark in some societies than in others. As the French anthropologist Claude Lévi-Strauss reported:

One of the deepest impressions which I retained from my first experiences in the field was the sight, in a central Brazilian native village, of a young man crouching for hours upon end in the corner of a hut, dismal, ill-cared for, fearfully thin, and seemingly in the most complete state of dejection. I observed him for several days. He rarely went out, except to go hunting by himself, and when the family meals began around the fires, he would as often as not have gone without if a female relative had not occasionally set a little food at his side, which he ate in silence. Intrigued by this strange fate, I finally asked who this person was, thinking that he suffered from some serious illness; my suppositions were laughed at and I was told, 'He is a bachelor.' This was indeed the sole reason for his apparent curse.[1]

Marriage may be the only route to sexual relations, full adult status, the services of a member of the opposite sex essential to a comfortable life if not to survival itself, alliances, honour and prestige, a household separate from kin, and socially approved children. These things may be sought for themselves alone or people may attempt to combine them with a relation which also provides sexual pleasure, emotional involvement and companionship. People may be able to have the latter without the former but the desire for what only marriage can bring inclines most to marry. Malinowski, for example, posed the question of why the Trobriand Islanders should wish to be bound in marriage 'even when marriage adds nothing to sexual freedom and, indeed, takes a great deal away from it, where two lovers can possess each other as long as they like without legal obligation'. In answer, he points out not only that marriage is associated with full adult status but that it brings, for men at least, considerable economic advantages as well as domestic services and children.[2] Women are less influenced by considerations of comfort or social status than by affection and the desire to have children in wedlock. In addition, Malinowski argues, lovers like to make certain of each other by the permanent ties marriage ideally creates and to have each other to themselves. Among the Trobriand Islanders it would appear that men have a more utilitarian interest in marriage than women;[3] more common in modern Western societies is the notion that women scheme for marriage while men attempt to evade it. Such an idea is by no means confined, however, to complex societies and in many simpler societies people may protest their antipathy to marriage, realizing its disadvantages as well as its attractions, while ultimately getting married.[4]

Generally speaking, people in Britain now have a greater choice about whether or not they marry than people in other societies, but most do get married. Some people may, however, have less choice than others. For example, for many of those living in close-knit communities, not to marry may still mean sexual frustration, dependence on parents, a less comfortable life and no family. To remain unmarried may be seen not as a matter of choice but of misfortune.

Many people feel that not only should a personally satisfying relationship precede and continue into marriage, but that this is what marriage is all about. Rather than regarding marriage as an institution concerned primarily with kinship, affines and children, people increasingly think of it as the legitimation of a personal relationship, a formal declaration of being a couple.

Marriage is culturally portrayed as the natural consequence of love. People look after their spouses, support them, sleep with them and have children because they love each other. To marry for any other reason – for money, status, sex, because the girl is pregnant, to get away from parents, to give up a tedious job or to ensure a more comfortable and secure life, is much less esteemed. 'To have to get married' not only suggests a breach of norms about premarital chastity or even the foolishness of 'getting caught', but can also be socially embarrassing simply because of the implication that the marriage is forced rather than desired and love may be missing.[5]

Many writers discussing how people select their spouses stress the importance of personal compatibility, the working through of relationships, attempts to sort out differences of opinions and values, the need for adjustment, the possibility of living together before marriage to test sexual and domestic harmony.[6] But in emphasizing personal compatibility, gratification of needs and the desire for rewards as part of a search for a spouse, two points are often overlooked: these are not the only emotions which now draw people of the opposite sex together; people often feel passionate about those who provide them with few rewards or whom they barely know. Many couples who live together do so with no thought of marriage, while others are more concerned with getting and being married than with the quality of the relationship on which the marriage will be based.[7] No intrinsic connection exists between either personal compatibility and marriage, or passion and marriage – why people feel the way they do about each other and why they get married are separate issues. Obviously, the more choice people have about getting married, the more diverse will be their reasons for so doing.

The reasons people have for marriage and their perceptions of marriage affect a further choice that all couples must make once they have decided to marry – that is, the kind of ceremony to have.

Formal weddings are many things. They are occasions for public displays of propriety and duty, affluence and prestige; they may demonstrate the fulfilment of a final parental obligation or a filial duty, reaffirm bonds of kinship, attest to the relative ranking of those involved. They are also occasions for licence and merriment, a time in which the couple getting married are the centre of attention – important and beautiful almost by definition, and upon which they may very well look back as one of the few, if not the only, times when this was true.

All wedding ceremonies are at least in part rites of passage, rituals which move people from one social status to another. Perhaps the most important difference between a formal church wedding and others is that it involves much more elaborate ritual, witnessed by more people. Such rites act on people's emotions, and at least some people who undergo a church ritual claim to feel married in a way they would not if they had only signed a document. Similarly, the rituals affect not only the central figures, but others whose social relations and statuses are being altered or reaffirmed by the event – the couple's kin and guests. These people, in turn, may also feel more strongly that the couple are truly married. In a register office this element is much reduced in favour of the purely legal character of the marriage contract.

The notion of rites of passage has been highly elaborated and has developed its own specialist terminology. The argument is that people are moved from one social status to another by means of a passage from an ordinary 'profane' existence to a 'sacred' state and back again. Basically the argument is asserting that the way people think and feel about each other and themselves is changed by rituals which first wipe out the ordinary, conceptually defined differences, statuses, regularities, thus moving people into an undifferentiated, or at least a less differentiated, state to which the term sacred is applied. After this is achieved, the ritual proceeds to impose a new set of statuses, by this means returning individuals to the profane, conceptually defined and regulated world, with new identities. A further point to the argument is that to experience the sacred, undifferentiated, amorphous state is to some extent dangerous and powerful. The point is significant because many aspects of the rituals can be understood as means of taming these powers, limiting these dangers, without undermining the effectiveness of the mechanisms.[8]

These considerations suggest two points. Firstly, that a couple are less likely to marry in church if, for them, the statuses 'married' and 'unmarried' are not sharply defined and opposed and hence getting married will alter their relation very little. Secondly, that they are less likely to marry in church if they are not enmeshed in an established network of kin and old friends. To understand why a virgin bride moving from her parents' home, support and protection to her husband's, and who will continue old relations in new ways with those around, should approach her wedding with trepidation and value ritual is easy; to understand why a couple who are already living together, who have no kin or close friends, should get up on the morning of their wedding and don bridal gown and morning suit to get married in church is more difficult.

In any case, people seldom repeatedly engage in meaningless behaviour. The meaning of a wedding may be to assert the couple's own social standing or to please others and fulfil obligations to them, or it may have deeper significance. In the following chapter Diana Leonard Barker, a sociologist, explores what the wedding ceremony meant to the couples she interviewed in Swansea.

A Proper Wedding

DIANA LEONARD BARKER

The conventional white wedding obviously does not symbolise what we, in the 1970s, mean by 'mutual society, help and comfort'. Few people take what it does symbolize seriously, but if not, why engage in an outdated charade at such a solemn moment of one's life?[1]

The question I raise in this chapter is one often posed by journalists who see Britain as a maxi London and by those sociologists who point with surprise or pride to the incidence of religious rites of passage in Britain today.[2] That question is 'Why do people in Britain bother to go on getting married?' The question has two parts, the first of which is 'Why do people marry and not simply live together?' The second, and the one with which I am primarily concerned, is 'Why do they have elaborate weddings?' Why, in an increasingly secular society, do so many couples continue to celebrate marriages in a way that is sometimes dubbed 'farcical' by the liberal intellectual middle classes – brides in virginal white, given away by their fathers and promising to obey their husbands before an audience of relatives they do not care for, decked out in finery bought for the occasion and never to be worn again? When the most the couple can hope for is that the wedding presents will at least equal the economic outlay, why do they not instead make their vows simply and privately and accept a gift of cash from their parents?

Implicit in the way these questions are often put is a belittlement of, and contempt for, ritual and religion, and a certain amount of anticlericalism.[3] But above all, the viewpoints they embrace portray an unwillingness to recognize the nature of marriage as an institution and its meaning to the majority of the population.

I want to suggest why the majority of people do continue to have church weddings and what some of the rituals mean to them. My discussion is based primarily on a study of couples getting married in Swansea, where I lived for four years. During the study I attended nearly a hundred weddings, several receptions and hen parties; I talked with vicars, ministers, priests and the superintendent registrar as well as with caterers, dress shop managers and taxi drivers. I interviewed more than fifty couples just before and just after they got married, and in some cases I talked with their parents.

THE POPULARITY OF MARRIAGE AND THE CHOICE OF LOCALE

Many authors have discussed the reasons people have for getting married.[4] I will simply say that the people I talked to in Swansea saw no alternative to marriage as a source of sexual gratification and no other means to establish a household separate from parents.[5] Here, as elsewhere in Britain, marriage is an increasingly popular institution: more people get married each year, the age at which people marry for the first time is decreasing, an increasing proportion of the population has been married at least once, and the majority of divorcees remarry.[6]

The upper and middle classes have celebrated weddings with great ceremony and conspicuous consumption for generations: more recently for the working class elaborate wedding rituals have superseded the funeral in this respect.[7] Weddings nowadays are a source of excitement and interest for women in particular and, together with births and christenings, deaths and funerals, form abiding topics of conversation in the home, factory and office. These are the main occasions on which kin may meet as a group and when husband and wife may participate jointly in social activities.[8] In this latter respect, weddings may serve as a reaffirmation of the marriages of guests attending them: husbands and wives who sit together in the service, hear the view of the church and state on marriage, and then attend a party of kin and friends as a couple. Certainly widows, widowers and divorcees find their sense of loss and incompleteness particularly marked at weddings.

Weddings are the only major ceremonials organized by most ordinary people, certainly by ordinary women. They are times of planning, saving, booking, choosing, checking details, and of endless expense. A 'proper' wedding usually takes at least three months' preparation, and nine months to a year is often regarded as reasonable time. One couple I interviewed had booked their reception fifteen months in advance; clergy had bookings for popular Saturdays eighteen months in advance; and an insurance salesman tried to sell us policies, to mature in fifteen years, on our daughters to pay for the cost of their weddings. (He assured us that these were very popular, though the one he had had for £350 on his daughter had not been large enough.)

Given that most people want to marry and are concerned about the way in which they get married, why do they choose a particular form of ceremony? Firstly, of course, their choice is limited by legal constraints – all weddings in England and Wales have to take place either in a register office or in an authorized place of worship licensed for marriages, for example, a Nonconfomist chapel, a Roman Catholic or Anglican church, a synagogue, Friends' Meeting House, Jehovah's Witness meeting hall, a Sikh temple.[9] In contrast, in America and elsewhere weddings can take place in private houses, gardens or hotels;[10] in other countries, such as France, a civic wedding must always take place, though couples may choose to follow it with a religious ceremony.

In England and Wales the proportion of civil marriages has risen since figures were first available in 1844. In 1967 they comprised 34 per cent of all weddings, in 1972, 45·5 per cent, though the proportion varies in different parts of the country.[11] During the same period the proportion of weddings conducted by the Anglican church has declined steadily, though it still officiates at almost 70 per cent of religious weddings (45 per cent of *all* weddings in 1967 and 37 per cent in 1972).[12] I should emphasize that 'church' weddings still outnumber civil weddings and that the Established, Anglican church officiates at more weddings than any other religious body.

THE MEANING OF 'A PROPER WEDDING'

In Swansea a very clear distinction is made between 'proper weddings' and those weddings for which there is less consensus as to title – referred to variously as 'civic do's', 'registry office weddings' and 'not proper weddings'.[13]

A 'proper wedding' is first and foremost a church (or chapel) wedding, but almost all such weddings are also 'white' – the bride wears a long white gown.[14] 'Proper weddings' follow a very standard form and the organizers make frequent references to experts on the ritual – etiquette books, bridal magazines, friends, relatives, colleagues, clergy, caterers, bakers, stationers, dress shop managers, florists and car hire firms – to make sure they get them right.[15] At the same time they try to make it personal by choosing particular details to their own taste. For example, though there will always be a cake, the number of tiers and the kind of decorations – shoes or doves, bride and groom figures or flowers on top, touches of pink or blue or silver – are matters of choice and great debate. To an outsider or to the uninterested (most men) such details are invisible. As one minister commented: 'After every wedding my wife says to me, "What did she (the bride) wear?", but for the life of me I can never remember. They all look alike.'

Weddings in register offices are more varied, and for these weddings there is generally less preparation, less publicity and less attention to detail. At one extreme are the couple I interviewed who had lived together for several years, marrying when the man got his divorce. Their 'secret' wedding took place three days after he was granted his decree absolute, and was by licence, which is quick as well as 'secret'.[16] His sister's husband acted as best man and drove the couple to the register office, collecting on the way the bride's friend to make the second witness necessary for a wedding. The groom wore a suit with a buttonhole, the bride an outfit she bought for a friend's wedding three years previously, with a new hat her only purchase. The bride's mother baby-sat with the couple's small daughter and prepared drinks and sandwiches for their return. The evening was spent at a dinner dance with the two witnesses and their spouses. There was no cake, no honeymoon, no joking and no publicity.

In more elaborate register office weddings the bride may wear a short white suit or coat, though most favour coloured clothes which are more useful afterwards.[17] She may have roses or ribbons woven into her hair, and carry a posy of flowers or have a spray pinned to her clothes. Small girls may be dressed up and counted as bridesmaids and there will be a best man to hand the ring to the groom and to pay the registrar for the licence after the ceremony. There may be a decorated car (even a hired limousine), guests may throw confetti, a photographer may be hired; the reception may be a sit-down meal for as many as twenty guests at a hotel or a buffet for forty at the house of either set of parents. However, the whole ceremonial always has much less formality and, for example, the reception at home is often referred to slightly disparagingly as 'a bit of a do', printed invitations are seldom sent out and people often invite themselves.

REASONS FOR GETTING MARRIED IN THE REGISTER OFFICE

Though some couples who marry in the register office vacillate for some time between a wedding in church and a wedding in the town hall,[18] there are two categories of people who marry in the register office primarily because their identities are spoilt from the point of view of marrying in church. Such couples are those in which the bride is pregnant and those in which at least one of the partners is divorced. Given that both these characteristics are seen as slightly discreditable, they are not always mentioned as reasons for choice of ceremony, but Swansea mores are very firm and in my sample of twenty register office weddings eight brides were pregnant and five of the men and four of the women had been married before.[19] Only seven out of twenty couples were in this sense 'eligible' to marry in church.

Although no formal impediment to a church wedding exists for the pregnant bride, many factors mitigate against such a choice. Couples want to marry quickly, before the pregnancy becomes too obvious and to give as long a period as possible between the marriage and the birth. They also want to marry quietly and without fuss so the wedding date is kept secret. ('It's not really something to be ashamed of, but equally it's not something to make a song and dance about.') The couple probably also need to save all ready cash – the precipitateness of the wedding usually means they have few savings, the bride may be unable to work immediately after marriage, and the expenses of the baby are already in sight. Finally, many are unwilling to reveal the pregnancy to the vicar, minister or priest, who would be expected to be (and felt to have the right to be) censorious. In contrast, the superintendent registrar is seen as a government official having no right to deny people the right to marry by licence, nor to inquire into the physical state of the bride.[20] All of these factors direct the couples to the register office.

Formal impediments to marriage in church affect mainly those who are divorced; Anglican and Roman Catholic churches are unwilling to remarry divorced people, while some Nonconformist ministers will perform the service only for 'innocent parties' in divorce cases. (In this latter case, ministers feel that to be sure persons asking to be married are really 'innocent parties' they need to know the individuals concerned, that is, these individuals need to be members of the church or to be known well to active members who could vouch for them.)[21]

A third factor causing couples to choose register office weddings may be unwillingness or inability of parents (specifically those of the bride) to meet the costs of the wedding. The couple are then faced with a number of alternatives. Either they wait and save for a long time to meet the costs of a wedding and a new home; or they have a proper wedding and make do with a furnished flat, the bride then working for several years to save for a house; or they dispense with the big wedding. This contingency sometimes occurs when the bride has several young brothers and sisters still at home, or when her father is out of work, or when relationships between the couple and the parents are simply bad. Under any of these conditions the girl may in any case be unwilling to have the spotlight of a big wedding turned on her family. (Three or four of the seven couples 'eligible' to marry in church in my sample were in this position.)

Civil weddings are also favoured by couples who want to marry quickly after an 'off-and-on' courtship or a short acquaintance (as did the other three couples in my sample). Such speedy weddings are again disfavoured – 'marry in haste, repent at leisure'. Finally, the register office may be chosen by those with a contempt for ritual. These people, however, were perceived by my sample as probably the most deviant of all, and I met no one in Swansea in this category outside the university.

Thus those who marry in the register office are seen to be those with little money or those who are 'tight' about spending it, those who are foolish enough to get pregnant, those who have already had one failed marriage, those who marry in indecent haste, or have bad relations with their families, or are generally immoral and lack respect for the important things of life. Consequently, register office weddings are second-class because people with spoilt identities use them; those who choose such weddings are scrutinized to see what 'forced' them into it. Local society is concerned with what is wrong with people who marry in the town hall, not with their relationships and social situation as a whole.[22] As one girl said: 'My mother was upset when she heard we wanted to get married in the registry office. Because, you see, my brother had to get married and she was worried that people would think there was something wrong with me too.'

Church weddings are normal: people have to have reasons for opting out of them – expense, fuss, worry, time. Most people who did opt out displayed no anticlericalism, and indeed there was considerable respect shown for the church.[23] One young woman said: 'We're not religious. I'd feel guilty about getting married in church. We don't go any more. Be hypocritical to use the church just for the one time.'

REASONS FOR MARRYING IN CHURCH

Church weddings, by contrast, show that couples are respectable, that no imputations can be made against them (hence, perhaps, the hilarity and gossip when something *is* uncovered). One meaning of a 'proper wedding' is therefore 'the way decent, decorous, correct, worthy, respectable people marry'. Individuals who are concerned with their good name within the community will choose a church wedding. (The greater number of civil weddings in conurbations than in rural areas may result from the reduction in pressure to conform experienced by those who move into big cities.[24])

Concern with the good name of the family may mean that, while the wedding is supposed to be the bride's big day and the kind of ceremony her choice, this may hold true only so long as she does choose to marry in church. If she does not so choose, she may come under pressure from her parents, the groom and/or his parents, on the basis that such a wedding is more respectable. The groom may himself be concerned that he be seen to be decorously and correctly married. I met young women who had not wanted to get engaged or to delay the wedding at all once the decision to marry had been made, but whose men had insisted on engagement and decent delay so that others would not think the wedding had had to be rushed. The concern for what others think is also demonstrated by the following interchange between a bride and groom over the bride's dress:

BRIDE: I fancied pink over white.
GROOM: But your mother said you couldn't possibly.
BRIDE: That's the trouble when you get married – you have to please people. Anyway, white doesn't represent virginity.
GROOM: People think it does.
BRIDE: I don't care what people think.
GROOM: Nor do I, but they do.
BRIDE: You must care or you'd have let me get married in pink – or cream, I fancied cream, but you wouldn't let me.

Perhaps a more important meaning of a 'proper wedding' is

that it is for many the 'only way of getting married which is really a wedding'. In other words, this is the form of ceremony to which the term 'wedding' properly belongs, the form of ritual which can *do* something which other sorts of wedding cannot. The registrar can make a legal contract; the church can make a mystical, binding union.

The register office is seen as very much part of this world: it is literally mundane. A large office in the town hall or in an old, converted building, it may be like a rather uncomfortable version of the front room of a private house and be similarly not in the least awe-inspiring. The church building, on the other hand, is set apart from everyday life: it is sacred. The more 'church-like' the building, the more popular it is likely to be for weddings – modern, prefabricated, temporary buildings and even Nonconformist chapels are less favoured than more elaborate buildings.

The registrar is just a man doing his job, a civil servant who stops for coffee breaks between weddings. A priest, on the other hand, has God-given authority and a pastoral interest in and responsibility for those he marries.

In ecclesiastical language the marriage ceremony is a *signa effectiva*, a symbol which really does something. This interpretation is shared by participants: the church can make a marriage more binding, it is a source of very potent magic. One vicar in Swansea explains the church's view of the sacramental nature of marriage to couples coming to him for preparation for marriage by saying that getting married in church enables the marriage to draw upon the strength of God to support it. He compares this to plugging in to the electricity supply and thereby 'getting all the force of Tyr John (the local power station) behind one'.

This second meaning of a 'proper wedding', emphasizing what a church wedding does that a civil wedding cannot do, overlaps to some extent with a third meaning, which concerns what the ritual *says*. This third element is that the ceremony is 'the form of ritual best suited to the purpose of marking the major status transition which is being made'. It expresses important values both in what it says explicitly and directly, and in its symbols.

The sanctity associated with the church and its officiants allows for other important behaviour patterns. In church, solemn, respectful behaviour is known to be appropriate and the transition from the 'normal' world is marked. For a register office wedding, new clothes, long white dresses, morning dress are not felt to be appropriate, but people are often very uncertain about what *is* appropriate, and people attending such weddings are often nervous about them. In church, dramaturgical elements are easier – the waiting groom, the bride's entrance with her father to the sound of organ music, the procession down the aisle, the bride's relations and friends to the left, the groom's to the right. Such acting out of the status passage may well help to impress it on the minds of those involved, a kind of 'learning by doing'.[25] In many chapels, however, side aisles prevent the demonstrable separation of the guests, and the bride's entrance is off-centre; at the front of the pews there is 'the big seat' below the lectern, so that the bride and groom and any attendants have to shuffle sideways awkwardly. In the register office the situation is even worse, in part because of the uncertainty. Civil weddings usually have few guests, so that most couples have never attended a register office wedding before their own; everyone waits together in a little room before moving into the 'wedding room' itself, so preventing a big entry for the principal actors; everyone arrives in the wedding room uncertain where to go and what to do.

Many see the religious service as more personal than others, at least in part because Swansea has some thirty-eight Anglican churches and one hundred and sixty-seven authorized places of worship, as against one register office. A couple marrying in church stand a high chance of being the only one being married in a particular building on that day, and even on popular Saturdays at popular churches weddings are booked at wide intervals so that parties do not overlap.[26] But in the register office, weddings can take place at fifteen-minute intervals. If guests arrive early or the bride for the previous wedding arrives late, they may have to wait in the waiting-room with the guests of the wedding ahead of theirs. The registrar is thus obviously seen not to be concentrating all his attentions on any one couple and the whole ceremony is felt to be hurried. As one informant said, the whole affair is like a 'glorified form of getting a new dog licence'.

Finally, the church or chapel is local to the home of one of the couple (traditionally, and still usually, that of the bride), thus lending a feeling of community and continuity, especially where the church is eponymous with the district.[27] The particular church is chosen because 'I was christened there and my parents were married there ... and I expect I'll be buried there'. In part this kind of statement could be seen as a validation produced by people who go irregularly, if at all, to church services, but who look around for some tenuous link to re-activate when they decide they want a church wedding. Such a view is, I think, unduly cynical and underestimates the continuing attachment felt by many people towards their denomination and their church.[28]

Thus the wedding ritual in part is saying that a major status change is being undertaken, a change to a highly valued state (marriage is popularly believed to be the major source of personal happiness and fulfilment today), a change which needs to be conducted in a sacred place, with due time and attention to the individual couple, in the solemn presence of neighbours, relatives and friends, as part of the families' continuing membership of the local community.

SYMBOLS – THE BRIDE AND HER DRESS

Many symbols are employed in a wedding, but here I shall confine myself just to the dominant symbol, the dress of the bride. The choice of this particular element for further exploration is justifiable in that the dress is the symbol by which a 'proper wedding' is alternatively designated: a white wedding.[29]

The cultural imperative is that a bride should look beautiful. A great deal of time, energy and money is spent to ensure she conforms as far as possible with this expectation. Bridal magazines suggest 'wedding countdowns' starting anything up to six months before the wedding, with diets and exercises to lose weight, firm muscles, improve hair and skin; they also supply advice on make-up, dress styles, head-dresses. Some such advice is read by most women planning weddings and it would be hard to overstate the attention to details (such as the colour of nail varnish, the kind of flowers) involved. Some slight personal imperfection on the day – a broken nail, a laddered stocking – is very upsetting and is reported to friends, neighbours, workmates (and visiting sociologists) weeks after the event.

The dress is often bought six months in advance and kept in the shop till the week before the wedding for lack of home storage or complete finance, or to keep it a secret. Often only a select few are allowed to see the dress, and in no case did the groom see the dress, much less the bride wearing the dress, before the day of the wedding. Most said that the latter was supposed to be unlucky. At least in part it seemed to be associated with making the wedding more of an occasion, like saving parcels for Christmas.

Surprise is the greater part of making that proud feeling. I want him to fall in love all over again.

Few wedding dresses are made at home (though many bridesmaids' dresses are), partly for the following kind of reason:

I was going to have it made and looked at patterns, but I work in a shop and in the lunch hour I tried one of ours on. I liked it so much I paid a bit more to be sure ... Rather than have it made and then decide I didn't like it.

The wedding dress itself should 'do something' for the bride-to-be when she tries it on – make her look beautiful, accentuate her best points, and this perhaps explains the rather surprising fact that many dresses were bought on impulse. A mother and daughter, for example, may be out shopping together and see something they fancy:

As soon as I saw it, I knew it was Susan's wedding dress.

The bridal magazines and their advertisers foster these ideas –

for example, see the blurb from an agency which hires out bridal gowns :

The most important dress you'll ever wear.
It can be perfect without being expensive

Your wedding gown
Every seam, every detail, must be impeccable ... The style must be uniquely you, not a mass-produced design. And yet, perfection and individuality are expensive. Such an ensemble could cost 75 guineas, probably more. Do you spend it, and perhaps sacrifice something that might have made your new home more beautiful, or settle for something less and forever regret that you didn't wear the finest on the most important day of your life?
There is another way ... [*hire* one of their dresses]

But hiring dresses or buying second-hand ones does not generally meet with approval, though some women interviewed said they might have considered it had there been better facilities in Swansea. All could cite 'horror stories' about friends of friends who had hired dresses which had proved to be too small, or stained with mud or wine. Many claimed that hiring was no cheaper; others wanted a dress they could keep. The comments of some were interesting:

I wouldn't fancy wearing what someone else had got married in.

If I was going to sink that low I'd have insisted on the registry office and not got married in white.

From the one girl who confessed to hiring a dress came the request to 'keep it quiet'.[30]

I haven't told people at work because they're a catty lot. They'd think of all the things they'd said about not wearing someone else's dress ... about it being dirty ...

The pollution felt to be involved in wearing clothes worn by someone else is particularly interesting since it does not seem to apply to men's clothes. The groom, the best man and the ushers almost invariably hire morning suits and even the shirts and shoes to go with them. In part the fear of pollution seems to be associated with the more intimate contact of the bride's dress, though rationally this is no greater than that of a man's suit or shirt. The attitudes emphasize that the bride is to be pure and unsullied in a way not applicable to the groom. One group of stores specializing in weddings uses this attitude as a big selling point when it claims:

'Every bride-to-be who purchases from our store enjoys the luxury of a brand new wedding gown *never tried on* by anyone before' [my italics].

The purity of the bride is, of course, also symbolized by the colour of her dress. Though people were very often vague about the meaning of other aspects of the ceremony[31] – confetti, horseshoes, etc. – about the whiteness of the dress there was agreement.

... I was going to get married in a gold dress and coat; but when I thought of it, white definitely meant something ... virginal ... purity ..

Studies on the sexual behaviour of young adults have shown that the majority of brides are not, in fact, sexually inexperienced at marriage,[32] but virginity as a concept is not necessarily as absolute as a literalist might suppose. As one young man put it:

There's virgins and virgins. There's girls who've lost their virginity to lots of fellows, and others who lost it only to the one they're marrying.

Thus virginal white seems to cover nubility and sexuality as well as virtue and irreproachability. But innocence and modesty are also indicated – the veiled face, the expectation of the 'blushing' bride, the covered-up style of her dress, the subdued make-up of a young girl. If jewellery is worn (and etiquette books suggest it really is not fitting), it must be real gold or silver, not paste or gilt. In all respects the bride is pure, young, fresh and lacking in artifice.

But 'white' has meanings other than purity. In our culture it is the opposite of black. Whilst 'nothing changes so markedly as the popular taste in colour',[33] black and white clothes have had invariable connotations for at least two hundred years. Black, and specifically lustreless black, is a sign of grief and age, like the black crepe of mourning; white is a sign of innocence, youth and joy.[34] Wedding dresses tend to be lustrous as well as white, suggesting radiance and spirituality in the bride, a radiance coming from inner happiness, tranquillity and purity of heart. As maker and physical symbol of the home she will thus provide a home which is a refuge and retreat for her husband and children from the depressing, corrupt and hurried world.[35]

Those few pregnant brides who do choose to marry in church illustrate some of these notions in their choice of outfits. The wedding may still be lavish, but the bride may not be in white. One mother described her discovery of the outfit for her pregnant daughter:

Well, actually, I seen it in David Evans' window . . . [my daughter] also seen it, and it took her eye. I 'phoned first to find the price – it was a model sent down from London for three days – it cost 72 guineas, and with a head-dress was a hundred pounds. It's gold brocade with mink cuffs.[36]

A couple reporting on the wedding of their friends (a wedding I missed because it was arranged at short notice) said it had taken place in February instead of June because the couple 'had slipped up'.

But she [the bride] had all the trimmings, though she wore cream, and she had planned white. But she wore a veil.

Of another informant's sister:

My sister, when she found she had to get married, my father wanted her to go down to the registry office next day, because he said the Minister wouldn't marry her like that. But she said she wanted a church wedding . . . then she wanted a long dress, to disguise it like so people wouldn't say at once she had to get married. In the end she had a long cream dress. But mam wouldn't let her have a veil or anything.[37]

In another case however:

She wasn't going to wear white, but when she went shopping there was nothing else she fancied. It wasn't an expensive dress though – only from C & A – and she didn't have any bridesmaids.

Thus when the bride is pregnant there are always refinements to the 'proper wedding dress', though often a discerning eye and close proximity to the bride is necessary to detect them. From the back of a church or in a wedding photograph such details are not obvious, and there is no consensus as to exactly what difference in dress is called for. The alterations do, however, have some importance for the actors and I suspect they serve the purpose of deflecting future criticism. 'Fancy her putting on all those airs when she was carrying' can be countered by 'but she didn't – she didn't have any bridesmaids', or whatever. More generally, the fact that a pregnant bride does not have a full white wedding serves to confirm the respectability and 'virginity' of those who do. (Youth is also important in white weddings. Very few brides who marry in church are over thirty – only about 5 per cent. A mature woman, even if marrying for the first time, will usually regard a long white dress and a lot of bridesmaids as girlish and inappropriate.)

Comparison of the woman's costume with that of the man underlines some of the differences in marriage for women and for men. Men at weddings dress formally, usually in dark (but not black) suits. The groom, best man, ushers and bride's father may hire morning dress, but in about half the weddings I studied the grooms simply wore suits – not necessarily new ones. The usual addition was a flower in the buttonhole, a decoration by no means exclusive to weddings.

The change in status from unmarried to married is much more marked in our culture for women than for men. The ritual dress of the bride marks out her transitional status,[38] and she usually keeps the dress as a memento and for luck.[39] The groom's costume is not particularly age-specific, and we would find ludicrous the idea that his clothing should signify anything about his sexuality or indicate whether or not he was a father-to-be as well as a husband-to-be. He is not singled out from other men present in terms of his costume, nor is the costume kept for luck, or regarded as being sacred in any way. However, differences between grooms are expressed in their clothes: upper-class men may own their own set of 'tails', the upper middle class hire them; the middle class and the skilled working class hire morning suits and do not wear top hats; the remainder wear ordinary suits of varying quality. In contrast, the brides, all of whom are becoming married women, housewives and mothers, do not express class differences in their dress.

CONCLUSION

Sociological explanations of why people marry in church have come predominantly from those interested in the churches: those who have looked at the problem in terms of why people have *religious* weddings in a *secular* society (though just how secular modern British society is remains a moot point). My argument is that for participants the choice is whether to have a 'proper wedding' or a 'civic centre do'. In Swansea, the question was not 'Why do so many people get married in church?', but 'Why do some people get married in the register office?' It is the people who have civil ceremonies who feel bound to justify their choice and who are scrutinized for stigma to explain their deviant behaviour.

One may speculate on why there has been an accelerating national trend towards register office weddings. The evidence from Swansea suggests that this is not simply related to decline in religious belief, though obviously if this is occurring it will affect the church's perceived capacity to make more binding marriages. (On the other hand, pregnant brides might well be less hesitant to use the church.) The move to the register office is perhaps due more to the decline in attendance at church and Sunday school, to people's unfamiliarity with the church buildings and clergy and their increasing uncertainty of correct behaviour in church in much the same way as described for the register office (see p. 65). The church also may be seen less as a symbol of the local community.[40] The couples themselves may now be increasingly concerned to save money. (My research was conducted at the end of a period of affluence.) However, the distinctions between the two types of wedding must decline if the stigmas of divorce and premarital pregnancy decline, and with them the 'unrespectability' of marrying in the register office. As more unstigmatized people marry in the register office, the distinction between the two types of wedding will decline still further.

To assess weddings only in terms of whether or not individuals have religious motivations for holding them in church is to neglect the meanings of the actual words and actions of the ritual, and the relationship between dogma and practice. Too often the observer decides that the gothic church or the bride's white dress have not been chosen for religious reasons and therefore dismisses them as 'well nigh meaningless', as anachronistic survivals or as outdated charades.[41]

But rituals or symbols are not unchanging. Participants may attempt to modify or manipulate them, to change them to express minor or major changes in the messages they convey (for example, the use of two rings to show both partners are married).[42] Rituals have to be repeated to reiterate, and rites of passage have to be repeated for each individual. Each repetition allows the accommodation of new developments and new interpretations so that change is endemic.

The form of words in the register office and the liturgy of some church services have statutory authority and change occurs slowly – more slowly, indeed, than many of the clergy would like. Many clergymen allow the bride to omit the promise to obey her husband; others have added blessings for both rings if the couple wish to exchange them; a vicar may wrap the end of his stole around the clasped right hands of the bride and groom, saying 'Those whom God has joined let no man put asunder', an action for which there is no rubric. (The latter is a popular action in the sense that at this point the congregation leans forward to watch, then relaxes with an audible sigh.)

In the wider sense most elements of a wedding are voluntary and chosen. Thus while an historical account may be sought for the origins of particular customs, and while the observer must be cautious not to attribute meanings to customs which derive from cultural values other than those of the actors, to say rituals are meaningless is empirically incorrect. To say they are 'survivals', continued through force of habit, is no explanation of their continued practice.

The analysis of rituals gives interesting insights into the

values and institutions of societies, for rituals 'say things which are difficult to think' – things the participants find difficult or embarrassing to articulate.[43] Rituals and symbols provide comprehensive signs for more or less abstract cultural values. Wedding ceremonies should give us insights into the 'things which are difficult to think' about marriage. Is there then any evidence which suggests that marriage as an institution has the meanings which seem to be carried by the symbols and the ceremonies associated with the start of a particular marriage?

Certainly, marital relationships and the family in our society are accorded a particular transcendental nature, a sacramental element. We do talk of 'the sanctity of the family', and forming a new family unit is very different from making other forms of contract.[44] A church wedding is thought more thorough because people believe that God can help in achieving the ideal – a binding, life-long, pervasive, holy union. The sacredness and the drama surrounding the acting out of the change of status of the participants impresses the status passage upon them and makes it known to the world at large.

The concern with the correctness of the ritual and with 'personalizing' the ceremony reflect and emphasize the cultural stress on individualism and free choice of spouse and of the decision to marry.[45] Cultural values about the power structure of the family and sex roles are reflected in the focus on the bride rather than the groom, underlining the fact that marriage involves a greater change of status for women than for men. The father of the bride in handing her over to the groom affirms who is the head of both her family of origin and the family being created by the marriage.[46] The very great difference between the clothing of female principals and male principals emphasizes the difference between the sexes.[47]

Some writers seem to suggest that the implications of a wife's submission carried by some of the symbols of the wedding – virginal white, the ring, the woman's change of name – do not correspond with marriage as we understand it today.[48] Obviously, the same symbol may mean different things to different groups or different things to the same group at different times; a bride, a groom, their relatives and the world at large may produce at any one time differing interpretations of the decision to conform to 'proper behaviour'. But overall, I believe these to be symbols of the general cultural values of the wife's submissiveness and I believe them to be in accord with marriage today.

The ideological stress often given by people writing about the family (both journalists and sociologists) to the attainment of equality between the sexes in marriage, masks and diverts attention from women's continuing dependent status. The labour market, statutory provisions, administrative and business practices and customary procedures combine to keep women dependent. The legal, economic and social position of women within the family has changed, but this does not mean that the sexes are now equal or that marital roles have the equality implied by the labels 'joint', 'complementary' and 'symmetrical'. For though the legal independence of married women has greatly increased since the turn of the century they still do not have the same legal rights as men; a wife may contribute considerable personal strength to a marriage but be unhappy to have a husband who is seen to be and spoken of as 'weaker' than she;[49] wives may be less deferential to their husbands than in the past but their earnings are often perceived as being only for 'little extras' (and while the wages of women remain on average about half those of men marriage remains the best way for a woman to attain a reasonable standard of living); certainly the dual standard of sexual behaviour is also still alive and well.[50] A wife is still expected to mould her life round her husband's, to live where it suits him, to keep his timetable and style of life, to care for their children and to provide him with sexual and domestic services.

In arguing that rituals provide symbols of cultural values and point up some frequently (and significantly) denied power structures in the society, I am not implying that rituals are mere reflections of the socio-political order. The symbolic system has an autonomy and viability of its own and there is a close, continual and dialectical relationship between it and the social relationships of individuals in the society.

Those who criticize people for having white weddings while

claiming that marriage as an institution is a 'Good Thing', may have in mind the personal relationships which do develop between two people, providing them both with long-term (and even life-long) support and love. However, these relationships are not restricted to marriage and indeed there is much in marriage as an institution which is antipathetic to them.[51]

On the other hand, if one does not support marriage as currently defined, to attack the ritual of the wedding is *not* to attack the shadow rather than the substance. For symbols are meaningful and effective. Social dramas

> try to effect a transformation in the psyches of the participants, conditioning their attitudes and sentiments, repetitively renewing beliefs, values and norms and thereby creating and re-creating the basic categorical imperatives on which the group depends for its existence.[52]

The social dramas of weddings re-create the 'categorical imperatives' of the family, the state and also usually the church.

To put this another way, participation in rituals and the use of symbols may cause people to feel particular sentiments, to accept norms and concepts, to objectify and thereby confirm social roles. The ceremonial may conjure up belief; attention to symbols may cause a value to be accepted or accepted more strongly; acting out a role may give that role more reality and importance. People may choose to marry in church because it is the 'done thing' and pressures are put on them to conform. But in participating in the ritual they will themselves be pushed towards accepting a traditional and conformist view of marriage.

Obviously, for the 'liberated' man or woman the trip down the aisle is not the equivalent of the road to Damascus, but the whole preparation for the wedding will cause changes in self-evaluation. Most obviously, the couple will be repeatedly told they are becoming a married couple with all that this entails. More generally, the gamut of values expressed in little girls wanting to be bridesmaids, the emphasis for girls on their prettiness, their youth, their sexual attractiveness (yet their chastity, too), as sources and evidence of their success as women, all find a focus in the image of the bride.

For a 'companionate', sexually libertarian couple to undergo the ceremony is, at the very least, a recognition of the continuing power of their parents, the community, the church and socially structured sex roles (in the sense of scripted, differentiated, unequal parts which exist as constraining forces even though the couple may try to work out their own interpretations).

Our feminist ire should not be aroused by the apparent anachronism of the rituals but by what they confirm and tell us about the continuing characteristics of marriage as an institution.

4. Marriage and Sex

People in all societies expect sex to be part of marriage, but sex outside marriage often causes trouble for married people. The problem seems to be less with sex itself than with the fact that adulterous physical intimacy often leads to long-lasting, strongly-felt attachments, and this personal sexual relation outside marriage can threaten the personal tie between husband and wife. Different people have solved this problem in different ways, including the familiar one of banning any kind of sex other than that between husband and wife. Encouraging lasting personal sexual relations with spouses and with other people simultaneously is thought by many to be the ideal solution, but this seems difficult in practice. Other attempts to reconcile marital and adulterous sex by permitting both have done so by making either the marital or the adulterous relation the personal relation to the exclusion of the other.

To seek sexual pleasure and companionship with one person while being married to another is perhaps more common than combining personal marital relations with institutionalized impersonal adultery, but examples of both can be found. When the former occurs, greater licence is often given to men than to their wives, for whom sexual attraction and romantic love must remain a spiritual rather than a carnal experience.[1] That men may need and desire sexual stimulation in and for itself may be given recognition, while 'nice' women may be supposed not to enjoy sex or to suffer it only so long as they will have the children they 'naturally' want as a result of it.

As a general rule, a modest woman seldom desires any sexual gratification for herself. She submits to her husband, but only to please him; and, but for the desire for maternity, would far rather be relieved from his attentions. The married woman has no wish to be treated on the footing of a mistress.[2]

Given this kind of disparity, wives will not be expected to be stimulating sexual companions, and men may seek sexual excitement and emotional satisfaction with women other than their wives. The socialization of women to accept these limitations on their own sexuality may mean that they do not object to their husband's activities, or at least suffer them with some equanimity.

This kind of sexual licence of married men may be accorded them only if their activities do not involve the wives of other men or women who will eventually become wives. Women may be divided into wives and potential wives on the one hand; entertainers, prostitutes and mistresses on the other. The means by which women become the latter are many and varied; parents may sell their daughters where female children are considered useless, a drain on resources and an expense to marry off;[3] daughters may be given as tribute to powerful men; women may 'fall from grace' because of their indiscretions or failure to conform to the behaviour appropriate to modest women; they may be the victims of financial hardship or deception, or deprived of male protection. The distinction between these women and virtuous ones may be extreme or fairly tenuous; their relations with men may be casual and mercenary or personal and enduring; though often condemned to a lowly social position devoid of honour and prestige, they may occasionally be more broadly and highly educated than those destined to become wives, being socially acceptable and influential in their own right as well as enjoying, for example, the reflected glory of being the suitable companions of philosophers, poets and statesmen, as they were in ancient Greece.

Under these circumstances the acceptability of a husband's adultery is quite different from a wife's. A wife's adultery may be highly problematic because it is seen as an infringement of the husband's rights or causes him loss of face and social standing. If this is the case, claims for compensation from the lover, punishment of the wife, steps taken by the husband and his kin to guard his honour, may serve to protect the marriage and re-establish the *status quo*.

The arrangements and attitudes I have outlined are typical where spouses are not couples, where marital relations are relatively impersonal and where men and women are different and unequal. However, as husbands and wives increasingly come to regard themselves as couples and to emphasize the personal quality of their relationship, extramarital sex of any kind may become more problematic. Mechanisms of the kind suggested above cannot protect a personal relation in the same way; experience cannot be wiped out, there is no return to the *status quo*. Many couples find they cannot adjust to this experience which threatens their identity as a couple : others, rather than banning extramarital sex or dealing with it as and when it occurs, agree to conditions under which it is permissible for both spouses. These rules often incorporate the traditional plea of adulterous spouses – 'it was only sex'. In other words, spouses are permitted sexual relations with others as long as these relations are limited, impersonal and do not lead to the formation of a competing couple.[4] While not insisting on fidelity, such spouses emphasize their own identity as a couple by trying to control the circumstances under which the boundaries may be transgressed. This emphasis on the couple suggests both that the rules must be the same for either partner and that they are applicable to both married and unmarried couples.

However, various more institutionalized forms of mate-swapping have developed in some western societies and for some spouses extramarital sex has become a kind of joint recreational activity, like tennis. The 'swingers' of the West coast of the U.S.A. provide a well-documented example. Husband and wife insist that other sexual relations occur only under specified circumstances – by private arrangement with other couples or at parties convened for the purpose and governed by their own rules of appropriate behaviour. Strangers, people of whom the couple have neither knowledge or experience, are preferred, and no personal relation should subsequently develop. To contact or to see a person with whom one 'swings' outside the approved context may be considered a great breach of swinging norms.[5]

Unattached people with no existing loyalty to spouses or lovers may be avoided and the couple may seek constantly to demonstrate that their own relation

... still does command their paramount loyalty. Willingness to forgo an attractive swinging opportunity because the spouse or lover is uninterested or opposed is one example of such a demonstration.[6]

As long as couples stress their emotional unity and the purely recreational nature of the extramarital sex it seems to pose little threat, and may even be seen as beneficial by those involved – 'those who swing together stay together'.[7]

Like the gentlemen of high status whose pursuits of great loves outside impersonal marriage contracts enliven the pages of many history books, swingers look for sexual pleasures outside marriage while hoping to keep the marriage intact, but they emphasize the equality of the sexes in their pursuit of sexual excitement as well as the fact that 'swinging' is something couples do together with other couples rather than something which individuals do independently.

A more traditional approach is embodied in Japanese society, a society in which men long enjoyed the social advantages of marriage to one woman and took their leisure and pleasure with others. The behaviour of Japanese women has long been marked by subservience to men and their desires and comforts – those who were to entertain men often being trained in music, dancing and the arts of conversation, accommodating the male in his search for relaxation and female companionship; those who married traditionally observed strict rules of etiquette and priority in the treatment of their husbands, arising before them in the mornings, bathing only after them, waiting on them at table, often eating inferior food, not sitting with them in the house or accompanying them to places of recreation and culture outside it, going to bed only after their husbands had retired for the night. After an arranged marriage, much more the concern of households than individuals, a bride became subject to the authority and whims of the men within the household to which she moved, controlled in everyday affairs by her mother-in-law.[8] The emphasis on the male line made the bride's position in the household relatively secure only when she had fulfilled her primary duty of producing a male heir to continue it and when she had become mistress of her own household.[9]

Many of these traditional aspects of Japanese family life have been changing, but traditional attitudes and practices usually only gradually give way to new ideas and patterns of behaviour and increasing industrialization may even for a time increase the importance of traditional practices.[10] Because it is a highly complex and industrialized society with a completely different cultural heritage from that of its western equivalents, the study of marital relations in Japan is particularly interesting in any comparative consideration of such relations. In the following chapter, 'Aspects of Japanese Marriage', Helmut Morsbach, a psychologist who lived and taught in Japan and studied the changing attitudes of young Japanese people, explores some aspects of Japanese marriage and the changes which have occurred.

Aspects of Japanese Marriage [1]

HELMUT MORSBACH

In many Western countries 'the couple' is a clearly identifiable unit, and has been so for many centuries. In Japan, by comparison, it is a new concept. Until the drastic post-war rewriting in 1948 of the Civil Code 'the couple' had no legally defined status inside the Japanese family system. For this reason a discussion of 'the couple' has to deal in some detail with aspects of the Japanese family system before the Second World War.

Certain difficulties arise when trying to compare any social aspect of 'the Japanese' with 'the West'. Western countries differ among themselves, and some of these differences which pertain to 'the couple' are described (or implied) in several of the other contributions to this volume. To represent 'the West' in a comparison with Japan, a gross over-simplification is necessary: the reader's concept of a hypothetical British couple of middle or upper-middle-class background will have to suffice.

CONTEMPLATING MARRIAGE

In the days before 1945 when a family member was of marriageable age, it was traditionally the household, 'stem family', or *ie* which made decisions as regards the choice of spouse and not the individual concerned.[2] Weddings were described as taking place between *ie* A and *ie* B – individuals were less important. However, this was not a symmetrical linking of family lines, but the recruitment of a female into a male line which could not continue to produce male descendants without her.[3] Households interested in finding spouses for their members were concerned to avoid anyone descended from outcastes,[4] or any *ie* of unsuitable rank in the community, or in which there were undesirable occupations, unpaid debts, religious wrangles or illness.[5]

This concern on both sides led to bargaining in which each party tended to exaggerate its assets and hide its liabilities. The chances of disagreement were therefore great, and a 'go-between' was (and still is) popular to minimize face-to-face conflicts during the search for a suitable match and while the arrangements for the wedding were being made. (These 'go-betweens' sometimes also helped the husband and wife to solve later problems in their married life.)[6]

Two factors made this system of arranged marriage, *miai kekkon*, popular, especially among the middle and upper-middle class. Firstly, premarital associations between boys and girls were frowned upon, and thus young people had little chance to meet suitable marriage partners on their own. Girls were especially protected and correspondingly inexperienced, while the only way for boys to gain heterosexual experience was to visit red-light districts with their seniors or peers. Since this cost money, the experience was limited in most cases.

The second important factor was the nature of relationships between parents and children, relations which have not greatly changed. Adolescents (and even grown-ups) are emotionally dependent on their parents, especially the mother. Child-rearing practices encourage this dependence, which usually lasts a lifetime and is seen at its strongest between the mother and her first-born son.

Contrary to middle-class practice in the U.S.A. and northern Europe, early independence of children is not encouraged in Japan. Simple pleasures, being cared for, taking hot baths together, are greatly enjoyed and potentially disruptive issues such as aggression, competition and sex are avoided. The psychological dependence between mother and child has been studied in great detail and compared with matched samples from Western countries.[7] One writer goes so far as to speak of 'Jewish mothering in Japan'.[8] Physical closeness is also emphasized, and even in relatively affluent families with large numbers of rooms in their houses, there is still a tendency (a) for parents and children to sleep in the same room and (b) for the youngest child to sleep under the covers with the mother and the second youngest with the father. Sometimes this pattern is continued until the child is ten years old.[9]

An important concept in this area is that of *amaeru*, which can be translated as 'to depend and presume on another's love', or 'to seek and bask in another's indulgence'.[10] In the West such behaviour would be seen as immature, appropriate only for babies, associated with the 'spoilt child'. In Japan it is acceptable even among adults in many situations.

From these general observations it follows that security was traditionally gained in marriage if a match (*o-miai*) was arranged by parents with the help of a go-between, although usually the prospective bride and groom had a say in the matter and could sometimes even veto a match they personally detested. In response to pictures of the Thematic Apperception Test,[11] people frequently told stories of unhappy marriages resulting from the fact that the couple had chosen each other on the basis of the selfish emotion of love. This reflects the attitudes of Tokugawa Japan when:

... the general value/attitudes considered a love marriage (*ren-ai kekkon*) as something improper, indecent, 'egoistic', or something similar to an extramarital affair in Western Christian moral codes. To be 'proper', a marriage needed to be arranged by parents and other elder members of the families concerned.[12]

On the whole, a pre-marital love affair between the couple was unacceptable in the Confucian-warrior value system of the time because it asserted individual interest rather than the more important group interest. Love matches were also regarded with suspicion because boys and girls of equivalent high-status families had almost no chance to meet secretly and fall in love. When love affairs did develop they usually therefore involved a relatively high-status boy and a servant girl – an 'impossible' match. Sometimes the only way out was a desperate but honourable one – double suicide. With such an act, aggression was turned inwards, individualism paid its gruesome price, and the family system remained unscathed.

Since the end of the Second World War, 'love marriages' have become increasingly popular, but although most present-day adolescents have the ideal of a love match, they soon find out how difficult it is to meet 'marriageable' partners on their own. Ideally the husband should be about three to five years older than his wife, which largely rules out love matches between childhood playmates, and also between, for example, students belonging to the same year of university entry. Secondly, as I mentioned previously, adolescents are taught very little about how to behave towards the opposite sex when they are alone together. Boys usually are too shy to take the initiative because they have been 'mothered'. In any case, boys and girls commonly meet others in a group, not singly. Traditionally, if a couple were seen alone in public, it was expected that they would make up their minds whether or not to marry after a few meetings. But privacy remains a scarce commodity in Japan. Casual home visits by persons other than family members and household friends are uncommon, leaving only coffee shops and cinemas as places to meet. The usual layout of coffee shops affords a semi-privacy, but sometimes there is a separate section (for example, the top floor) where sofas with high backs are turned in such a way that couples are relatively invisible to others.

The results of attitude surveys among present-day adolescents give the strong impression that almost all of them were planning to marry mainly for love. However, as the time approaches when the individual is old enough to marry, another consideration is added: the increasing realization that the couple will be financially dependent on the parents for several years after marriage and therefore cannot go much against their wishes. A complete break with one's family is to be avoided, and, as a result, many so-called 'love marriages' are often no more than semi-arranged ones where the couple have somewhat more chance than usual to get to know each other before the wedding day.[13]

Traditionally, the kind of premarital 'love' seen as non-threatening to future stability of the marriage was of a special kind:

When my Hiroshima professor-interpreter heard that one of his nephews had fallen in love, he feared the worst. Nevertheless, he agreed to serve as a matchmaker and began his investigation:

'I was pleasantly surprised to find that this was a pure love based only on occasional glances at each other on the street-car which both rode every day. There were no conversations, no dates, no intimacy. I felt that such a couple *should* marry because this was not a sordid love affair involving pleasure and self-indulgence in which people have already reaped rewards. Rather this was a restrained, self-disciplined, spiritual love.'[14]

But love frequently did not enter into the picture at all, as the following quote shows:

I was the youngest among my brothers and sisters. They were all married and I was left alone as a single woman. My mother got high blood pressure from worry about my being unmarried. My family were anxious to arrange a marriage as soon as possible and showed my mother the picture of my prospective husband. I was thus in haste to marry. After the *miai* I did not love my partner but I married him. It was not for my sake but because I wanted to relieve my mother and my family of their anxiety that I decided to marry.[15]

WEDDING AND MARRIAGE REGISTRATION

Since a wedding united two previously unrelated households it was (and still is) a costly ceremony of great social importance. In traditional farming communities the household receiving the spouse carried the greater part of the expense, since it would be the one to gain a full-time worker. People often talked of 'to get *tema* (labour)' rather than 'to get a bride'.[16] The ties created between households were considered more important than the union between bride and groom.

Traditionally, no religious sanctions were required and no priests were present. Wedding ceremonies where a Shinto priest officiates have become common only during the last fifty years.[17] The custom started among the urban populations and spread to rural areas after the war. However, even though the implications of marriage have recently become more similar to those in the West, to announce a wedding as 'wedding ceremony of *ie* X and *ie* Y' is still common.

The great importance of the household is also expressed symbolically in the traditional kimono worn by brides in rural areas:

When she [the bride] leaves her parental house, she is dressed up in a *white* ceremonial kimono, the same colour as the shroud in which corpses are dressed. The meaning of this is that she will not return to her parental household alive; by her marriage she changes her membership forever from the household of her father to that of her husband. In fact she will be buried in the grave of her husband's family, never in that of her parents, unless she is divorced without remarriage.[18]

The headgear worn by the bride also expresses her subordinate position. Called *tsunokakushi*, which can be translated as 'horn-hiding head-dress', it served to hide the horns of jealousy or signified the bride's eager wish to be free of jealousy, despite the fact that she would probably be given good reason for it.[19]

Only the registration of marriage is legally binding in Japan, and not the wedding ceremony itself. Very often in the past a marriage was registered only when the wife had fulfilled her main obligation towards her new family by giving birth to an heir. Often, too, registration was delayed to see how well the new wife got on with her husband's family in general and her mother-in-law in particular. In any dispute the bride could expect no help from her husband, who had been taught since childhood to obey his parents' wishes and who therefore took their side rather than hers.

Registration became increasingly important with a post-war law stating that a registered bride could claim half the family property.[20] But since young girls often were, and are, ignorant of the necessity to register the marriage or could do little to facilitate its registration even if they did know, many 'marriages' ended in separation before they ever legally existed.

MARRIED LIFE

In the traditional system and for the eldest sons in 'traditional' farming communities today, life does not change very much after marriage since the strong relationship with the mother remains unbroken. Even if they leave their mothers on marriage, such sons show a strong tendency to continue the mother–son role with a new person, their wife.

So accustomed are men to getting maximum satisfaction from a maternal source that many seem to seek in marriage also a maternal relation. The husband is markedly dependent on his wife, she reciprocates with the same watchful care she will eventually give to her child, and all the world around them reinforces this relationship with praise. Sex need not be the focus of such a relationship. Sociologically speaking, a strong sexual relationship is potentially harmful to the vertical unity of a stem family and is discouraged; psychologically speaking, tests give little evidence of a strong sexual bond between husband and wife. (Yet it is hazardous to conclude merely from sparse or absent testimony that the bond is unimportant.)[21]

A husband may, for example, *amaeru* to his wife, or vice versa, or both to each other. Failure to *amaeru* or to respond to it is seen as a handicap in such marital relations. Westerners might conclude that a person seeking to *amaeru* puts himself or herself in a submissive position, thus emphasizing the hierarchical relationship. However, *amaeru* mitigates the 'harshness' of the vertical relationship based on dominance and submission:[22] it could be said to be the female principle which enters the male principle of authority relationships, possibly making such relationships in Japan essentially different from those in the West.[23]

For the bride there is no such relatively smooth continuation of previous life patterns when she marries. For her, marriage is essentially entry into another family group and not the establishment of a couple relationship with a particular man.[24] Traditionally the term applied to her is *yome* (married woman of the youngest generation) rather than the Japanese term for wife. A young bride faces many problems of adjustment and her feelings of loneliness are often aggravated by the fact that she can expect little help from others in the neighbourhood experiencing the same conditions.

In Japan ... the mother-in-law and daughter-in-law problem is preferably solved inside the household, and the luckless bride has to struggle through in isolation, without help from her own family, relatives or neighbours. By comparison, in agricultural villages in India not only can the bride make long visits to her parental home but her brother may frequently visit her and help her out in various ways. Mother-in-law and daughter-in-law quarrels are conducted in raised voices that can be heard all over the neighbourhood, and when such shouting is heard all the women (of the same caste) in the neighbourhood come over to help out. The mutual assistance among the wives who came from other villages is a quite enviable factor completely unimaginable among Japanese women.[25]

The bride traditionally occupies the lowest social position inside the household and falls under the direct supervision of her mother-in-law, who sees to it that the newcomer is explicitly instructed in the 'ways of the family' which stress the importance of family solidarity and continuity. Frequently this dominance–submission relationship is tinged with cruelty, which is, perhaps, not surprising given that the elder woman herself underwent the same 'hazing' when she came in from the outside as a stranger. Conflict between mother-in-law and daughter-in-law is considered almost normal;[26] the former's proverbial jealousy tends to imperil the emergence of a strong 'couple' feeling between the newlyweds. A mother finds it hard to lose some of her son's love, one of the few satisfactions of her life.

The young wife's role competes with hers: she is a young *mother* intended to comfort and serve the husband in a maternal role. If she wins him, the mother might well be the loser.[27]

The husband's sister(s) also frequently harboured negative feelings towards the bride and one proverb warns that to have one sister-in-law is like having a hundred devils.

The bride can gain status only by giving birth to a child, preferably a boy. This also relieves her loneliness, for she is at last able to express unreserved love towards another human being. If the child is a boy, she has the pleasant prospect of living with him for the rest of her life.

She was taught to serve men – here she can do it gladly ... The same protective relations, the same reluctance to have him do for himself any household service she can do for him, extends to her husband. Coupled with her sexlessness in dress and manner before the men of the house, this maternalism sets the boy's image of what a woman should be in the house. The magic is applied to any woman he respects.[28]

Real security and status are usually achieved only when the mother-in-law retires by 'handing over the spoon', an event which commonly coincides with the formal retirement *inkyo* of the head of the household, or after his death. It is quite understandable that the younger woman, having had to wait so long to reach her goal, should then, in turn, make it heavy going for the successor her own son brings to the household.

Except perhaps in old age the husband–wife relation is rarely one of partnership. The husband has exclusive sexual rights to his wife, but the prevailing Confucian ethic sees to it that the reverse is not the case. Sometimes in the past a husband even had the obligation to keep a mistress if his wife was infertile, because continuation of the family name was of paramount importance. Aizawa Seishisai, scholar of the late Tokugawa period, was scornful of Westerners, whom he saw as being little better than beasts: they would rather die without heirs than take a concubine to ensure their succession.[29]

In the modern and largely urban setting, more and more families are of the nuclear type, and the 'mother-in-law problem' thus loses some of its threat. This development no doubt helps to strengthen the 'couple' bond, at least during the early years of marriage. But other factors now intrude, because the typical Japanese 'salaryman' (white-collar worker) must, on the whole, devote more mental and physical energy to his firm than his Western counterpart. This holds especially true after normal office hours, because the Western attitude 'that is not my business' in response to a non-routine request by superiors is severely frowned upon.[30] The in-group involvement is very strong, and with life-long employment security inside one particular firm the saying, 'It is easier to change one's wife than one's firm' is more than a mere joke. The hold which the firm has on the husband tends to increase as he moves up the promotion ladder where he can command bigger expense accounts for 'after-hour' entertainment of clients – a time when the atmosphere is relaxed and business deals can be discussed informally. Furthermore, nights on the town with his peer group allow the average 'salaryman' to enjoy life with the aid of alcohol and bar hostesses, whereas at home relaxation in the crowded *danchi* (high-rise flat) or tiny house is less easily achieved. In modern times the young couple, just married, has of course many romantic, Western notions of doing things together, but the bond between the husband and his firm becomes increasingly strong as the years go by. The wife will naturally tend to resent the time after office hours which is spent away from home, but, by and by, has to reconcile herself to a life largely independent from his. This weakening of the bond is hastened by the arrival of her first child, which allows her to turn her love to the baby so obviously in need of care.

Through extensive emotional and time-consuming commitment to his in-group at the place of work, the average Japanese male leaves his wife (and mother) relatively free to rule over household affairs.[31] This role dualism has its origins in *samurai* traditions: since men in that class seldom bothered themselves with money matters, it was up to their wives to balance income and expenditure. As it was below a man's dignity to involve himself in the woman's sphere, her authority inside the home was rarely challenged.[32] In matters concerning outsiders (for example, marriage of children) she could not show open disagreement with her husband, but usually influenced his decision behind the scenes. Other classes showed different patterns, depending, in part, on the extent to which the *samurai* ethics were adopted. The tendency of women to control the purse-strings persists to the present day, especially in urban families where the husband is a company employee. The term 'hundred-yen husband',[33] popular in the sixties, well illustrates this: the husband hands over his entire salary to his wife and is then allocated about one hundred yen (approximately 20p) in pocket money per day which he takes to work. He very often has no idea how his salary is being allocated and does not particularly care to know, since this is traditionally his wife's concern. She keeps the account book up to date every night before retiring, and new account books are regularly included as December supplements of women's magazines.

A daily allowance of one hundred yen might have been sufficient to pay the average Japanese husband's extra expenses twelve years ago, but it is no longer so in most cases. However, the change is a numerical and not a qualitative one: the basic assumption is not affected by inflation. The existence of such a concept highlights a rather important difference in the relationships of couples between Japan and Western societies:

We must ... remember how European views of history and women have warped our understanding of the role of women in Japanese history. With the coming of the Middle Ages in Europe, the position of women underwent a great change. The growth of chivalry meant that women were either revered as princesses or used as servants. There was no in-between. Whether a woman was the object for a man's devotion of whether she was regarded as someone to be used, her ability was either underestimated or ignored. In Europe, women have never become household managers. Even in the Middle Ages, however, Japanese women had a great deal of power inside the house ... If a woman took one step outside the house, however, she moved outside her sphere of activity and everything was left to the man ... it is feasible to think that because the women were so excellent at running the home, the men were freed from such worries. They were thus able to give their undivided loyalty to their overlords.[34]

This ability of Japanese women (as well as men) to play a variety of roles more convincingly than average Westerners tends to give the casual Western observer a one-sided picture, since he or she is likely to see only one role of many and tends to generalize on the basis of it.

In Japanese society the capacity to endure in order to succeed reaches its apotheosis in the role of the married woman; as does the capacity to identify with one's 'superior'. Women identify readily with males carrying out their expected role behaviour, an identification that is an essential part of the capacity to feel a deep sense of accomplishment as a mother. This capacity for endurance on the part of the Japanese woman permits her to go through what seems to be almost incredible acts of metamorphosis in later stages of her life cycle.

As we have suggested ... the maid can be construed as at a larval stage and the meek bride as at the pupal stage of a later horrendous mother-in-law. So, too, the eager male apprentice, for good or ill, is potentially the larval stage of a future dominant master, albeit many males carry on a continuing larval existence as more-or-less well cared-for drones.[35]

While the wife is usually powerful at home, the husband is fairly free to do what he likes outside it, provided that he regularly brings home his pay. If the wife does control the money earned, the husband is rarely able to paint the town red with the 'allowance' available, unless he is able to keep bonus payments secret from his wife or has a substantial expense account at his place of work.

In Japanese business circles, female entertainers are often used to break the ice of after-hours business discussions by skilful conversation and the liberal pouring of drinks. Sooner or later a man in the city is likely to have some attachment with one or more women in the entertainment world. This might simply be an occasional visit to her establishment, where he specifically asks for her by name (she thereby becoming his *shimei*, i.e. the 'designated one', which increases her earnings); or he might have enough money and authority over his wife to set her up as his mistress in a separate household. (The Chinese custom of having the wife and one or more concubines living in the same house has not been practised in Japan.)

The traditional Japanese wife simply had to bear this situation and find her solace elsewhere:

My father made a fortune in the stock market and needed to be notified of business emergencies, so he always told my mother where he was going when he went with his concubine. My mother says she never felt any jealousy. Of course, hers was not a love match. She was interested only in her parents and her children. Her husband was only a source of money for her to use for her children. She is a perfect Japanese wife, uncomplaining, and spoiling her husband.[36]

In fact, a man in his middle years who has attained wealth and power is still frequently expected to sport a mistress as a status symbol and display of 'conspicuous consumption'. Such a man even risks being called '*hara ga chiisai*' ('weak-stomached') if he does not get involved:

One Japanese informer told of a lawyer who wanted to run for the national Diet but was advised against it because, 'You don't have the guts to have a concubine.' According to this informant, 'People *expect* a prominent politician or businessman to have a concubine' and wonder what is wrong if he doesn't.[37]

Japanese men generally keep their home life separate from the business sphere. Since mistresses usually belong to the latter, their major attraction is frequently not only sex, but the way in which they can be used to impress others. Some writers have called this a 'little boy mode of behaviour which Freudians might label "phallic phase"', ascribing it to the tendency in Japanese culture to tolerate self-centred, juvenile dependency in males who generally pay little attention to women except as maternal figures who give them comfort.[38]

Unlike European countries, where mistress-keeping is mostly secret and often associated with feelings of guilt, there can be striking openness in Japan, though the kind of incident described below is probably rare:

I remember how one well-known Japanese academic in Kyoto would come to my parties in the company now of his dowdy but highly intelligent wife and now of his elegant but bird-brained mistress. Naïvely, I used to wonder if the wife were aware that she had to take her turn; until at my farewell party, a trio came up my steps – husband in front, and behind, twittering to each other, the two ladies in Kimono and *zōri* (formal sandals). In no other country of the world can sexual pleasure, in however bizarre a form, be both so accessible and so little alloyed with fuss, guilt or anger.[39]

While the hierarchical relationship between 'superior' males and 'inferior' females seems fairly clear-cut in public, a deep-down ambivalence and anxiety about this state of affairs seems to remain in many males.[40]

CHANGES SINCE THE SECOND WORLD WAR

The new law after the Second World War, abolishing the legal status of the *ie* and substituting the nuclear family, caused a great change in Japanese social life. Japanese society had of course changed considerably in other ways (e.g. in industry) during the preceding seventy odd years, and the *ie* had not remained unaffected. During this period the number of persons living as members of an extended family under one roof had gradually decreased, and with rapid urbanization the number of nuclear families increased, especially in the cities. Although this might in many cases have led to a decreased authority of the *ie* head, his legal powers were unaffected. The family hierarchy with its strong emphasis on verticality was reflected (and often consciously praised as a model) in the hierarchial structuring of business firms, especially the large *zaibatsu* (conglomerates). Here, so-called *oyabun–kobun* (parent–child) relationships were stressed as being the cornerstone of stability and growth and good relationships inside the firm.[41]

Under the new law the wife (and not only the husband) is now able to divorce the spouse on grounds of infidelity. Furthermore, the category of *shoshi* has been abolished. This was the term for the husband's illegitimate children which, until that time, his wife had to accept as her own.[42] 'Cooperation' became the new slogan, at least in theory, concerning decisions such as where the couple would live and how they should exercise their parental rights. The increasing popularity of *renai kekkon* (love marriage) did not, however, necessarily indicate a greater equality in the couple relationship:

... the association (between greater 'merging and sharing' and love marriage) is only a weak one. This suggests the qualification that the 'love' insisted on for the 'love' marriage is not necessarily a love between equals implying equal regard for the wishes of both partners and the sharing of responsibilities and interests which is the Western romantic ideal. It can be no more than an assertion by the man of the right of individual choice of the woman who shall be his bond-maid. A love marriage is not a precondition for greater sharing of interests and responsibilities; this trend affects the relations of couples married by arrangement too.[43]

A major factor influencing the couple relationship is the improved post-war education of women generally. The experience of being on their own in some job for a few years between the end of their education and marriage makes it less likely that husbands will treat their wives as extreme inferiors. However, with baby-sitting by non-kin still strongly disapproved of, if the mother wants to work part-time outside the home relatives must mind the children. Many Japanese women also think that they ought to be full-time mothers. Even when they have to work for financial reasons they want to stop work as soon as possible to become full-time mothers.[44] Those who do keep working (if their mothers or mothers-in-law are baby-sitting and cooking for them) often feel guilty about this state of affairs and suffer from inner conflicts.[45]

When asked about their future plans, only one in a sample of thirty adolescent Japanese girls mentioned that she wanted to have a job outside the home while married, contrasting strongly with the 57 per cent of American girls in a comparable sample who did want such a job.[46]

While many Western customs have been taken over by the Japanese, those concerning the ideal of 'putting women on a pedestal' have created confusion among Japanese couples. Should the husband now be more polite to his wife in public? And how does this tally with their behaviour behind closed doors? In spite of Western ideals concerning equality and love in marriage, to live this way in Japan is problematic. What is lacking above all is the pre-marital training on how to behave in a relaxed way with a person of the opposite sex. Old behaviour patterns are not likely to change fast, as the following observation indicates:

When talking with us, many (Japanese women) expressed envy of American wives who go out with husbands, and many were curious as to what it would be like. Several went so far as to try it for the first time during our stay, but reported that they were too tense to enjoy themselves. When out with husbands and their friends, they have to be so careful to behave properly that it is difficult to go beyond polite pleasantries. Moreover, they must be so retiring that they generally prefer the more relaxed times with their lady friends. One wife, upon hearing about a husband and a wife going on a trip for a few days, responded, 'How nice', but after a moment's reflection she added, 'but what would they talk about for so long?'[47]

5. Marital Harmony and Conflict

However personal or impersonal the relation between husband and wife in any society, or however limited or encompassing, marriage is usually considered a long-term commitment. But this commitment is one that can almost invariably be reduced or ended under specified circumstances.[1] Marriage ends when a contract is dissolved and the most common grounds for dissolution may simply be breach of contract – failure to fulfil obligations, overstepping of rights. Often only the person whose rights have been infringed may seek divorce, may repudiate the partner who has committed the offence or not fulfilled the obligations.[2] Only in some societies is dissatisfaction of one or both parties with the personal relation between them recognized as sufficient grounds for divorce. In England only as recently as 1971 has recognition been given to the fact that the existence of a normal marital relation and the ability of two people to get along together is an important criterion in deciding whether or not they should stay married to each other, and that there is little to be gained from preserving the 'marriage' in a minimal legal sense.[3]

Certain forms of behaviour like adultery and cruelty may strain, if not end, both some marriage contracts and some personal relations between husbands and wives. But very often the kinds of strains to which more personal marital relations are subject are quite different from those to which relations more limited to and focused on obligation and duty are subject, particularly if people with these relatively impersonal marital relations are otherwise enmeshed in a variety of personal relations offering them companionship and support.

To take southern Spain as my example again, husbands and wives often quarrel over the alleged inadequacy of one spouse in their duties and obligations, or over their deviation from proper behaviour of men and women respectively. But wives are usually content if their husbands give them sufficient money, do not abuse them physically, treat the children well and do not bring the family into disrepute by drunkenness and attentions to other women. Husbands are similarly satisfied if their wives are thrifty managers, keep a clean home and their children under control, provide regular meals and are mindful of their social position. When they do quarrel over failure to comply with these expectations and obligations, the women at least usually regard the quarrels firstly as being only what is expected of marriage and, secondly, as being insignificant. Wives are not at all reluctant to make marital disagreements known or to report on the weaknesses of their husbands and almost invariably draw strength from the sympathy and support they automatically expect and receive from other women. Husbands' complaints and criticisms are seldom taken to indicate anything about wives' inadequacies, for men are, by definition, arbitrary, unreasonable, stubborn and lacking in sensitivity. These intrinsically male characteristics account for the unreasonableness of the demands they are prone to make and suggest that to argue with them is simply a waste of time and energy. Submission to their husbands' demands is equated to the need to indulge a recalcitrant child, demanding patient tolerance and the condescension appropriate to dealings with people who cannot be expected to know any better.

Undoubtedly the men have their own version.[4] In some ways both men and women seem to accept that in most disagreements no one can win or that both win in their own ways, simply because they are of opposite sex and can only be expected to see things differently. The fact that spouses can largely ignore each other and can count on the support of others means that conflict in most instances causes no threat to the relationship and little feeling of personal offence. With no divorce possible and with legal separation difficult, this has, perhaps, its advantages.[5]

This capacity for ignoring spouses and concentrating on

other relations characteristic of some wives in southern Spain is reflected in the comment of a woman from a traditional established community in Britain: 'I couldn't get on without me mother. I could get on without my husband. I don't notice him.'[6] But for many women in Britain today, moving around the country has increased their dependence on their husbands and the importance of the marital relation, as I became acutely aware when interviewing managers and their wives in various parts of England.[7]

When a couple move, both have the problem of establishing new social relations, of making new friends, but these problems are far greater for non-working wives than for their husbands. Most of the ways open – joining clubs and organizations, attending adult education classes, meeting the mothers of children's friends (should there be children), involve a very deliberate and concerted effort, for which some wives may have less confidence, ability or perseverance than others.[8] The husband's new colleagues often do not become good friends. As one woman I interviewed put it:

I don't really see many people – only sometimes the wives of my husband's colleagues. But I don't think you can really mix work and entertaining – if there are differences of opinion at work it can be very embarrassing meeting them in their own homes and wives can be very nasty about this. It's not really wise to get to know the wives – but if you don't know them, who else is there?

For those whose husbands move frequently, making friends may not seem worthwhile if they are only to move again and have to repeat the process – 'When my husband moves I lose friends, so I'm very wary of getting involved.' The resulting isolation for many wives is examplified by these remarks:

I don't know them (her neighbours) very intimately. They're friendly in a general way. Two of them are particular friends and I may go and have tea *every other week or so*, but that's all. They are my *best friends*.

I didn't make friends at all when we first came here, though I eventually went to work and met a few girls but it took me a long time to get to know them. I did get very lonely. I missed my friends from Brighton, I wished I had friends here. I was four years here before I had someone I would call a friend. The woman on one side used to stop and chat occasionally but nobody ever asked me in for coffee or anything. I've stopped work a while ago and my husband won't let me take a job again.

If husbands are reluctant to let their wives go out to work or to attend such things as evening classes, wives may become dependent for any conversation and companionship on their husbands.[9] Men absorbed in careers, often to the point of spending every evening working, may have little time to devote to their wives, which may mean the latter have little conversation and hardly ever go out at all. The interviews I conducted with couples of this kind demonstrated to me how much many of the women simply wanted someone – anyone – with whom to talk about their lives and problems, even a wandering interviewer. After one such interview, the husband took me aside and told me how glad he was that I had come to interview them, his wife had not had such a lot of company for a long time and it had probably done her the world of good!

These couples were all relatively wealthy, and could afford most of the luxuries of middle class life – their impoverishment was one of social relations rather than money. This impoverishment affected the women more than the men, accentuating the differential dependence of the two on the relation and imbuing any dissatisfaction in the relation with tremendous importance.[10]

The importance attached to this one relationship by these kinds of couples simply underlines the generally increasing expectations people have of marriage as a source of personal fulfilment, love, companionship, sexual satisfaction and excitement. These expectations are highlighted by the general importance attached to couples as social units in our society and by demographic changes – as people marry younger, live longer and have fewer children, couples who stay married not only have a greater span of married life than people elsewhere but spend much of it alone.[11] That people are often disappointed with marriage is, perhaps, hardly surprising.

Nevertheless, personal relations between husband and wife

seem to be able to tolerate an extraordinary amount of strain and dissatisfaction without the couple contemplating divorce. One couple told me together that their marriage was a failure; the husband told me that he thought his wife 'hated the sight of him'; the wife described her marriage in the following way:

... in a way I expected it to be all lovey dovey and thought it would be a merging of two people, merging their personalities and getting the best out of the relationship. Oh hell, I thought marriage would give me more happiness than it has, and it's not really given me any happiness, not the marriage itself ... It always go back to this thing of my husband seeing me as one of his other possessions ... But in a marriage you usually have at least one thing in common, and that's sex, and if there's not that, there's really nothing to keep you together ... At the beginning it should have played a biggish part in early marriage, but with my husband it never played a big part. He was either too tired, too busy, or too anything, and over the years I've become not interested. I didn't really worry about it until now. In a way I'm relieved but I feel I shouldn't be like this. If you want something for over twenty years and not get it it's time to give up. I've never been sexually satisfied in all my married life. For me it's always been a duty, and if you were married to my husband, you'd think so too. As I said, I'm his possession. He doesn't want to be unkind, but he's touchy. We can't even have a row as he won't talk about it. He'll talk work problems, but not the most important one that he has closed his eyes to all these years.

However, she also claimed that she derived her sense of security primarily from her husband.

Knowing that no matter what happens, that he will be there. Not just providing for me – that means nothing, but just being here with me. He is more important than the provision he makes ... I suppose this sounds as though I'm contradicting myself but I definitely feel it's true ... It's our need for each other. I think you can need each other without sex. After he studied and qualified he went into bigger and better jobs and after the sort of background we both had we needed each other to face the consequences of this.

Even eternal and continuing marital strife does not necessarily lead married couples to part. J. F. Cüber and P. B. Harroff, for example, recorded this interview with an American husband who had what they termed a 'conflict-habituated' marriage.[12] The couple had been married for twenty-five years and had never seriously thought of parting.

As I look back at it, I can't remember specific quarrels; it's more like a running guerrilla fight with intermediate periods, sometimes quite long, of pretty good fun and some damn good sex ... It's hard to know what it is we fight about most of the time. You name it and we'll fight about it ... Now these fights get pretty damned colourful. You called them arguments a while ago – I have to correct you – they're brawls. There's never a bit of physical violence – at least not directed at each other – but the verbal gunfire gets pretty thick ... Of course we don't settle any of the issues. It's sort of a matter of principle not to. Because somebody would have to give in and then lose face for the next encounter ... I feel a little foolish about it. I wouldn't tolerate such a condition in any other relationship in my life and yet here I do and always have ...

Each personal relation is unique and people vary greatly in their expectations, prejudices, abilities to adjust to change. Consequently, the circumstances under which any individual finds a personal relation in which he or she is involved intolerable are also varied. But to end such relationships can be a very painful process.

The dissolution of a marriage contract is something which causes consternation in most societies, affecting as it does the relations of people other than the husband and wife, and often involving domestic rearrangement, property divisions, concern for children, and a sense of disgrace. When a personal relation is also involved, the transition from married – associated with achievement and happiness, to divorce – associated often with a sense of total personal failure, may not only be an extremely distressing experience but a very prolonged one. At least in part, the distress and time involved result from a lack of coincidence between the dissolution of a marriage; the break-up of a couple; the end of a personal relation.

In the following chapter, 'Marital Breakdown as a Personal Crisis', Nicky Hart discusses the problems people encounter in ending their marriages, the effects of this on their relations with other people and the difference made by the support of friends and relatives in this transition like so many others. Her discussion is based primarily upon interviews with and observations of people belonging to a divorced persons' club in a Midlands university town and illustrates why such clubs should exist at all.

Marital Breakdown as a Personal Crisis

NICKY HART

INTRODUCTION

The relationship between a husband and wife is expected to be both highly personal and enduring. It may be terminated either through the death of one of them or by their separation. The ending of a marriage in either way involves a change in status for both partners: after the death of one spouse the remaining one becomes a widow or widower, in the case of marital breakdown the estranged partners become divorcees.[1] Changes in status such as these can result in a whole new set of circumstances for the individual, and the way in which men and women respond to these changes is of particular significance to the student of social behaviour. Changes of this kind are usually referred to by anthropologists and sociologists as 'status passages', and this chapter is concerned with some of the more problematic aspects of the status passage which occurs when married couples part.

Every member of society is likely to occupy a series of social positions during his or her life, each of which involves the individual in complex relationships with other people. Some of these social positions or statuses can be anticipated from the day the person is born. In these cases a change from one status to another is unproblematic and usually involves a prior expectation on the part of the individual, as well as those closely associated with him, that at some future date he will occupy the particular social position. Everyone involved is thus able to plan and prepare for the event, and for some important status transitions elaborate *rites-de-passage* may exist to mark the occasion and to provide behavioural guidelines for the key participants.[2]

For example, in Britain as in most societies, the great majority of adults exchange bachelorhood for wedlock.[3] The celebration of marriage remains one of the few status passages for which an institutionalized rite still exists and is, moreover, still widely practised in an otherwise relatively ritual-free society. The wedding day usually marks a number of important changes in the lives of the marrying couple. The woman takes a new name, both partners leave their natal families to form a new domestic group, possibly moving into a new home, and the relationships which each shared as individuals must now be redefined to take account of the fact that they are a married couple. Each partner may previously have been involved in relationships of varying intensity with other people, but few of these relationships are likely to have achieved the intimacy which usually develops between the conjugal pair who live together, eat together, sleep together and pool all, or most, of their resources in a lifetime's commitment.

The great majority of adults who decide to get married in Britain today can still expect to remain together until one of them dies. One commentator on recent trends in the stability of marriage in this country has suggested that, notwithstanding the new reforms in the divorce law, something like four fifths of all marriages are likely to survive to widowhood.[4] This leaves 20 per cent to be terminated by separation or divorce, which although a minority, is still a sizeable increase over the level of marital breakdown earlier in this century. Throughout the 1960s[5] the rate of divorce doubled to 4·1 per 1,000 married population, and in 1971, the year in which the new act became effective,[6] the number of petitions for divorce showed an increase of 50 per cent on the previous year. Much of this increase was probably due to an accumulation of cases which, under the old laws, were ineligible for divorce, but even so it seems safe to assume that in the future the breakdown of marriage is likely to be the experience of an increasing number of couples in Britain.

Getting out of wedlock is entirely different from entering it. Both may be equally momentous for the individual, but whereas one is a happy and well planned occasion, the other is often abrupt and traumatic. The death of a spouse usually marks the end of a long life together, and even though there may be abundant support, as well as a ritualized sequence to help the bereaved in their time of grief, adjustment to a life on one's own is often a painful experience. Marital breakdown also entails adjustment to a new single existence, but unlike the status passage between marriage and widowhood, becoming a divorcee is a process fraught with uncertainty and guilt, as well as indifference or perhaps even hostility on the part of the individual's close kin and friends. The following analysis will trace some of these difficulties as they were reported to me by men and women who were members of a club for the divorced and separated in a Midlands city.[7]

Their reminiscences no doubt reflect that they were all largely passive agents in the breakdown of their marriages. For them adjustment to a new partnerless existence was hampered by the fact that they had mostly been married for quite a long time (mean – 11·9 years), that they tended to have custody of larger than average broken families, and that they were somewhat older than the average divorcee. They were, by and large, the ones who got left behind, and while this may bias their accounts, these nevertheless provide many insights into those aspects of marital breakdown which cause acute personal distress.

THE CHARACTER OF THE STATUS PASSAGE

Nearly all those who remarked upon their reaction to becoming separated stressed a total lack of long-term anticipation. Without exception they had never considered (at least initially) the possibility of their own marriages breaking up.

Well I suppose I had thought about it before, I mean I had friends who had split up. But I never seriously thought that something like that would happen to us.

I never believed it, I mean not until he actually moved out of the house, and even then I thought we would make it up. You know we often had rows and threatened to do something like this, but it was never serious on my part. I never wanted to break up the marriage – I still don't.

It is like an accident. No one ever thinks that they will be knocked over by a bus, do they? How can you anticipate something like that, I mean it's like courting disaster. If someone did try to prepare themselves for such a possibility, people would think that they were a bit odd. You just have to go on as though these things are not going to happen to you. And marriage is just the same. It simply isn't something that you can be half-hearted about. You have to believe that nothing can go wrong or you would never get married in the first place.

This last reaction illustrates, perhaps, the hub of the problem. How can one ever anticipate a disaster? By definition a disaster is such because it is unexpected; this is what gives it its impact. Divorce amounted to such a disaster for most of those I interviewed.

When two people marry, they make a long-term commitment to each other on the basis of which they pool their individual assets in a lifetime's investment. The selection of a spouse must therefore be counted as amongst life's most crucial decisions for the individual, and it can be assumed that, when the choice is made, all doubts will have been resolved. How else can the individual persuade himself upon the rightness of such an important decision, and otherwise how can he implement it? Marriage is not normally considered in experimental terms; indeed, such an orientation is a luxury limited to those with a surplus of investment assets (using the term 'assets' in its widest sense). Very few can ever contemplate the possibility of a mistake, and certainly no one in my sample had. All of them were almost completely unprepared for the breakdown of their marriages: the adverse personal and social attitudes surrounding divorce, perceived and held by most, accentuated their difficulties.

I am very ashamed of what has happened to me. (Divorced female: 49, nurse)

I don't like the word divorce. (Separated male: 27, school-teacher)

Yes I would like to re-marry, but only to a bachelor or perhaps a young widower. I would not marry a divorced man; you just would not know if there was something wrong with him. (Divorced female: 28, mother/part-time clerk)

Other people, not the divorced and separated, look down upon you as inferior. (Divorced male: 43, factory worker)

People look down on us far more than the unmarried mother; it's like living with a label on. (Separated female: 24, mother)

Marital breakdown was viewed with apprehension and guilt, a sense of failure, rejection and defeat, as abnormal and freakish, in short, with dismay. The prospect of separation and divorce was unwelcome in the extreme, and this, compounded by the almost universal lack of expectation, made the transition from the married to the divorced state highly traumatic.

THE CHARACTER OF THE STATUS PASSAGE

Passage from one status to another is rarely a clearcut process. The status change may be marked by a ritual enactment and by an abrupt change of title or behaviour, but in most cases the boundary between status lost and status gained is blurred. Not only is the new status often partially experienced before the public rite of passage, but also the life associated with the old status may never be completely discarded. Thus, before the public celebration of marriage, a couple may behave in many ways as though married (joint budgeting, co-habitation, etc.) and, after the event, old life styles and associations may persist. The same applies with even greater force to the end of a marriage.

The bond uniting a husband and wife can only be legitimately severed through legal channels. Either or both spouses may seek to dissolve their marriage in the courts either through legal separation or divorce.[8] However, by the time a case reaches the matrimonial courts, a couple may have long since ceased to live together and may also have abandoned many other aspects of their relationship. The divorce decree, in this country in particular, plays almost no guiding role in the dynamics of the status passage from married to separated/divorced person – it is more like a post-mortem defining, in retrospect, the causes and the distribution of blame.

I have already suggested that the public definition of the

transition does not coincide with the personal experience of changeover, which in fact usually occurs at some point prior to the legal dismantling of the marriage.[9] Locating the exact point of breakdown is difficult. A physical separation of spouses is always subject to possible reconciliation, and the sociological observer is probably seldom in a position to identify with any accuracy the point at which the marriage has ended in fact if not in law. But the problems which this process of changeover poses are not confined to the analytic problems of the observer. Those involved are also likely to be confused by the timing and pacing of the change, for marital breakdown is a messy and at best ill organized affair.

In one analysis of marital dissolution in the U.S.A., divorce is seen as the end point of a cyclical process of alienation between the spouses.[10] The process involves crisis after crisis, after each of which the relationship is redefined at a level of greater alienation and instability. This process of alienation, which seems to lay great stress upon the role of personal conflict between spouses as the motivating force in separation, might be conceptualized as a form of preparatory socialization for the ensuing change of status.

Within my sample there were several marriages which seemed to exhibit this process of conflict generated through a series of successive crises which reached their final denouement in separation and ultimately divorce. But no one amongst those who described their experiences in this way found it prepared them in any way for what was to come. Indeed the development of this interpersonal conflict was a process which many seemed to recognize as such only after separation had occurred. Most also felt that some friction between husbands and wives characterized any marriage – why should theirs be different? After the event, they began to see things differently. If the marriages of others survived, when theirs had collapsed, then something must have been wrong. They must have known greater conflict than other people. The history of one man, Mr Bolan, provides a good illustration of this. Despite the fact that his wife had left him and then returned on several occasions, he still did not think of their marital relationship as out of the ordinary. They had their disagreements, true, but doesn't everyone? His wife's frequent trips to her mother were just part of the ups and downs of married life. It took Mr Bolan a very long time to accept that his wife and son were really not coming back finally and, when I interviewed him, more than six years later, he still treasured vague hopes of a reconciliation.

The process of alienation in the Bolan case, if it existed at all, was one-sided. One spouse grew farther and farther away whilst the other remained constant, and when the final split came the one who had made the least adjustment no doubt suffered the greatest shock. The precipitating causes of the separation were unknown to Mr Bolan, who felt that his marriage was no different from anybody else's.

'At the time I felt that we were no different from anyone else, but looking back on it, I suppose we must have had more problems than most.' This state of affairs was common in the recollections of club members, the majority of whom were the passive partners in their marital breakdown. Separation was thus unanticipated, not only in terms of long-term socialization but also from the shorter-term perspective. The more or less immediate crises which led up to dissolution went unrecognized by those intimately involved in them. The exact nature of 'normal' marital interaction was unknown – those interviewed had no way of knowing if their own experience was different from that of others. For these people separation was something foisted upon them as a *fait accompli* and their confused reactions were an attempt at personal comprehension of an unexpected turn of events. For the passive partners separation came as an abrupt change of circumstances: the spouse taking the initiative perhaps benefited from a more gradual preparation for the idea of separation.

Others who had experienced a degree of alienation from the conjugal relationship were perhaps somewhat better prepared. They had at least been forewarned of what might happen. In these cases the development of disaffection by one spouse was based largely upon behavioural indiscretions of the other. Repeated infidelity, alcoholism, cruelty and financial mismanagement were the main precipitants, although in a few cases the growth of dissatisfaction had a more philosophical basis – such as the wife who felt that marriage had blocked her own personal fulfilment. Nevertheless, the decision to take steps to terminate a marriage and therefore break up a home is not one to be taken lightly and those placed in this difficult position resolved to do so only after a considerable period of uncertainty. Even after making such a decision some subsequently changed their minds.

Mrs Walters was in her late twenties when she left her husband and returned with her two infants to her natal home in England. Much of her married life had been spent abroad, mainly in the Middle East where her husband's work with an oil company took him. When she first joined the club she was very enthusiastic about its aims, and within a month she found herself voted on to the executive, of which she remained an active member throughout the whole period of my fieldwork.

Her marriage was first threatened when the Middle East war broke out in 1966. At this time all the wives and children of expatriates employed in her husband's firm were sent home to England for safety, and it was some months before she returned to her spouse. Her husband, however, had not been lonely in her absence; he had become enamoured of a Swiss secretary, whom he had met after his wife had left. By the time his young family returned to him, he was involved in what his wife described as 'an intense love affair'. Mrs Walters was initially shocked, and her reaction turned to anger when her husband refused to give up his lover and asked her to be patient with him. He did not want her to leave him and he refused to consent to divorce. After six months of trying to persuade him, Mrs Walters decided to pack her bags and go home. She took with her some incriminating letters written by the other woman, which she had found amongst her husband's clothes. This evidence, however, was insufficient for divorce; she had to prove that her husband reciprocated the sentiments contained in the letters and she could not even prove that he had replied to them. Unable to get a divorce on the grounds of adultery, she resorted to legal separation. Mrs Walters had many months to consider her decision. In her case, the level of friction was a manifest preparation for separation and, when she finally left her husband, she had given herself the time to visualize alternatives to marriage. To me, she always seemed a woman intent upon divorce, and, had she had corroborative evidence, she would surely have gone through with it.

The couple lived separately for about two years, the wife living with her kin. However, some time after completing my fieldwork, I heard in a letter from the club's secretary that Mrs Walters had been reconciled with her husband; the club had lost one of its most promising leaders.

All of the signs indicated that Mrs Walters's marriage was over when I knew her, but time was to prove my assumption wrong. Perhaps the only absolutely water-tight definition of terminated marriage is when a decree absolute has been conferred; but this ignores those separated couples who are partners to a contract which is effectively as dead as any union whose termination has received a legal blessing. Several respondents had 'felt divorced' months before a judge ratified their feelings. To these the divorce case was extraneous to the process of status passage.

The difficult question is, when does the individual begin the passage from one status to the other? Did Mrs Walters, for instance, make any progress along the status passage 'married to divorced' during the eighteen months or so that I knew her? When did Mr Bolan first start to think of himself as a man whose marriage had broken up, and when did he begin to adjust to the new state of affairs? The analytic problems inherent in these questions are also problems which beset the individuals concerned. Decisions to separate and divorce are taken over considerable time spans, during which people probably begin the lengthy transition to the new status. Potential divorcees who eventually reconcile differences with their spouses may well begin or even complete the married-separated-married passage during the period of living apart. Perhaps Mrs Walters did. For a time her identification with the club and its members seemed total. To this extent she may have experienced life as a divorcee before being reincorporated into the ranks of the married. She had experienced the 'reality' of estrangement. Legally separated, she had felt the impact of life without a husband, of being typed a marital failure, of coping single-handed with the demands of two young sons.

WILLING AND UNWILLING PARTIES

The extent to which separation constitutes a time of uncertainty depends largely on the individual's attitude to the breakdown of his marriage. Some variation could, in part, be traced to feelings and intentions when the couple first began to live separately. Whether the individual had played an active or passive part in the separation was an important factor.

Two distinct types of people seem to exist among those who initiate separation. Firstly, there are those for whom marriage has become a prison from which they earnestly desire to escape. Some of these may already be committed to a relationship with another person, in which case separation constitutes little more than an exchange of one conjugal arrangement for another. No one in my sample could be classified in this way, but possibly for such people any uncertainty they felt about leaving their spouses was mitigated by the fact that separation was also a positive step towards a desired relation with another person.

Of course, not everyone who desires release from marriage takes action because of the existence of a more attractive alternative partner. Within the sample were a number of people who wanted to be free of their spouse, even though it might mean considerable hardship and loneliness. For this second type the marital relationship had become intolerable and, no matter what the cost, separation was the only solution. These cases involved physical and mental cruelty, continuous and flaunted infidelity, homosexuality, and extreme cases of financial mismanagement and bankruptcy. Those who saw separation and possibly divorce as the only way out of such situations had, as it were, reached the end of their tethers. For them, separation was not an abrupt transition – but one considered over months, years and sometimes even decades. Some middle-aged women claimed in retrospect to have remained with their husband only for the sake of their children. Theirs had been a sacrifice of more than a decade and there is every likelihood that some form of anticipatory socialization may have taken place.

Some people in this category had few or no economic problems after separation; two women claimed that social security, on which they had become dependent, was a better and more reliable income than that to which they had been accustomed during married life. For others, however, living apart meant a considerable fall in living standards. Difficulties about where to live were often acute for a deserting spouse, and this was compounded, especially for women, by shortages of cash. For everyone there were problems of isolation and loneliness. Separation was a devastating experience in its initial stages, and when I asked people to describe it to me, they would laugh and say that it was impossible to describe, the words did not exist. Expressed in these terms the value of anticipatory socialization becomes somewhat diluted, but it throws into sharp relief what might be the experience of those who, before the event of separation, had no acquaintance with the idea at all.

Another group who might be classified as taking the initiating action were those who did not necessarily perceive separation as in any sense a permanent state of affairs, or as one which would ultimately lead to divorce. Some of these people were not at all sure what they eventually intended, but saw separation as a short-term solution to conflict. Others perhaps saw the utility of separation as a form of threat aimed at the reformation of a recalcitrant spouse. For both categories, the outcome of separation was possibly perceived as reconciliation; and some respondents had experienced a string of such separations followed by reconciliations. For this group, separation had an almost experimental flavour. At the outset, few may have seriously considered divorce, but, depending upon their experiences of being separated, some came to view it, possibly after a series of separations, as an ultimate solution. It would be wrong to equate the pattern of repeated separation followed by reconciliation as a game in which all the players can predict the next move. Each time a couple part, they may experience trauma and fears for the future, and there is no guarantee that those who have forgiven and forgotten in the past will do so again.

When a separation occurs but some doubt still exists on both sides about the future viability of the union, the relationship between the spouses is unlikely to reach the same degree of estrangement reached when one or both partners are determined to go through with it. In this form the experience of separation might be viewed as a gradual preparation for divorce – a taste of what may be in store but with fewer economic sanctions and less bitterness. The act of separation seen in these terms may be similar to the kind of conjugal crisis suggested earlier, in which, after a number of separations, the marital relationship becomes gradually redefined and the partners more inured to the idea of divorce. Life apart can even provide the incentive for divorce. Those in the sample who decided to end their marriage after they had already been living apart for occupational reasons were not faced with a sudden disruption of conjugal arrangements. To some extent, their problems of adjustment had been partially solved whilst the marriage was still outwardly intact. When this was the case, a long period of separation before divorce was frustrating. Once people were sure that they wanted a divorce, they felt irritated and constrained at being locked in an interstitial status in which their rights, duties and obligations were ill-defined. They wanted quick results and the process of law often appeared cumbersome and ineffectual for the price. Clearly some felt ill at ease, especially with the opposite sex, while they were separated and awaiting a divorce case. Even those who already 'felt divorced' and who claimed that the court hearing was no more than an expensive formality, still felt anxious to get it over. As one woman put it:

I will be very relieved when my divorce comes through. It feels wrong somehow going out with other men whilst I am still married to Tom and besides the neighbours talk so much.

Some people felt that they could not really begin the process of building their life again until they cut off all links with the past; for them a lengthy separation only delayed the process.

I just want to get it all over and done with, and then I will be able to start my life afresh.

For those who had been forced to wait five years for a desertion order, separation was an interstitial status of some permanence.

However, separation is not the precursor to divorce for every-one. Many were very distressed by the experience of living apart, and for some the impact of separation may itself be a disincentive to divorce, providing an interlude which allows them to evaluate the benefits as well as the costs of their con-tinued relationship.

In all, just over a quarter of those interviewed could be classi-fied as the initiators of separation. Because they took the first active steps to dissolve the marriage they had the opportunity to consider beforehand the possible repercussions of their actions. Despite the advantage of forewarning, separation was still a traumatic experience and one which entailed long months of adjustment.[11]

To know exactly how a separated respondent felt about his marriage and his future was often difficult (cf. Mrs Walters). The attitudes of those considering divorce were in a constant state of flux, so that one week a respondent might say one thing, only to contradict himself the next. The preceding section has attempted to cover the range of orientations of those who can be described as initiators of separation, but to say that a particular respondent had a particular orientation is difficult – some people changed their minds frequently. The separated person is taking one of the biggest steps in his whole life, and the sociolo-gist must forgive him if his vacillating behaviour does not fit into neat boxes.

In only 5 per cent of the sample had husband and wife dis-cussed separation. Most of the remainder portrayed themselves as 'acted against' rather than 'active' in the break-up and were all the more unprepared for what took place. Their response was often one of disbelief; they were unable to grasp the reality of what had happened. Several, particularly men, in their reluctance to admit the fact that they had been deserted, went so far as to report their errant spouses to the police as missing persons and possible accident victims. Others were likewise unable to anticipate the separation, believing their married life to be quite normal; but when it came to the point, they were at least capable of recognizing separation for what it was. Finally, there were some others in this group of 'unwilling parties' who, although they acknowledged the existence of conflict in their married lives, felt that there was too much at stake for either spouse to risk a final break-up. Thus separation and extra-marital affairs were thought of as temporary aberrations, to be expunged when the other partner came back to his or her senses.

From the accounts of those who portrayed themselves as unwilling victims, it seemed that absolute marital breakdown was never expected and only reluctantly recognized, even when the spouses were living apart. The state of uncertainty induced by this failure to come to terms with the reality of separation may be likened to a 'no-man's-land' between marriage and divorce, where the individual is thoroughly perplexed as to the likely outcome. This period may last for a long time. Amongst club members were people separated for years, who still hoped for a reunion with their spouses; some, guided by religious principles, felt this to be the only acceptable solution, and they insisted that they were still in love and earnestly believed that one day things would return to normal. They thus lived out the present as though it was a temporary state of emergency, due to be terminated when the old pattern of life was resumed. One separated woman in her late forties had spent three years apart from her husband: she became widowed while she was still waiting for a reconciliation. Another middle-aged woman had been separated for seven years, but still refused to admit that her husband, who had left the country, would not come back to her. A devout Catholic, she did not believe in divorce even though she was the club's secretary and its representative on the National organization. Since her husband's departure she had been hospitalized several times following nervous breakdowns, and two of her children had been sent to a remand home. Other club members interpreted her mental disorder as a function of her failure to face reality, and they may have been right.

For most people the interval between the actual parting and divorce was many months, and, given the intricacies of the legal processes, a period of several years was quite usual. The use of the word 'failure' to describe the inability of separated people to recognize separation as a precursor to divorce need not imply any widespread incidence of self-deception on the part of those personally involved. Reconciliation was always a possibility, constituting in some people's eyes the easiest solution to what was an extremely difficult state of affairs. That so many respondents took months and even years to rule it out completely as a viable solution is not surprising. In some cases, only after the individual had finalized some other plans for the future – another partner, or perhaps a new occupation or career – could the old life be completely abandoned and arrangements for the legal dissolution of the marriage made.

COPING WITH UNCERTAINTY

The character of the status passage for those who are initially unwilling or unsure is one of attenuated uncertainty. The individual is set upon a course whose outcome is unknown, and the process of adjustment must be adjourned until a more definite stage has been reached in the transition. The status passage in this case is devoid of one of the single most important components of a status transfer – it lacks inevitability. Only when a person is certain from the outset, or at least from an early stage, of the unavoidability of what is about to happen, may he understand the process for what it is and hence begin to plan and make adjustments to what is at best a difficult personal crisis.

To some extent the widowed find themselves in a similar situation.[12] Even though the other partner is definitely lost, the widow still finds it extremely difficult to believe in it and get used to his absence. The domestic life of a couple is at the very core of their existence and seems to have an almost everlasting quality. When disrupted prematurely, a great strain is placed upon the person who is forced to make a rapid adjustment to the change. For the separated person, these problems are compounded by the uncertainty of the new situation, the possibility that life may revert to its old pattern.

The shorter the length of time since the couple parted, the more likely it was that feelings of affection or even just tolerance would be expressed for the other partner. Those in the club whose acquaintance I first made when they were newly separated appeared to be going through a period of indecision. At this stage they were more likely to be ambivalent about whose fault it all was, and, if a third party was involved, there was a marked tendency to attribute blame to this source. As time went on and it became more apparent that there would be no return to the *status quo*, feelings towards the former loved one began to harden. A sudden awakening to the irreversibility of breakdown was sometimes wrought when a rejected wife went to abuse or plead with her husband's lover. Several women claimed that, following such an encounter, the husband had returned and beaten them up (and this response was not confined to working-class men).

In general, the most negative descriptions of the 'ex' came from those who had either initiated the break-up, or were divorced or nearly divorced. A common theme in the reminiscences of this group was, 'Looking back on it, I do not think I ever really loved him,' or 'I should have known right from the beginning; I just blinded myself to her faults.' Acknowledgement that the marriage was 'dead' went hand in hand with a reorganization of attitudes towards the former spouse, and the quality of married life. But it took the individual some time to reach the point at which such feelings could be expressed, and they were usually confined to those who had finally severed all links with their former 'partner in life'.

For one spouse to have actively considered and pursued the termination of the marriage, whilst the other was ostensibly ignorant of what was developing, was common amongst club members. Few people reported that both partners had perceived the ending of the marriage was inevitable. The extent to which two people interpret the same events in a diverse way is illustrated in the above account of the independence of thoughts and actions between the conjugal pair. The married couple who jointly inhabit a small, confined and intimate world, even though they are likely to experience the same events with ample opportunity for mutual discussion, are still capable of perceiving two very different realities. For one, the marital relationship is unsuccessful and reaching breaking point; for the other the relationship is normal, not deviating from the usual run of conjugal experience, and its future is not seriously threatened (cf. Mr Bolan).

Any individual construction of reality is subject to change and, over time, an individual's view of the world he inhabits and of his place in it may become transformed. But this process seldom involves a sudden transformation, for the stability of the individual personality is dependent upon some level of consistency in everyday life. The way in which any view of reality becomes transformed is through interaction with others. Each of us strives to confirm that the way we view things is correct and though we can, with ease, make minor alterations in our constructions of reality, we may be reluctant to perceive dramatic transformations of the picture. The hesitation of people who are faced suddenly with separation and the prospect of a broken marriage may be understood in these terms. In postponing the acceptance of separation as the 'beginning of the end', they not only make provision for the possibility of a mistake; they allow themselves time to etch out more gradually a new view of their immediate world, a view more in accord with the constraints of their current existence.

CONCEALING THE RIFT

The separation of a couple invariably creates problems in interaction with others who are indirectly involved. No matter what the attitudes of husband and wife are to the event, relationships with other people (children, kin, close friends) are almost always affected, and perhaps the greatest strains are experienced by those for whom separation is not seen as a first step to an inevitable divorce.

When separation is viewed as a temporary phase in a couple's otherwise normal relationship, considerable problems of information control may arise.[13] Well over half the sample thought at some stage in the separation that a reconciliation was a real possibility, and sought to hide the fact that conflict existed until their differences came to be seen as irrevocable. As long as a return to conjugality could be envisaged, they did not want to undermine the relationship in the eyes of other people, which meant that the current state of the marriage was kept a secret. In this way the 'back stage' of the relationship was protected from exposure so that in future interaction with kin, in-laws, children, neighbours and friends, the couple would continue to portray a united front. The sources of conflict between partners, especially behavioural indiscretions, remained safely within the confines of the conjugal relationship. The so-called 'innocent' party, often at great personal strain, attempted to maintain a front of normality, when in actual fact he or she desperately needed a shoulder to cry on.

The maintenance of normal relationships with close associates could present considerable difficulties. When a couple had moved around the country during their marriage, keeping the knowledge of what was happening from kin and friends presented no immediate problems. One woman, for example, had been deserted more than two years previously and still had not revealed her 'circumstances' to her family, who lived no more than two hours away in London. On family visits she would claim that her husband was away on business, and even though her mother and sister had not seen their in-law for years, their view of her marriage was of one still intact.

When kin reside closer to home, however, there are greater difficulties in maintaining the pretence. Even so, many did manage to keep their secret intact, although the elaborate excuses and performances this entailed often seemed fantastic, when related to me after the event. The mechanism most commonly employed for explaining the absence of a spouse was that he or she was away on business or on a social visit to friends or in-laws. Those couples whose friends and relatives had little to do with each other reaped the benefits of anonymity in this situation, while those who had lived in a social environment in which everyone knew everyone else found that their lame excuses were often quickly exposed when their spouse was seen locally on the arm of a lover.

Children were the hardest of all to protect from premature exposure to the news of their parents' separation. Obviously children were quick to notice the absence of a parent and their persistent queries as to the whereabouts of the missing person were a preview for the remaining parent of what life as a single parent would mean. Even those determined not to have their spouse back would sometimes delay for months the unpleasant task of breaking the news to young children. Their prevarications took a similar line to those of more hesitant parents. A frequent excuse was that the other missing parent was ill and away in hospital. The anxiety of children when a couple part may be one of the strongest incentives for reconciliation and several respondents claimed to have delayed a parting until the time when their children were 'old enough to understand'. One or two older respondents reported that the separation had been a joint family decision and, in one case, two teenage children had testified for their mother in a contested cruelty case.

Relationships with friends and acquaintances were also affected by the need to 'conceal the rift'. Close personal friends were sometimes the ones to whom the individual preferred to turn for advice and guidance. But mostly the individual felt that these relationships, being of a lesser significance than the conjugal one, should not be made privy to what had happened until such a time that divorce or permanent separation seemed a certain outcome. The act of concealment, however, often necessitated more or less complete withdrawal from social interaction, especially when husband and wife shared the same friends. If the individual cherished hopes for a reconciliation and thus sought to hide the fact of the other partner's absence, he or she was obliged to follow a policy of deliberate isolation, only turning to the help and companionship of kin and friends when a more final stage of affairs had been reached.

Another source of anxiety for newly-separated people in their relationships with kin and friends was the shame and sense of failure they felt. Fears of disappointing and even alienating others were a considerable obstacle to those faced with the need to disclose the news of the marriage breakdown. The separation itself and the usually unpleasant events leading up to it were made worse by a sense of personal shame which led to an erosion of self-confidence in interpersonal relationships. A reluctance to reveal the news may have stemmed in part from these sources. One woman who reported her experience almost immediately to her mother was rewarded with a reaction of shocked amazement. The parents, who lived some distance away from their daughter, wanted her to pretend, for the benefit of friends and neighbours, that nothing had happened when she came to visit. When she refused to take part in this masquerade, she was deprived of their emotional and potentially considerable financial support. When I interviewed her, she had not communicated with her kin for over two years. The fear of such a reaction may have persuaded many to hide the fact of separation for as long as possible. However, deliberate deception in interaction placed people under considerable stress, and the need for this insincerity only added to the anxiety of an already unhappy situation.

Controlling information in the early or indefinite stage of separation presented acute difficulties and often placed individuals on the brink of embarrassing exposure. The fact that others found out or were told by the other partner forced many to come to terms with the inevitability of permanent separation, and gave some the final impetus to decide to seek divorce. Only then was the individual free to seek the support of others, but he was still likely to encounter difficulties.

THE RESPONSE OF OTHERS

People respond in various ways to the announcement by a friend or relative that his marriage is over and that he is in the throes of legal action. In a minority of cases in the sample, the individual's decision was received with relief by natal kin, friends, and even in-laws. When told, they often revealed that they had known all along that things were not going well. In cases of infidelity the 'injured' party might well now discover that he or she was the last person to find out about the spouse's indiscretions. When a person was fearful of the reaction of others, their complacent acceptance of the announcement often did much to dissipate his distress. But when friends greeted the decision with disapproval, the revelation that others had known all along what was happening produced a very different response.

Not only were these others claiming a right to express an opinion on what was perceived as a purely personal decision, but they were also admitting to the possession of incriminating evidence about the spouse which they had not divulged to the person most deeply affected by it. Their 'insincerity' was likely to produce a reaction of withdrawal – the individual interpreting their antipathy to the news as an attempt to protect themselves from bad publicity, or from future possibility of embarrassment caused by dual loyalties. Nuclear and affinal kin were most often cast in these roles, but more impartial observers were also prone to dissuade the individual from his chosen course. Joint conjugal friends, themselves on the horns of a dilemma over which side to take, sometimes attempted to peruade their friends to change their minds in order to reduce the conflict of their own position. Alternatively, and this was especially the case with more impersonal acquaintances, sheer embarrassment and confusion led to a withdrawal from interaction by both parties.

Lost all of my friends; my fault really; I just could not tolerate anyone when I was first separated.

After divorce, I suddenly realized that I had no friends. I think I must have lost them when the marriage was breaking up.

Other more formal agencies to which people resorted also seemed bent upon the preservation of the marriage. The Samaritans, the medical profession, the Marriage Guidance Council and even the Department of Health and Social Security, each in their own way tried to dissuade people from their chosen course or at least communicated disapproval of it. As far as they were concerned any kind of marriage was better than being divorced, and they attempted to make their clients try for a reconciliation as the lesser of two evils.[14] But very often by the time the individual looked for help, especially from those close to him, he might already have been through months of indecision. Those in whom he confided had not had a similar length of time to make an adjustment to the idea, and, when the news was sprung on them, their negative response was predictable.

To the divorcee in need of positive sanctions for his actions, therefore, the attitude of those to whom he made a direct appeal was often disappointing. He found himself alone without any ally, in a situation over which he had little or no control. The only agencies who did not attempt to reintroduce uncertainty into the issue were the Citizens' Advice Bureau and the various agencies of the law. The advice and guidance they were able to provide, however, was of a purely procedural kind, and to someone in need of sympathy and approval it often smacked of indifference.

At this stage, the newly separated, deprived of the support of kin and friends, felt most alone. In the absence of sympathy from those close to him, the individual went to government departments expecting perhaps a little more than the direct and impersonal information which they were prepared and able to give.

The forms of support which the individual needed differed. From nuclear kin, older children, and close friends, he hoped for positive sanctions, help, affection, sympathy and approval. Instead, he sometimes found that he gained no sustenance whatsoever from these people, who, far from endorsing his position, tried to induce a state of uncertainty. Each for various reasons was ill-equipped to extend the kind of support needed. Family members were likely to feel that they themselves had been disgraced by the fate of their parent, child or sibling. Feeling that the humiliation of divorce may well rub off on them, they sought to avoid it. In some cases, however, kin did provide abundant material help as well as sympathy and respect for the individual's position, a reaction especially characteristic of kin among whom there had been previous divorces.

Not everyone, of course, had access to close kin who cared. Older people, especially those whose parents were dead, often knew hardly anyone who was genuinely concerned, and even those who did felt that others were insensitive to their needs. The distress of divorce was too difficult to comprehend for those not directly involved. Many of those getting divorced found it difficult to communicate their feelings, and those around them may well have felt impotent, unable to help. Their apparent indifference may have simply expressed their incapacity – if divorce was something new to them, they may have had no idea of what they could or should do.[15]

Whatever the cause, most people found themselves alone with their problems and most had to negotiate the passage from married person to separated/divorced person without the benefit of support from others.

CONCLUDING REMARKS

Movement from one social position to another often presents difficulties. Changes of status are frequently unexpected and the transition may be beset with uncertainty and disorder. Even the change from 'single' to 'married' carries many unknowns, despite anticipation and organized ritual. Most people seem to be able to cope with these difficulties. Why then is the process of marital breakdown so problematic for many?

As I have suggested, this status passage is likely to be most difficult for those who never wanted their marriage to end and who subsequently felt rejected by the person they valued most. Those deserted for younger, more attractive or more affluent partners felt they had been cast off as scrap. Their self-confidence, now more necessary than ever to build a new life, had been severely damaged. The change had a terrible significance which exacerbated the lack of structure and anticipation in the situation.

Status changes occurring at transitional points in the life cycle nearly always mark the end of relationships and established patterns of behaviour as well as the initiation of new ones. The changes are normally compartmentalized so that routine patterns of social interaction remain largely unaffected. The change of status at the end of marriage is more pervasive. The extent to which people's lives are disrupted varies, but for many of those I studied, breakdown of their marriage constituted a complete reversal of customary expectations, leaving them in a state of shock and depression. Routine behaviour lost its meaning, the pattern of life was undermined, problems of coping with the unknown and unexpected assumed overwhelming proportions. Their competence at home, work and in their social life was sometimes seriously affected, and a heightened sense of personal inadequacy was common. Friendships ended and relationships with kin were threatened, frequently isolating the divorcee both inside and outside the home. Opportunities for interaction seemed much curtailed for single people, so loss of a spouse removed a bulwark of social as well as of private existence. Apart from being lonely, club members felt marginal, stigmatized and discriminated against. Uncertainty as to whether these perceived slights had a subjective or objective basis merely compounded the distress of individuals who now found themselves to be deviants. All were conscious of being in some way abnormal, although the stress laid on this varied. Many felt they were no longer respectable; some discovered that they held long-dormant stereotypes of the statuses in which they now found themselves. Most suffered considerable material deprivation – loss of income and home and corresponding changes for the worse in life-style caused great dissatisfaction and discomfort. Struggles over children highlighted the travesty of conjugality that their lives had become. Perhaps not surprisingly, these elements sometimes induced a sense of profound psychological ill-being which occasionally led to suicide attempts or merged into physiological deterioration.

Reconciliation was often seen as the only salvation, but hopes for such an outcome only delayed for months or years the process of learning to identify with the new status. Even those who were sure their marriage had ended did not welcome the label 'divorcee', and none saw the status as in any sense permanent. But although most sought escape in remarriage, only a minority of club members were likely to realize this ambition.[16] Most found they had little chance of making new acquaintances, never mind meeting a second mate; they were likely to spend the rest of their lives in the supposedly transitional status 'divorcee'.

However objectively unsatisfactory their marriages had been, separation and divorce was a personal tragedy – to label their difficulties 'problems' is to risk serious understatement. Yet despite this, they are unassisted by any kind of institutionalized support. The most problematic stages of the status passage have already been negotiated by the time of legal divorce; separation without divorce may be a long-drawn-out process, lacking even the final resolution of a court's decision. Whereas elaborate customs exist to help widows in their grief and to prepare brides for marriage, newly separated people must sort out their problems alone.[17] The public stigma associated with divorce proceedings and their report in the local press, the general lack of sympathetic advice, the absence of institutionalized material and emotional aid, all exemplify the inadequacy of the social milieu. The suggestion has been made that divorcees in the U.S.A. are punished and left without support, or at least treated in an ambiguous fashion, because they, unlike victims of bereavement, have themselves initiated the tragedy and their acts, unlike those of brides, transgress against canons of social convention.[18] But for those whose marriages end through no wish of their own – the 'passive' third of divorcees – marital failure does not appear a voluntary act. They see themselves as victims, and are bewildered to find that disentangling themselves from a broken marriage is unaided and may be hindered by those agencies (private and public) to which they would normally look for support.

A broken marriage also represents a considerable blow to individual identity. A person's social identity might be conceptualized as a blend of all the social positions that person has previously held, currently holds and expects to hold in the future. This complex of statuses and the social relationships they involve combine to produce the individual's notion of 'self', his sense of who he is and where he belongs in society. Marriage, linking together the statuses of spouse and parent, is expected to span many years and consume a great deal of an individual's stock of resources in time, energy and funds. As such, its loss may involve not only a reorganization of day-to-day activities but also a reorganization of self.

The association between separation and symptoms of personal disorganization such as physical illness, mental breakdown and attempted suicide point to the crucial part played by the conjugal relationship in the construction and maintenance of a stable pattern of everyday life. Those who have experienced marital breakdown know only too well that the loss of a partner means disruptions not just to their economic and social life but also to their sense of personal well-being in modern society.

6. After Divorce

Despite the fact that divorce rates are rising in Britain and in the U.S.A., people seem to be more disillusioned with a particular marriage or a particular person than with marriage itself, for very many divorced people, despite the trauma of divorce, do get married again. 'Divorced' is an undesirable status and the only way to lose it is to remarry. Many people who do remarry marry other divorced people, and sometimes ex-spouses even remarry each other. The uncertainty some people may feel about the end of their relation and indeed their marriage is reflected in the kind of bizarre situation, reported by J. C. Westman and D. W. Cline, of an American couple who separated seventeen times, divorced three times and experienced eighteen reconciliations.[1]

The disapproval with which people greet divorce may be especially marked when a couple have children, and custody and visiting rights may often prolong the relation and the conflict between parents even after their marriage has legally ended.[2] Children are also a constraint on new sexual relations; the parent with custody of them may be more inclined to remarry, seeking a partner who is prepared to take on a ready-made family and who will get on with the children and be a good parent to them.

Whether or not they have children, divorced people seek to remarry for many reasons. The disparity between the earnings and prestige accorded jobs available to women and men tends to mean that women whose income and social standing decline with divorce are often especially anxious to remarry, particularly those who find it difficult to re-establish themselves in paid employment after years at home. Many divorced people find they lack the experience and confidence to cope with those areas of life previously controlled by the spouse, and some fear becoming socially peripheral, given the importance of couples to many social occasions. Those who are older and who were married for some time may be particularly concerned, unwilling to face old age alone and having lost touch with the usual ways in which new sexual relations are established.[3]

Obviously, people's reasons for wanting involvement with someone of the opposite sex are not always reasons for wanting to remarry. But the desire for respectability and the approval of kin and friends, for proof to themselves that they 'can make a marriage work', for security of companionship as they grow old, serves to make other relationships less satisfactory. For the formerly married as well as for the single, the commitment implied by marriage makes it attractive. As one sociologist put it:

> Marriage *feels* permanent, and that's the important thing. It's buying instead of rental. It's even-if-you-are-acting-like-an-s.o.b. – we'll stick it through. It's going home at night to somebody you don't have to keep winning. It's having *decided*. In a way, you know, the happiest people in prison are the lifers.[4]

In the following chapter, 'Couple Relationships', Robert Weiss discusses four different kinds of sexual relationships in which both the previously married and the unmarried may become involved, and considers some of the factors which lead to one kind of relation rather than another. Many of his observations are based on talks with widowed and divorced women, and to illustrate his general discussion he follows through the case history of a divorced woman with two children.

There are some relationships of men and women in which the well-being of each participant is not dependent on the presence of the other or assurance of the other's accessibility. The participants may be fond of one another but they are not in this sense emotionally attached. There are other relationships of men and women in which the other's inaccessibility gives rise to distress. Marriage is one such relationship, but it is not the only one. My concern in this chapter is to describe the forms assumed by relationships containing emotional attachment as one component, to contrast them with cross-sex relationships which do not contain emotional attachment, and finally to consider what may be the source and the implications of emotional attachment.[1]

The work on which I am here drawing was for the most part conducted within the programme of the Laboratory of Community Psychiatry, Harvard Medical School. The work includes studies of small samples of individuals in various circumstances, including mothers on their own, married couples, widows and widowers, and the recently separated. Our approach in most of our studies has been to interview our respondents regularly at intervals ranging from two weeks to several months over periods ranging from a few months to two or three years. An exception to this has been our work with the newly separated, where three times a year we provided a series of lectures and opportunities for group discussion as a way of helping formerly married individuals manage the transition to their new status. I also draw on observations made in a study of the contributions to its membership of an organization of single parents.[2]

Although the forms of couple relationships described are based on work with heterosexual couples, I would expect those of homosexual couples to be similar. The forms can be shown to develop from alternative resolutions of issues which arise in emotional attachments, and should, therefore, represent the alternatives available to homosexuals as well as to heterosexuals. The relative frequencies of the forms might, however, be expected to differ, even leaving aside the fact that homosexuals cannot marry.

FORMS OF COUPLE RELATIONSHIPS

Some relationships of couples do not sustain emotional attachment. In the settings in which we worked some women found it difficult to go out in the evenings without a man to escort them; and, in turn, some men felt ill at ease without a woman to escort. Other women wanted a man's view on the way to handle finances, bring up boys, or deal with a car; while some men found that advising a woman in these ways helped them to recognize their own areas of competence and worth. We designated as 'comradeship', those relations in which men and women wanted nothing more than the exchange of those services appropriate between friends.

In comradeship a man and woman may keep one another company, may ask favours of one another, can each count on the other as a friend, but are not emotionally attached. They may hope that eventually emotional attachment will develop, or they may not. But its absence in reality is easily recognizable. The participants are relatively indifferent to temporary separation; they do not feel lonely or anxious if days or weeks go by during which they neither see the other nor hear from the other. They do not regularly share their moods with one another, although they may on infrequent occasions confide in one another in what is recognized as a break from the usual tenor of the relationship. Neither feels identified with the other nor expects the other to be identified with them. They each may feel lonely despite the existence of the relationship. Should the relationship fade there may be regret, but there will not be grief.

Central to these relationships was a community of interests: an area of shared concern, which might be work or sociability, or an area in which friendly exchange could be mutually profitable. Individuals who maintained no cross-sex relationship which provided emotional attachment often had relationships of this sort which furnished them with an opportunity they might otherwise not have for cross-sex exchange. Women who worked or who had other bases for specialist interest also had such relations with men who shared their interests, whether or not they had concurrent emotional attachments.

Individuals did not think of themselves and the others with whom they maintained comradeships as 'couples'. For one individual to claim that another was 'just a friend' communicated to others that their relationship had no special significance as a cross-sex relationship. Where there was no sharing of specialist interests comradeships were apt to be dropped should either the man or the woman develop a cross-sex emotional attachment with someone else.

The following excerpt from an interview describes a comradeship:

There is one fellow, I've known him since we were kids. We go to the movies once a week, maybe every couple of weeks. I told him right away that there is no possibility of marriage. We just go out together when we don't have anything to do. He'll call up, 'Hey, want to take in a show tonight?' So I go. He's just like a brother. And then we always come straight home after the movies, just like a brother.

Relationships in which there was emotional attachment were of critical importance in an individual's life. Whereas an individual would be content to see a 'comrade' only infrequently, if there was an emotional attachment an individual might feel uneasy if even a single evening passed during which the other had not at least been talked with by phone. To know that the other was accessible and that one had not been even temporarily abandoned was especially important. One of the husbands we knew worked nights and could not fall asleep when he returned home unless his wife was in the house; it seems reasonable to suppose that he became too anxious.

Emotional attachment usually involves a general desire to please the other and, of course, desire to be responded to by the other with affection and commitment. Each wants to satisfy the other's wants and each expects the other to display the same feelings. Emotional attachment, unlike comradeship, was accompanied by sexual intimacy, almost as a matter of course, among the couples in our study.

The first issue facing an 'emotionally attached' couple is how to arrange to be accessible to each other. One possibility is to live together. Another is to maintain separate residences but nevertheless to see each other with the frequency attachment implies: i.e., simply 'to go together'.

Couples seemed to have a number of rather different kinds of reasons for choosing 'to go together' rather than to live together. Firstly, the couple, perhaps especially the woman, were often unwilling to make public the sexual nature of the relationship. As long as separate residences were maintained, the man did not evidently stay overnight, and there was no pregnancy, those of our respondents who were going with someone were able to maintain the position of *honi soit qui mal y pense*. They could consider their respectability to continue essentially undamaged, whatever others might think. Secondly, either the man or woman or both were unwilling to become deeply enmeshed in the relationship, despite their attachment, either because they feared that it would end sooner or later, or because they felt it was somehow inappropriate or undesirable and so *should* end. The third kind of reason had to do with the desire of the woman, especially, to retain independence in the management of her affairs and of the man, especially, to retain autonomy and a limit to responsibility. One woman described going together as a most desirable relationship just because it would provide attachment without the problems of shared routines and living arrangements. She said:

You know what I think ideally I would do. Meet a man who has been married and has some kids. So he knows what it is all about. Fall in love, and all that goes with it ... But 'You live in your house and I'll live in my house – and don't get under my feet.'

When a couple were going together each continued to be

responsible for management of a separate household and a separate financial economy. As the relationship developed there might be an extensive exchange of favours: for example, the woman might invite the man to dinner fairly regularly and the man, on his part, might help the woman with her shopping, take her out for an evening or for coffee, perhaps paying the baby-sitter, and now and then bring the woman flowers or small quantities of food. But these exchanges were understood as gifts, freely offered testimonies to the attachment rather than dutiful expressions of responsibilities.

Accompanying absence of responsibility for each other's household was an absence of rights within it. In particular, the man could not require that the woman observe household routines or ways of managing children that he thought desirable. This was one of the attractions of going together for some women, including those who had had unhappy marriages and were pleased to be close to someone yet to remain independent, and those strongly attracted to men with whom they were not willing to establish an economic partnership or to whom they did not want to cede authority over their children. But this meant that the man had only the status of a guest in the setting in which the couple spent most of their time; he had no genuine rights there. 'Going together' had other disadvantages, too, for the woman as well as for the man. The frequent to and fro between separate households, the need to make dates and arrangements, the awkwardness of arranging shared activities, made it uneconomic of time as well as money. The sense, for both man and woman, that they were managing routines only for themselves made chores seem pointless and unrewarding.

Living together solved a number of these problems: it was more economic; it made being together a matter of course rather than something to be arranged and rearranged; it solved, at least partially, the man's problem of not having rights in the space in which he spent much of his time; and it made routine responsibility a shared concern. The following quotation suggests how living together may give routine responsibility greater significance. The man with whom the respondent lived was sometimes away, sometimes with her. She said, about the times he was with her:

Then I'm an altogether different person. I'm smiling, I'm happy ... It gives me a lift. It makes me want to live. He makes me want to clean and cook. I cook and cook and cook. I cook so much when he's around – stuffed peppers, stuffed eggs – I love to cook.

And in addition to having someone to do things for, there was someone who would do things for her:

He seems to take a burden off my shoulders when he's around. Even with the kids, I don't have to keep checking on them ... He'll take the kids for a walk, take them for an ice cream, play with them ...

Perhaps because living together is not entirely compatible with respectability, only a few of our respondents currently did so or had done so in the past.[3] Nevertheless, a couple who were living together were getting along. Generally there seemed to be great mutual considerateness in their management of their shared division of labour – very likely in order to protect the continuation of the critically important emotional attachment. However, living together also seemed to provide some basis for fear of exploitation. Each could suspect the other of demanding too much or of giving too little, and each might fear that in the long run the books would be unbalanced to his or her disfavour. One respondent complained that the man with whom she was living wanted her to put up his visiting sister and her six children; another said that a man with whom she had once lived had spent his evenings with friends rather than with her, so that she felt she was important to him only as a cook and housekeeper. Men, we would suppose, might be concerned about the woman's use of the funds they contributed to the household, possibly suspecting that they were being squandered or used to help the woman's kin or being put aside by the woman for her own later use.[4]

Marriage seems to reduce both the likelihood of great considerateness and the fear of exploitation. For while living together is understood to involve no special commitment to permanence, marriage, despite recognition of the accessibility of divorce, is understood to obligate each partner to a continuing and permanent responsibility for the other's well-being: to help the other when needed, if helping is possible; to act as an ally by exhibiting loyalty and support; and to recognize these obligations irrespective of potential reciprocity and even of liking.

Acceptance of these obligations constitutes the core of the marriage ceremony – each partner vowing to care for the other no matter what may happen – even if the other should become ill or impoverished or less attractive as a mate in still other ways. Acceptance of these obligations brings rights to speak and act for the other – obligations and rights acknowledged and reinforced by the laws and customs of the society. For example, each marriage partner is required to provide support for the other if the other is in need and can make decisions for the other where the other is adjudged incompetent.

These obligations and rights are essentially those of near kin, and it seems proper to see marriage as a way of establishing a kinship tie between two previously unrelated individuals – both the law and social understanding accepting them as next-of-kin. The man's kin recognize that his wife is also their kin; and the woman's kin in turn recognize the new bond to the man. The permanence expected of marriage is based in this sense of marriage as bringing individuals into kinship to one another.

It is the introduction of kinship and its implied rights and obligations that makes for the difference between marriage and living together. Because it is understood that each has a right to the other's concern, mutual concern is obligatory; the considerateness which may seem entirely natural as a component of the relationship of a couple living together may appear studied and unnatural in marriage. Each participant is required by vow to contribute to the corporate well-being and therefore the contributions each makes might ordinarily be taken for granted, though with occasional recognition of special competence or special effort.[5] At the same time possible exploitation is less of an issue: each participant is obligated to contribute in ways that are appropriate to the socially defined roles of husband and wife. For example, our respondent who told the man with whom she lived that she would not put up his visiting sister and her six children said that if she and the man had been married she would have had to agree to house his kin.

The reasons people have for getting married rather than simply living together bear this out. The woman may want a relationship she can really count on, even though she is quite aware that desertion or divorce are regular occurrences. She wants to know that there is a bond between her and the man beyond that of mere affection. The man may want to *have* a family, and not simply to live with a family – to have the woman and the children socially recognized as his. Marriage may be attractive for many other reasons, including notably the social desirability of the roles of husband and wife, but the sense of security based on an understanding of permanence would seem to be the major interactional one.[6]

Our study of bereavement gives some evidence for the existence – and the persistence – of kin obligation in marriage. A surviving spouse ordinarily continues to display loyalty to the memory of the dead partner in a way which would not be true had they only been living together. Widows who were considering giving up mourning costume or attending a potentially lively gathering for the first time since their husbands' deaths might first seek permission from the parents or siblings of their husbands. A widow, planning an outing to a movie, said, 'I called my mother-in-law to explain it was for the children, and she said it was all right.' Widows repudiate for months and sometimes for years any hint of interest in a new sexual tie, and explain that their continued loyalty to their husband's memory makes any such thought impossible. That it is loyalty and not immobilization of feeling because of loss that is responsible for this moratorium is suggested by the observation that divorcees do not observe a period of withdrawal from the world of men and gaiety, nor do they consult their former in-laws about anything whatsoever.[7]

Widowers also display continued responsibility to the memories of their wives, but do so differently. In particular, they do not observe a taboo on fantasies of dating and remarriage. One respondent reported having such fantasies three days after his wife's death, several men discussed the possibility of remarriage within the first month after the wife's death, many had remarried by the first anniversary of the wife's death, and more had remarried by the second. Widowers expressed continued loyalty in ways which did not constrain their behaviour: they felt responsible for visits to the wife's grave, though they did not always make them; if they were believing Catholics, they arranged for prayers to be said regularly; they were concerned that their children remember their mothers, even when the children had new stepmothers to care for them.

One of our respondents had been living with a man who then died. The man had kept a room in his mother's apartment and sometimes stayed there, but except for this he shared a residence with our respondent, for which he paid most of the rent, where he was man of the house. He and our respondent had had a child together. After his death the man's family, who had always disapproved of the relationship, cut off ties with the woman. Her own family had also been embarrassed by the relationship and though they sympathized with her loss, they were awkward in expressing their sympathy. She was made to feel uncomfortable by the man's family at the burial, later did not wear mourning, and felt no expectation on the part of others that she would display any continued loyalty to the man's memory. Her grief was as great as it would have been had she and the man been married, but since they had not been, it was a social embarrassment. Attitudes to the widowed express as much our recognition of the loyalty they owe their lost next-of-kin as our recognition of their grief.

So far I have described four forms of heterosexual relationship, comradeship, going together, living together, and marriage, and I have proposed that it is attachment which gives the latter three their critical importance for the emotional life of the individual. The following case history suggests some of the qualities of the various forms and the way in which the importance of emotional attachment displays itself.

Mrs Davis was just recently thirty, slim, very attractive. She had two children, a girl aged twelve and a boy aged eight. When we first met her she was going with Harold, a man about twelve years older than she whom she had met at the beach. Harold was separated from his wife but not as yet divorced. Mrs Davis at that point said about Harold, 'We're lucky to have him. He's wonderful to us. He takes us everywhere – out to dinner, the kids to the zoo and the Science Museum.' Still Mrs Davis was unsure about marrying Harold when he became free to remarry. Harold had an ulcer condition and Mrs Davis' younger child, the boy, sometimes upset him. There had already been a stormy scene when Harold spanked the boy and scolded his older sister. The boy had taken the sister's skates without her permission after Harold had told him not to, and the sister, when she learned of Harold's ruling, had said that the skates were hers and her brother could use them if he wanted to. Mrs Davis defended Harold, saying, 'It's all right for Harold to take you everywhere, take you out to dinner, take you to nice places, but if he scolds you, you don't like it.' But the incident made her uneasy about marriage.

Had Mrs Davis and Harold been living together instead of going together the question of his authority in the home would very likely have been settled another way: by Mrs Davis at least requiring her children to accept that Harold had the right to insist that they be orderly and reasonably quiet. As it was, Mrs Davis sided with Harold but implicitly acknowledged that he had no intrinsic rights in relation to the children by arguing that the children owed him respect because of the things he did for them.

Nevertheless Mrs Davis depended on Harold in many ways. She spent most of her evenings with him and when he couldn't come for dinner or take her out she found life dull and herself dispirited. Once, when Harold was spending his evenings with his hospitalized mother, Mrs Davis said she was dreadfully bored; without Harold she felt herself unable to go anywhere or do anything. Harold was also important in other ways: when Mrs Davis had a dispute with the owner of a furniture store over a television set she had bought, she eventually asked Harold to see if he could get the owner to repair the set, and somehow he was able to.

Mrs Davis was ambivalent about her sexual relationship with Harold. After the relationship had ended, she said:

He was so warm and loving. I think this is what I miss most of all. It would be 'honey' this and 'honey' that. No matter what we were doing, he would be romantic. Drinking a cup of coffee, watching television, even if I was washing dishes he would come and put his arms around me and give me a kiss on the back of the neck . . .

He knew how to satisfy a woman. Making love with him was beautiful. He would fondle me and I would fondle him. I used to say to him, 'Imagine what I could be like if I were your wife and really relaxed.' . . . He was always thinking of me.

While in some ways she found the relationship intensely gratifying, Mrs Davis was also terrified that the sexual relationship would be discovered, bringing shame to herself and her family. At one point, just before the relationship with Harold ended, Mrs Davis said to the interviewer:

I'm going to tell you this. I can't tell this to even my own sister. I've been having relations with Harold. Isn't that terrible? Me! I told you how I feel about religion and morals. I've been on pills. Can you imagine that? I had to do something. I don't like a prophylactic or a diaphragm. I never felt they were foolproof . . . But I'd kill myself if I got pregnant. Do you know what that would do to my family, to my children? When everyone thinks so much of me? My family thinks I'm wonderful.

When I heard that Harold was having trouble getting a divorce I knew it had to stop. I threw the pills away. I threw them in a container in the subway, I was so upset. I didn't realize until afterwards that my name was on the box. I don't think anyone goes looking through trash . . .

This is why my mother keeps asking me when Harold and I are going to get married. She doesn't like long engagements. She says to me, 'Rose, you're such a good girl, I know I don't have to worry about you.' I know she is worried. I feel like such a hypocrite.

About this time Mrs Davis began to want to marry Harold. Marriage seemed the only way out of her dilemma: the only way to maintain both the relationship and her respectability. Her need for Harold was becoming more evident to her, and she began arguing with herself that Harold would be a kind and considerate husband.

He likes to go shopping. He helps me in the kitchen. He has a good disposition and he's good to the kids.

Mrs Davis told Harold that they couldn't go on as they had: that they would have to go forward to marriage or break off. About a month later, quite without warning, Harold called Mrs Davis to say that he had just learned that he could not possibly get a divorce and he did not think it fair to Mrs Davis to see her again. His lawyer, he said, also advised him to move out of the State to escape his wife's financial demands. (Later it appeared that Harold had shifted his affections to a new woman, but it was some time before Mrs Davis learned this.) Mrs Davis's reactions were indicative of the critical role her attachment to Harold played in her life.

She reacted with shock, distress, an over-alertness and anxiety which for one thing prevented her from sleeping, and a need for the sympathy and support of others. Describing what had happened, she said:

I am so miserable and upset. Harold called me and told me he is leaving the state. His lawyer has advised him to do this. I was so upset after he spoke to me that I cried and cried. In fact I cried over the telephone while he was talking to me. It was very late and I wanted somebody to talk to. I remembered that my sister once said, 'Whenever you get upset, no matter what hour it is, call me.' So I called her and I spoke to her until two-thirty this morning. I was so exhausted, and so emotionally upset, that I didn't sleep during the night. I called in to work and told them I was sick.

With Harold gone Mrs Davis felt 'lost and empty' – the feelings many other respondents also associated with loneliness. She imagined what it would be like to have Harold walk in the door again – she felt compelled to come again into contact with him. In these ways Mrs Davis's feelings and behaviour were very much like those of women whose husbands had died; she, like them, was responding to the loss of the figure to whom there was emotional attachment.

You know, Harold and I are really through. I don't get the calls and

I don't get the visits. It just ended abruptly. I can't get over it. But I have to get over it. I called him Wednesday, at work, and I told him that it embarrassed me to call, that I don't like to, but that we were more than just friends, what we meant to each other, and that was the reason I was calling. And he said 'Why prolong it?' and that there was nothing that he could do and there was no future in it. He said I should pretend that he was a bastard and just forget him. And I said, 'How can I pretend you were bad when you were far from it? I just remember all the beautiful things, and I miss hearing your voice and seeing you at the door.' And I said how he was a stranger now and even friends call to say hello. So I said, 'You should be able to understand how I feel and how hurt I am, because you were so wonderful to me.' And after that phone call I bawled a little more. And I just won't call him again. And naturally I feel so lost and empty.

At this time Mrs Davis became extremely short-tempered with her children. She tried to explain to them that she wasn't herself, and at one point wrote her daughter a letter apologizing to her for having exploded with rage the evening before. Mrs Davis found it helpful to talk to our interviewer and sometimes called our interviewer during the supper hour.

After a few weeks Mrs Davis got in touch with Ronnie, a man with whom she had maintained a comradeship before becoming involved with Harold. She remembered how much fun Ronnie had been – and how understanding:

The good times I had with Ronnie – he was just a marvellous guy. I gave him up because I wanted to show Harold what a nice girl I was, that I would go steady with him, be his girl ... Of course with Ronnie we never got into any kind of overly warm thing. I mean it was a shake of the hand, goodnight kiss, 'See you later,' you know? I could never be that warm with Ronnie because he just wasn't that kind of a guy. But I'd sit next to him and we'd dance close and he'd kind of hold me close and that was all right. And there was nothing beyond that.

Mrs Davis sent Ronnie a birthday card. Ronnie understood the overture and called, and they had a friendly and flirtatious conversation, agreeing to meet when Ronnie returned from a business trip. Ronnie never asked about Harold. While on his trip Ronnie sent Mrs Davis a postcard and when he returned he called to say he would be busy for a while, but would take her to dinner in two weeks or so. Mrs Davis seemed content with this. But before it could happen Mrs Davis met somebody else. How rapidly the new emotional attachment became established is especially noteworthy.

My sister kept telling me that this wonderful guy, Ed, works with my brother-in-law, and she'd love me to meet him and just go out with him, he's such a fine person. Ed is legally separated. After Harold, I said, 'I don't want to date anybody unless he's either single or already divorced.' I just felt, what if I get to like him, why start something that can't be finished?

Well, to make a long story short, the couple downstairs were taking me out for a drink and I mentioned this to my sister. So lo and behold who came into the place but my sister and brother-in-law and Ed. So we were all sitting around together and Ed asked me to dance and we all came back to the house for Chinese food and from that night on he started to call ... We started going out and it just seemed as though – it almost seems crazy to say we hit it off as well as we did. I just can't believe how I feel about this guy, and how he feels about me. Can you believe it? Honest to God, I'm really crazy about him. I can really honestly, truthfully, say that ... I can honestly say I'm in love with him. I know it. I'm in love with him.

Mrs Davis made the above statement when she had known Ed for about three weeks and because of the relationship she was entirely her old self again; ebullient, positive, energetic. We happen to know how this story continued. Ed did get his divorce and he and Mrs Davis were married. We may hope she will not have to deal again with the loss of an emotional attachment for many years.

This story illustrates some of the contributions and difficulties of going together, some of the attractions of marriage, the consequences of loss of an emotional attachment, some of the ways in which comradeships can be useful, and the consequences of re-establishing an emotional attachment. It also suggests several characteristics of emotional attachment: the value of the attachment for a sense of well-being, the loss of such attachment resulting in the syndrome of feeling lost and empty, of experiencing difficulties with restlessness and anxiety, of expressing fluctuating and volatile moods; the association of emotional attachment and sexual accessibility; the rapidity with which new emotional attachments may be formed. Though these phenomena are only illustrated and not demonstrated by this single case, our other materials corroborate their generality. How can we explain them?

One of the most striking characteristics of emotional attachment is that it fosters security. As one respondent put it, with emotional attachment there is:

This feeling of being able to talk to somebody, of knowing that somebody is listening, there's a feeling of safety there ... of safety and security.

Some time later this respondent lost the relationship that had given rise to the above description, and then said she felt hollow and anxious, very much as Mrs Davis described herself feeling lost and empty. Attachment appears to be a bond which provides security, whose absence provokes feelings of emptiness and hollowness, suggestive of hunger, and of loss and anxiety, suggestive of abandonment. Adult emotional attachment would seem to have much in common, then, with attachment in infants: when the infant's mother, or other attachment figure, is present or at least accessible there is security; when the attachment figure appears to be inaccessible there is anxiety stemming from feelings of abandonment. Security is associated with the presence of the attachment figure; anxiety with its absence.

Attachment seems to have an all-or-nothing quality; when it happens, it happens all at once. This is not to say that attachment must occur immediately on acquaintance or not at all, but rather that instead of developing gradually it seems suddenly to exist in full force. From this it appears that the attachment feelings are already present in full force in the individual and the only question is whether they should properly be directed to a particular other. To answer this question may demand some time, though often not a great deal. This odd all-or-nothing quality can be explained if we assume that attachment in adults involves the invoking of an already developed system of feelings in response to a new stimulus. Attachment, it would appear, is fundamentally transference.

This view also suggests an explanation for the phenomena of loss and loneliness. If attachment re-establishes a system of feelings developed in the individual's infancy, then the loss of an attachment should bring with it infantile fears associated with abandonment. Such fears indeed seem to be the core of the experience first of loss and later of loneliness. In loss there is the anxiety which might be appropriate to an infant alone in a meaningless and perhaps hostile world; in loneliness there is the sense that warmth, understanding, and nurturance have fled, and that one is alone in a barren world.

Individuals differ in their readiness to establish emotional attachments, in their ability to maintain constancy in emotional attachments and in the extremity of their distress on the loss of such attachments. That those who have suffered early loss are more tentative in their subsequent attachments and more severely disorganized by experience of loss is an appealing hypothesis. To my knowledge, too little information as yet exists for us to judge whether this hypothesis is true.

Most relationships in which there is emotional attachment and in which sexual involvement is possible seem to become sexual relationships even if there are fairly strong resistances, so long as these are not outright prohibitions. Identification with the other and concern for the other's well-being makes each participant responsive to the other's needs quite aside from the very likely association of attachment strivings and sexual striving. Women especially, though occasionally men as well, disparage sexual involvement except in relationships in which there is attachment. Even when there is attachment, women for whom respectability is important are uncomfortable with a sexual relationship with a man who is not permanently obligated to remain with them, as in marriage. Women who are going with a man may attempt to disguise the sexual nature of the relationship by not letting the man come to see them late in the evening, or not letting him stay overnight. Women who are living with a man may present the relationship as one which has all the stability of marriage; one of our respondents told her neighbours that she and the man she was living with would have gotten married except for his illness, which required occasional hospitalization (although at one point she let us know she had serious doubts about marrying the man and was pleased that marriage was for the time being impractical).

CONCLUSION

Concern for respectability may be losing some of its force, especially among the young, and more and more couples may choose to go together or live together rather than to marry. These are alternative ways of establishing emotional attachments and there seems no reason for asserting that they are inherently less satisfactory forms than marriage. What we may be certain of is that though the relative popularity of one form or another may change, relationships sustaining emotional attachments will continue. We may also be certain that those of us who have secure attachments will be relatively content in at least one area of our lives while those of us who have lost attachments will be distressed and lonely, and that most of us can expect sometimes to be within the one group, sometimes within the other.

7. The Choice Not to Marry

The more marriage is confined to legitimizing an established couple relation the more pertinent becomes the question, 'Why get married?'

I suggested earlier that marriage was basically concerned with kinship classifications, and to some extent it must follow that the less important these classifications become the less important marriage becomes. In complex modern societies, kinship classifications have little of the importance attached to them in other societies – although they still determine a range of people who cannot marry each other, the number of people barred for any one individual by kinship is a very small proportion of potential spouses; though relations with the wider range of kin often remain channels for support, information, help and companionship, kinship categories do not specify who owes what obligations to whom, and how people behave towards their kin is very much a matter of their experience of them as individuals. Similarly, kinship is decreasingly concerned with who has rights to what resources and social positions as increasingly status results from achievement and not ascription.[1] To be without a full range of kin in complex societies is of little consequence to most people, and even if they have them they may have relatively little to do with them. As well as the wider range of kin, 'father'[2] has become of less significance with attempts in some societies to introduce legislation establishing that all children have the same rights regardless of legitimacy.[3]

If, in addition, sex and living together are possible without marriage; growing equality of the sexes places less of a premium on men as husbands and women as wives; the relations of married people are in general little different from those of unmarried couples and little structured by the fact of marriage and of being husband and wife, what, then, does marriage offer?

Married people may still acquire rights in each other's property and that accumulated during marriage, and their 'investment' in the relation in terms of labour and money is to some extent protected. Marriage may be felt to create a greater sense of permanence and obligation, and public acknowledgement of the legitimacy of the relation may lend an air of greater respectability.

However, marriage and respectability are not intrinsically connected; the sense of permanence and obligation which may be created by no means ensures the relation will be permanent. In any case, the more impersonal obligations to behave in certain ways which may arise from marriage are themselves distasteful to people who believe that personal involvement rather than contract should be the basis of relations between the sexes. Property rights are of greater importance to some people than to others; individuals may prefer to maintain greater independence by not forming a joint household in the way demanded by marriage; the protection of investment may be balanced by the costs when other choices are available.

Under conditions of this kind, the legalities of marriage are more a deterrent than an encouragement to many people to marry; any steps taken to reduce legal obligations and make marriage more like other couple relations may simply further reduce the incentive to marry. To the extent that marriage does become simply and only a more legitimate form of a personal, sexual relation that is possible without marriage, fewer people will marry, though the numbers engaged in relatively enduring and exclusive couple relations may remain the same.

Sweden is a country often mentioned in discussions of sexual permissiveness and egalitarian marital relations, and certainly marriage in Sweden is interesting from this point of view. But in Sweden, unlike Britain and the U.S.A., marriage rates are declining, suggesting that rather than allowing people to base their marriages on sexual equality and on greater experience of each other, the changes which have occurred have primarily allowed people greater freedom not to marry at all. In the following article, Jan Trost, a Swedish sociologist, analyses the changes in Sweden's marriage rates and looks at recent legislation on marriage and how people may perceive the costs of marriage.

Married and Unmarried Cohabitation in Sweden

JAN TROST

In the middle of the nineteenth century Eilert Sundt published a book of great importance called *Om Giftermaal i Norge* (On Marriages in Norway). Sundt was a Lutheran minister, but he was also the first real sociologist in Norway. He used anthropological and demographic methods of outstanding quality for his time, and even for today. Using both these methods, he showed that rise and fall in marriage rates is mainly due to the numbers of children born twenty-five to thirty years earlier.[1] He thus refuted the more usual explanation of these changes, that is, that they are caused by wars and economic crises. It would be a slight exaggeration to say these factors are of no importance, but their importance is minor.

If Sundt's findings for the middle of the last century are valid, and valid for modern times, marriage rates in Sweden should have increased during the last five to ten years. However, there has been an enormous *decrease* in Swedish marriage rates over the last few years.[2] What has happened since 1966 is extraordinary.

Marriages in Sweden 1966–73

1966	61,101
1967	56,561
1968	52,534
1969	48,357
1970	43,278
1971	39,918
1972	39,000
1973	37,500

Thus over seven years the absolute numbers have decreased by 40 per cent, despite the fact that the number of possible spouses – the number of unmarried men and women – has increased. (The birth rate in Sweden reached a peak in the mid 1940s – not only a peak but, for Sweden, a very high rate.) Does this enormous decrease in marriage rates indicate that Sundt was wrong? If we define marriage as he did – which was reasonable at the time – he was wrong. But he was not wrong in principle if we are prepared to define marriage somewhat differently.

For a long time Sweden has had a low marriage rate compared to other countries, though not the lowest. Again, war and economic crisis do not really account for this – Sweden has had no wars for over 150 years and is neither a poor country nor one that has suffered economic crises. The steady and comparatively low marriage rate could, however, be explained by the fact that some hundred years ago many couples who were not married lived together, with or without children. This tradition, fairly common in rural districts, has never totally disappeared.[3] Ten to twenty years ago, cohabiting unmarried couples comprised only an estimated 1 per cent of the total of married and unmarried cohabiting couples.[4] We can assume from available data that the number of unmarried couples living together in 1970 was about 7 per cent of the total, while in 1974 the figure seemed to have increased to about 12 per cent.[5] The decrease in the marriage rate is thus dependent upon an increase in the number of unmarried couples living together. If we do not define marriage in the normal legal way, but as 'syndyasmos' – all long-lasting cohabiting couples (man and woman) irrespective of legal marriage, Sundt's proposition is still correct.[6] In other words, if we speak about marriages and *de facto* marriages together, that is, syndyasmos, instead of only marriages, there has been no change in the 'marriage rate'. The syndyasmos is no less popular than it was ten years ago, but legal marriage is much less popular.

COHABITING UNMARRIED COUPLES

Two related questions await answers: why this increase in unmarried couples living together (why have they not married?), and what types of couples are they in comparison to those who marry?

Couples who live together without marriage may themselves perceive many reasons for not marrying, though most reasons can be categorized in one of three ways – legal, economic and ideological. The terms are labels for internally different reasons, but the labelling structures the reality.

The legal motives for not marrying are ostensibly the fact that one or both partners are already married to someone else; a lack of acceptance that the marriage law expressly claims fidelity; that getting married is too complicated; that getting a divorce is too complicated; experience of divorce.

The economic motives for not marrying centre on economic independence; taxation; widower's pensions; social subsidies; the costs of the wedding ceremony.

The 'ideological' motives are that people want to be free and independent; are not religious or have political reasons or motives; that love is strong enough without marriage; that partners are more careful to keep the syndyasmos intact when not married.

The partners of a couple who live together without marriage may have motives which fall into one, two, all or none of these categories. Where none of the categories is relevant, the reason most often given is simply, 'it just happened that we didn't marry', or one of the partners has a motive but not the other.

Sometimes one or both partners decide they will marry later. Some marry because the situation changes, for example, economic conditions improve, the married one gets a divorce, they have a child and do not want it classified as born out of wedlock. Some decide to marry because of social pressures, despite their motives for not marrying and, of course, some simply change their minds. Others may marry only after they have had the opportunity to find out if they are compatible (sometimes called 'trial' marriage), delaying their marriage for ideological reasons.

In many cases a couple's perception of reality is 'wrong'. Those with 'legal' motives for not marrying often have a perception of the law which is incorrect (perhaps the easiest kind of case in which to talk of 'wrong' perceptions). So, for example, a couple may think that to marry one has to be religious, which is not true – the civil ceremony has been an alternative to the religious since 1908. (This motive was previously described as 'ideological', but is a mixture of 'ideological' and 'legal'.)

Obviously people have a great variety of reasons for not being married at any particular time and some people have no real motive at all. As yet we do not know how common these different situations are. However, there seem to be two main reasons for the enormous increase in the number of cohabiting unmarried couples. One is the greater openmindedness we suppose or feel has come about during the last ten years. Ten or fifteen years ago unmarried couples seldom admitted to living together, and parents and relatives were unlikely to know about the relationships to the extent they do today. If they did know, they hesitated to talk about them. Today, partners and their relatives do talk about the relation and almost no one looks upon cohabitation as something negative or immoral. Similarly, newspapers freely discuss these points, and some unmarried couples advertise in the newspapers when they start to live together in the same way that other couples advertise when they marry. They usually do so under the heading 'conscience marriage' rather than the normal 'marriage'. ('Conscience marriage' has been a term for these arrangements since the beginning of this century when some couples lived together without marriage as a protest against the existing society. Being very radical at that time, such couples told anybody who wanted to listen. Today the label seems in most cases irrelevant.)

The second main reason for the increase in cohabiting unmarried couples is simply that it has become fashionable not to marry. However, a majority still do marry, although if present trends continue those who do will shortly be in a minority.

Unmarried couples who live together tend to have certain characteristics. Firstly, such couples are much younger than married ones, which is to be expected given that the divorce rate has not been higher than 5 to 7 divorces per 1,000 existing marriages, and that most people are between twenty and thirty years old when they start a syndyasmos.[7] Secondly, unmarried couples are less stable than married ones, taking the number of dissolutions as an indicator. Taking account of differences in age and duration, unmarried cohabiting couples have an estimated dissolution rate seven to eight times that of married couples.[8] Many of them, of course, 'dissolve' as unmarried couples to become married ones. The differences, however, between married and unmarried cohabiting couples are referable to differences in age and the self-evident differences in duration of the dyad.

SWEDISH MARRIAGE LAW

Parts of the Swedish law on marriage are important for an understanding of marriage rates and the reasons people have for marrying or not marrying. Some important changes were made in the law from 1 January 1974 and, where relevant, I refer both to the present system and the system before 1974.[9]

Under the old law a couple were legally engaged when they had mutually decided to marry, though socially (rather than legally) the engagement date was the time at which rings were exchanged or an equivalent informal ceremony held. Under present law, engagement no longer has any legal meaning. Prior to 1974 it did have, especially for children conceived or born during the engagement. If the parents were not engaged at the time of conception or birth, the child could not inherit from the father, nor have his surname (which could be important for some individuals). If one partner broke off the engagement, a court could decide to award economic compensation for the emotional and economic damages sustained. In modern thought, such compensation does not seem reasonable, and engagement now has no effect on children either, since all have the same inheritance rights and so forth, irrespective of the circumstances under which they are conceived or born. Even the informal, non-legal engagement is out of date, being no longer a necessary excuse for sex or living together.

The new law has abolished some impediments to marriage, mental illness or retardation, for example. The main reasons for this are: firstly, only some mentally ill or retarded people are defined as such by the society and secondly, there is nothing to prevent them living together, so why should they not marry? Marriage between half-brother and half-sister is now allowed by exemption of the Government, there seemingly being no greater genetic risk to their offspring than to those of the marriage of a person and the children of a brother or sister (a marriage allowed by exemption under the old law). The committee investigating these matters in fact found no medical or social objections to marriage between a sister or brother and the other's children, but the government proposed that social objections still existed and that such marriages should continue to be allowed only by exemption.

The 1974 law retains the notion that marriage should be preceded by an investigation of impediments to marriage, but the only really important ones are the age limit – eighteen years for both men and women; marital status – bigamy is not allowed; prohibitions on close relatives; the requirement that spouses are of opposite sex.

The wedding itself may be either religious or civil and the ceremony very simple. In 1971, about 15 per cent of all marriages were civil, the high figure for religious ceremonies probably being more due to tradition than religious feeling.[10] (Brides especially seem to want religious ceremonies.) Under both old and new laws, religious marriage demands only the presence of a clergyman, a witness and the couple themselves. Civil marriage can be similarly simple and the new law provides an alternative formulation for those who want an even shorter and more simple ceremony. Judges usually officiate at civil ceremonies, but in every district there is at least one 'common' man or woman who is given the right by the court to conduct weddings.

With the exception of the new alternative mentioned, in both religious and civil ceremonies the official asks first the man and then the woman if he or she is willing to take the other as spouse and love him/her, and so forth. The entire ceremony may last only two or three minutes if the couple so wish. No identity control is needed; no papers are signed. The new short alternative consists only of a question to the partners if they wish to be married, their consent and the official's statement that they are married. None of these alternatives involves compulsory costs for the couple. Those who give 'high cost' as a reason for not marrying seem either not to know this or to be thinking of the unnecessary costs of making a wedding a highly ceremonious occasion.

Once married, both spouses, under both old and new law, have to contribute according to their means to the family's survival, either by earning money through gainful employment or through activities in the home. The intention here is to guarantee the housewife or househusband a fair standard of living without need for gratitude for money contributed by the employed partner. If one of the spouses buys on credit articles necessary for everyday life or for the upbringing of children, both spouses are held equally responsible. At the same time, the property and income of each spouse is theirs and each is allowed to dispose of it as wished, within the limits about common contribution to the family.

However, when a marriage is dissolved by death or divorce each spouse is considered to own half the total property, irrespective of who earned it, owned it before marriage, or inherited it. In principle, all property held at the time of death or divorce is considered joint and divided into two irrespective of its origins; in practice, settlements contrary to this fifty-fifty principle are possible. Under the new law, a court may split the property in another way if it finds a fifty-fifty division unreasonable in the light of the economic situation of the spouses and the duration of the marriage. Behind this rule lies the notion that, especially in new marriages where there is no economic communion, equal division of property might have the effect of allowing people to marry and divorce in order to obtain money.

According to the law before 1974, a couple could get a divorce either directly or, more usually, through a legal separation. If both parties agreed, the court gave them a separation; if only one partner wanted to separate they had, formally, to prove they were unhappy together, though in practice the separation was usually granted. But before they were allowed to separate they were supposed to undergo 'mediation': they would discuss with a mediator (either a layman or a family counsellor) the reasons for divorce and the mediator would try to help the couple to continue to live together. In practice, mediation mostly meant that the mediator signed a paper saying mediation had been done. After at least a year of legal separation either spouse could apply to the court for a divorce, which was given without hesitation.

To get a divorce without separation one of the spouses had to show the court that the other had committed adultery, was an alcoholic, or had been sentenced to serve at least six months in prison, or some similar 'offence'. In 1970, 85 per cent of all divorcing couples had a legal separation; about 10 per cent of cases involved adultery, and the remainder claimed some other reason for immediate divorce. To get a divorce under the old law was easy, but most people preferred to wait a year for the final, legal dissolution.

The new law clearly embodies firstly the idea that if one or both spouses no longer want to be married they should not be forced by law to stay together (in practice, of course, the law can force people only to stay married, not to live together) and, secondly, the idea that if divorce is simple people should be hindered from rushing into it. Consequently, if both spouses now agree to a divorce they will be immediately granted one if they have no children aged sixteen or below. Application is made to the court, which makes its decision immediately. If only one spouse wants a divorce, or if the couple do have children aged sixteen or below, they must separate for six months before applying for a divorce. If neither party applies within twelve months, the case is annulled, which means that if either wants a divorce after that period they must start the procedure over again. Under this law, people wanting a divorce need never give the court their reasons and, therefore, the legal procedure is very simple.

But, of course, divorce raises problems for most couples. If they have small children the court must decide which parent should have custody of them, though usually the court simply confirms the decision made by the spouses themselves. The spouse who does not get custody of the children must pay money to the other partner for their support, and often decisions over the amounts involved are very complex. In principle, ex-spouses should not pay alimony to each other, though such payments are sometimes made. For example, if one partner (normally the wife) has worked at home during a long marriage and cannot be expected to get a job, the other will be ordered by the court to pay a certain amount of money over a number of years or even for ever. Importantly, the law does not differentiate between the sexes in any of these respects. The possibility of a woman paying alimony to her ex-husband exists, though mostly alimony is paid to ex-wives when it is paid at all.

The past housing shortage in Sweden means that most Swedes live in apartments (the main shortage today being of apartments at a reasonable price) and that the court's decision on who should have the apartment after divorce is an important one.

Until January 1974, there were no rules at all for unmarried couples who lived together. Since then, a rule about residence has been established – the partner with most need of the apartment (usually the woman if she has a child) can claim the right to it even if the other is the rent holder or the owner. In all other respects unmarried couples are still not protected by legal rules, which means that the dissolution of such a relationship may often be more complicated than the dissolution of a marriage. Another motive for not marrying – the complications of divorce – is also a misconception.

Some rules of the welfare system do, however, favour living together without marriage. For instance, a one-parent family has a much higher chance of getting an apartment at a reasonable price or rent than a two-parent family. Officially, and if the couple do not tell the clerks, an unmarried couple with a child is a one-parent family. A one-parent family finds it easier to get subsidies for housing costs and to get a place for a child or children in a day-care home. Taxes are also still somewhat lower for one-parent families (though less so now than a couple of years ago). Against these advantages for unmarried couples are balanced a number of disadvantages in addition to those already mentioned in relation to rules at dissolution. They have, for example, no possibility of exercising a right of pre-emption – pensions and insurances do not usually accept an unmarried partner as a spouse; one partner cannot inherit from the other without a will; a partner with no children has no right to the apartment if the contract was in the other's name. When they separate, whoever has the receipt for the television set, the sofa, the refrigerator, or whatever, owns them.

These are only a few of the rules which might be of relevance to changes in marriages rates, but they seem to be among the most important ones.

MARRIAGE IN THE FUTURE

Some people assume, on the basis of decreasing marriage rates and the kinds of changes in the law that I have summarized, that marriage will disappear as a social institution. However, a number of alternative assumptions can be made. We can assume either: (a) that the new fashion for cohabitation without marriage will spread and become accepted by a greater proportion of the population; or (b) that the new fashion is not an objection to marriage as such, but simply a renewal of a cultural tradition to cohabit for some time before marriage; or (c) that the new fashion is just a fashion and therefore is likely to disappear.

Should the first assumption be correct, the marriage rate will continue to decrease, the level reached probably being dependent on the number of young people who believe that marriage is instituted by God and not society. Only they will marry. This would mean, if there are no changes, that the number of marriages would be almost zero, since Swedes by tradition have never let the church decide their behaviour to any great extent.[11] Should the second assumption be correct, there will be a renewed tradition of 'trial' or 'engagement' marriages which would effect a rapid increase in the marriage rate in a couple of years, a high rate for some years, followed by a decrease to 'normal' levels. (The peak, of course, would result from the marriages of those who, under 'normal' conditions would have married during the last few years.) If the third assumption is correct, the result would be almost the same.

I believe in the second assumption, though it is hard to find concrete grounds for this belief which, if reality follows belief, could be called an intuitive feeling.

At the same time, to isolate marriage rates from other social influences is impossible. The mass media and perhaps the state will spread information on the new laws, which should alter people's perceptions of them. This new cognition, based on simplified laws and better information, will make irrelevant some of the perceived motives for not marrying. Similarly, the spread of information will increase knowledge of the latent problems of unmarried cohabitation, especially important for those with children. I would predict that these 'forces', taken together with all the other factors mentioned, will lead to a renewed tradition of pre-marital cohabitation, an increase in marriage rates, and stabilization of rates in several years to a level only slightly lower than that before the change in the law.

8. Homosexual Couples

That liking and companionability, love and affection, should exist between two people of the same sex is usually taken for granted, but passionate or romantic love and sexual interest between them is most often regarded as unnatural in Western societies, the consummation of such attractions as a perversion, the result of psychic disorder. But for at least some people, couple relations with members of their own sex provide a viable and desirable alternative to any kind of sexual relation with those of the opposite sex.

Homosexual interest and intercourse has met with many different responses in different societies. Some regard homosexuality as a criminal offence punishable by death, or imprisonment; many treat it with repugnance and ridicule; some accept its inevitability for a small minority of people within the society or consider that it constitutes a second best when other avenues of sexual gratification are barred; and a few have glorified it. Very often sexual relations between men are regarded with greater animosity than those between women, perhaps not only because of different reactions to the specifically sexual nature of such relations but because, in Western societies at least, physical contact and expression of tenderness between men is more contrary to norms of masculinity than the equivalent between women is to norms of femininity. Lesbianism seldom suffers the same legal sanctions as male homosexuality, and, though it is still often regarded as a perversion, much less attention has been paid to it.[1]

In England, legislation making homosexual acts legal under certain conditions removed one major problem for homosexuals.

Both gay liberation and women's liberation movements have attacked Western notions of 'masculinity' and 'femininity', emphasizing that there is no intrinsic reason why biological gender, itself a concept of degree, should determine the social behaviour and attitudes of individuals. The two movements together seek, in other words, to divest 'man' and 'woman' of as much of their social meaning as possible, and, in doing so, both help homosexuality to become more socially acceptable.

Even so, homosexuals encounter difficulties in our society. Many people are reluctant to treat homosexual couples informally in the same way as any other couple. Even more would resist, for many reasons, the notion that homosexuals should be able to marry and raise a family.

If marriage is regarded fundamentally as a means of providing children with a standard complement of kinsmen and giving them a place, an identity, in that complement, and if these kinship categories embody gender differences as they do in our society, homosexual marriages would be extremely anomalous. Such marriages would not only institutionalize male 'mothers' and female 'fathers', but also make possible, by extension, male 'sisters', 'aunts', 'nieces' and 'daughters', as well as female 'brothers', 'uncles', 'nephews' and 'sons' unless the classification were adapted.[2] Obviously, to permit homosexuals to marry is not to insist that they become parents, but there is no reason to assume that because people have particular kinds of sexual interests they will have no wish to have children. To say that a couple may 'marry' but to prevent them from becoming legal parents by adoption, or to claim that a child of one party could stand in no special relation to the other and his/her kin, would be to make complete nonsense of this most fundamental aspect of marriage.

Leaving aside kinship *per se* and turning to raising a family, further difficulties and objections are encountered. Heterosexual couples, of course, can and do have and bring up children without marriage, though usually the children are their own (or at least offspring of one of the partners), such couples having much more difficulty than married ones in adopting or fostering children. Homosexual couples cannot legally adopt or foster children. Female homosexuals may bear children resulting from heterosexual liaisons and raise them with their homosexual partner. Male homosexuals are at a greater disadvantage; the only way in which they can 'easily' acquire children is through a heterosexual marriage. Even were these problems surmountable a further objection might lie in the supposed detrimental effects on children of being brought up in a household lacking approved gender models.

To the extent that biological gender, male and female, become divested of their social meaning, to that extent objections to homosexuals raising children should diminish. How they acquire these children, particularly male homosexuals, may remain something of a problem. If homosexual 'parentage' were legally accepted, homosexual marriage might be insisted upon as a precondition for adoption or fostering, as it is for heterosexuals. Should they be able to acquire children in other ways, marriage is, of course, no more necessary to the founding of families by homosexuals than it is to their founding by heterosexuals.

In our culture, gender distinctions are an essential feature of the kinship system, but this is neither intrinsic nor necessary to kinship. It is, therefore, perfectly feasible to have kinship systems which incorporate homosexual marriages and treat them as quite acceptable means of legitimizing children. However, in as much as kinship itself is becoming less relevant and necessary and easier to ignore in our society, there seems little reason why homosexual couples any more than heterosexual couples should need to marry for kinship reasons.

Taken in conjunction these two changes – the decreasing social importance of gender and kinship – would suggest that the formation of homosexual families may become easier. If some form of marriage remains an integral/usual part of such families it is unlikely to be because of kinship. Instead it will be some form of contract to form a household with legal responsibility for children.

The next chapter, 'Men in Love: Observations on Male Homosexual Couples', by Ken Plummer, is based on the author's participant observation among homosexuals in London and on interviews with homosexual couples. As well as giving an account of attitudes towards homosexuality, the difficulties faced by homosexuals and how some couples feel both about their own relationships and about marriage, the chapter highlights just how many assumptions are generally made about 'man' and 'woman' and about 'a man and a woman' in social relationships in general.

Men in Love: Observations on Male Homosexual Couples

KEN PLUMMER

It is, perhaps, a sign of the times that a book on 'The Couple' should include a chapter on homosexual couples. While nothing seems more natural than to discuss heterosexuality in terms of relationships and couples, homosexuality has been thought of as a condition requiring special causal explanations and special devices for controlling it. Only recently in this culture has homosexuality come to be viewed increasingly as a legitimate alternative way of life, and as a relationship.

This chapter is concerned only with male homosexual couples in contemporary England (and America). It deals with the nature and prevalence of 'gay' couples, and the social context which engulfs the homosexual experience, making such couples relatively infrequent.[1] The particular experiences of nine gay couples are used to illustrate the way some homosexuals have overcome the problems faced. Throughout, data are drawn from the fragmented and limited literature in this field, from fieldwork in the homosexual community of London in the late sixties; from interviews with the nine couples mentioned above; and from personal experience. The discussion remains on the level of exploration.[2]

WHAT IS A GAY COUPLE?

Two approaches to identifying 'a couple' are possible – the subjective and the conventional. The former suggests that a gay couple exists when a homosexual defines somebody as his partner. How an outsider defines the relationship is irrelevant; the important thing is the meanings that individuals attach to their own relationships. By this kind of definition, for example, a husband and wife living together in marital disharmony for thirty years and who do not see themselves as a couple, are not a couple; while two homosexuals who fall in love but part within weeks are a couple during the time they define their relationship in this way. Such an approach has difficulties, though it does direct attention towards what people themselves mean by couples.

The second kind of definition is more conventional and attempts to establish independent criteria by which any relationship can be assessed as a couple or not. Such criteria may include the emotional, social and sexual nature of the relationship, its duration, its exclusivity and whether or not the two people live together. By such criteria one definition of a 'gay couple' would be *a fairly permanent, more or less exclusive relationship, based upon a social, emotional and sexual foundation, between two people of the same sex who sometimes share a common home.* This would be an ideal type from which many variations could be derived. The main feature of the definition is that it includes several criteria, any one of which, if taken alone, would not depict a couple. Men may have long-term emotional commitments to other men; they may set up house with other men; they may have permanent sexual relationships with each other – all these would not be couples. Outsiders often make mistaken assumptions about the relationships of others: they may assume that two homosexuals who demonstrate a close friendship are also lovers, but generally this is not true. (Indeed, as Leznoff and Westley observed in their study of a Canadian homosexual community, a kind of 'incest-taboo' appears to exist amongst homosexuals, such that friends are prohibited as sexual partners.[3] Many homosexuals call their close friends 'sisters', depicting a strong, non-sexual bond.) Similarly, outsiders may assume a love affair when two homosexuals set up house together, but homosexuals often do this out of convenience, practical considerations being more important than romantic ones. In other words, a range of relationships does exist in the homosexual world, but only a few could be labelled 'couples' according to the above definition.

KINDS OF COUPLES

There are many variations in homosexual couples, as there are
in heterosexual ones. Carol Warren, in a study of a middle-class
American gay community, suggested three kinds: those model-
led on heterosexual marriage, those based upon a more flexible
concept of an 'open marriage' where 'extra-marital' relationships are welcomed, and those based on 'three-way relationships' – stable relationships built up among three men.[4] More
generally three forms can be distinguished – 'marriage', the 'boy
friend' and the 'partnership', forms which correspond more or
less to the distinctions made by Weiss elsewhere in this book for
heterosexual couples (see pp. 138–43).

Homosexual 'Marriage': Homosexuals sometimes, but rarely, attempt to imitate the rituals establishing heterosexual marriages –
an engagement party, a 'marriage' ceremony, a wedding party,
an exchange of rings and vows, a honeymoon.[5] The relationship
itself may develop on the basis of the male–female dichotomy,
with one partner having a professional occupation, earning most
of the money and playing the active role in sex, while the other
plays a generally subordinate role, has a lower income and a less
responsible job, and plays the passive role in sex.

Some of these 'marriages' are romantically ritualistic and
serve primarily as an excuse for a party and a good time. Such
marriages do not seem to last very long and are unstable – the
ritual being more important than the relationship.[6] Others may
be more serious. In England some gay priests are frequently
approached to conduct marriage ceremonies for lovers seeking
recognition from the church. Sometimes their requests are
granted in as much as a simple exchange of vows takes place. In
America one ecumenical, revivalistic homosexual church (Troy
Perry's Metropolitan Community Church) publicly conducts
and witnesses its own 'marriage' ceremonies.[7] There have even
been some successful attempts to find loopholes in the law by
which gay 'marriages' can become legal and enjoy the benefits of
tax relief associated with heterosexual marriage.[8]

Boyfriends: This refers simply to a love relationship between homosexuals who do not live together as, for example, one ageing respondent and his friend whose relationship had lasted almost twenty years but who slept and lived together only at weekends. This pattern is often a compromise solution to the problem of courting when one or both wish to maintain their autonomy or when parental and work restrictions make living together impossible. Sometimes these relationships do develop into homosexual partnerships.

Homosexual Partnerships: In such partnerships two men live together and try to establish a life-style particular to their own needs. They shun any attempt to mimic heterosexuals, especially rigid male and female roles. As one respondent put it, 'Your butch and femme types is just not on. We do everything jointly.' Thus all the middle-class respondents shared their incomes, took turns doing household chores and cooking, did not restrict their sexual behaviour to stereotyped role patterns, and held roughly similar occupational positions. Interestingly, the two more working-class respondents did display a clearer separation of gender roles, a separation which may reflect class variation found among heterosexual married couples.

Most of my discussion is concerned with 'marriages' and with partnerships.

THE INFREQUENCY OF HOMOSEXUAL COUPLES

In 1948 Kinsey concluded that 'long-term relationships between two males are notably few', and subsequent research has largely validated this observation.[9] Many homosexuals (between 40 per cent and 60 per cent of most samples) do form stable relationships of over a year's duration, but very few last more than ten years and almost none celebrate a 'silver anniversary'.[10] These findings, of course, are all subject to methodological flaws, since to obtain a random sample of homosexuals is impossible. Generalizations about the prevalance of homosexual couples cannot, therefore, be made with any accuracy, though Schofield's work does suggest that the rate of formation of couples may differ from one homosexual group to another.[11] In his sample of 150 homosexuals, couples were very common amongst homosexuals in the community at large, though those who had been in prison very seldom formed couples and those who had visited psychiatrists formed them even less frequently. Even though generalizations cannot be made on the basis of these findings, that couples should emerge more frequently amongst homosexuals in the community than amongst those who visit psychiatrists seems plausible. Yet regrettably, most research on homosexuality comes from clinical studies.

Those homosexuals who do meet a partner, settle down, and isolate themselves from effective involvement in the homosexual world, are least likely to fall into the narrow sweep of the researcher's net. Conventional sampling sources for research on homosexuals may thus be of restricted value in understanding couples. Those involved have no need for the help of psychiatrists since they are well adjusted; they have little need for casual sex as they are sexually satisfied; they have little need for homophile organizations since they eschew protest and change; and they often have minimal involvement in the gay world. The small number of homosexual couples discovered by researchers may, therefore, be entirely unrepresentative of actual numbers, so creating difficult problems for research and generalization.

Even allowing for sampling problems, however, I have little doubt that male homosexuals less frequently form lasting couple relationships than heterosexuals. Several explanations for this exist in the literature.

Some biologists suggest that the infrequency of such relationships is a consequence of man's innate predatory and promiscuous sexual instinct, of the fact that man is more readily conditionable to any sexual stimulus than woman. (This explanation would also be used to account for the greater stability usually attributed to lesbian relationships.) The explanation claims that men, unlike women, are 'by nature' concerned with sexual stimulation rather than romantic attachment, which is thought more conducive to long-lasting relationships. Even if we accept that gender differences are largely the consequence of social learning (as I do) and not directly of biology, the conclusions drawn are the same – in this culture men are conventionally 'sexier' than women, which may make it difficult for a man to settle down with another man.

Some clinicians (probably a minority) stress that homosexuality is a sickness, a behavioural disorder making homosexuals incapable of stability and permanence in their relationships. Thus Bergler could argue that homosexuals are unconscious masochists seeking painful relationships in order to eliminate their guilt,[12] while Socarides more recently (1972) suggested:

Instead of co-operation, solace, stimulation, emotional enrichment and a maximum opportunity for creative interpersonal maturation and realistic fulfilment, there are multiple underlying factors which threaten any ongoing homosexual relationship: destruction, mutual defeat, exploitation of the partner and the self, oral sadistic incorporation, aggressive onslaughts and attempts to alleviate anxiety – all comprising a pseudo-solution to the aggressive and libidinal conflicts that dominate and torment the individuals concerned.[13]

Robbins, in an earlier paper on 'Homosexual Marriages' drawing on two case studies, describes homosexual relationships as characterized by 'the parasitic boring of one member into the other, regardless of personal consequence in response to an imperative craving'.[14] This craving is 'the impulse to enslave and cruelly exploit another'. 'This sadism,' he continues, 'responsible for creating the actual need for the merger, functions throughout the entire relationship.' Bieber, probably the most scholarly of these workers, is less extreme and sees difficulties ensuing from the high anxiety state generated in the homosexual, an anxiety state which is 'similar to the anxiety surrounding the sexual and possessive feelings toward a mother figure'.[15]

At best these arguments linking homosexuality with sickness are scientifically debatable. At worst, they are ideological distortions which serve to contain homosexuality in this society. Though homosexuals may develop pathological symptoms, Freedman, after reviewing a substantial body of work on the adjustment of homosexuals, concludes that 'homosexuality is compatible with positive psychological functioning':

They demonstrate that most of the homosexually orientated individuals evaluated in the studies function as well as comparable groups of heterosexually oriented individuals; that their functioning could be typically characterised as normal; and that in some cases, their function even approximates that of self-actualizing people. Cumulatively these studies dealt with more than 600 homosexually oriented subjects, whereas the studies with negative or mixed results had only about 150 homosexually oriented subjects in all.[16]

Clinical explanations of the infrequency of homosexual couples are insufficient, firstly, because there is no doubt that many homosexuals are well adjusted, and secondly, even allowing for some degree of pathology, social rather than psychic factors cannot be ignored.[17] In other words, the formation of homosexual couples may best be understood as a consequence of certain kinds of society. As one author rather crudely put it, 'the reason that males who are homosexually inclined cannot form stable relationships with each other is that society does not want them to'.[18] It is to this society that I now turn.

THE SOCIAL CONTEXT OF HOMOSEXUALITY

My argument here draws from the broader one (developed in my book *Sexual Stigma*)[19] that no adequate understanding of homosexuality, and indeed all sexuality, is possible without relating it to broader socio-historical contexts. Homosexuality or any pattern of sexuality has no absolute, automatic or trans-situational meaning – it takes its meaning and forms from its context. Such an observation is no more than an often overlooked truism; but it is a significant truism. It means that while homosexuality exists in this culture as a real and identifiable condition, this need not be so; that while the process of becoming a homosexual may be characterized by problems of guilt, access and identity (and sometimes, concomitantly, pathology), this need not be so; that while a subculture of homosexuality emerges, this need not be so (or at least not in the form it takes); that while the everyday experience of homosexuals may be characterized by 'passing as straight' and 'avoiding stigma', this need not be so. Most importantly here, it means that while homosexual relationships in general and couples in particular may be inhibited in this culture, again this need not be so.

The experience of homosexuality is situationally shaped, assuming its meanings from the context in which it arises, a context which comprises both *direct* responses to homosexuality and *indirect* responses which, while not directly aimed at homosexuals, nevertheless play a powerful role.

Negative or *direct* responses have received most attention. Recent studies have stressed the pervasiveness of homophobia. Condemned as a sin, sickness, crime or simply a sorrowful state, homosexuality has been responded to in a highly stigmatizing fashion. At worst, homosexuals have been slaughtered in concentration camps, murdered by 'queer-bashers' or killed by aversion therapy: more moderately, they have been hospitalized as sick, imprisoned as criminals, discriminated against in employment, mocked by media and acquaintances.

Homosexuals are confronted by an experience that is devalued and rendered illegitimate for them by their society. As a result, a homosexual may come to see his own experiences as wrong, feeling guilt and shame and a desire to conceal the experiences from others. He may subsequently find difficulty in meeting other homosexuals and in accepting his position in society as a homosexual. Through guilt and secrecy, the experience may be heightened until it becomes a pivotal part of his life and he develops an exaggerated concern with issues of masculinity and sexuality. These consequences of social hostility may inhibit the development of couple relations.

The *indirect* responses are also important. Such responses are the ideologies and institutions found in the mainstream of society which provides expectations and models of appropriate behaviour and attitudes for members of that society, expectations and models which run counter to homosexuality. Among these three stand out: the broad institutions of marriage and the family with its accompanying belief system of romantic love, familism and coupling; gender variation associated with the ideology of 'sexism'; and procreative sexuality linked to sex negativism – the belief that sexuality constitutes a powerful natural drive linked to procreation and in need of constant control. All of these raise problems for homosexuals. The belief that it is natural, obvious, better to live one's life with a partner than without one is a taken-for-granted view that homosexuals have to confront. Status is given to the couple, suspicion is cast upon the single. All people should at least aspire towards these relationships even if they do not achieve them, and marriage, of course, is the norm. (In 1966 87·2 per cent of all people in England aged between thirty and forty were married.) As Ralph Turner commented:

> Marriage is one of the key devices ... for validating personal adequacy, heterosexual normality and personal maturity. Learning this connection explicitly or implicitly, most individuals expect to become married on reaching maturity. Turning the relations around, they become anxious about their own adequacy, normality and maturity when marriage is unduly delayed.[20]

While other writers do not necessarily stress marriage, they place even more importance on couple relationships as a means of self-actualization, fulfilment, and as a condition for healthy development.[21]

To have a stable partner is perceived as normal and mature; not to have one as worrying and unhealthy. Such a powerful ideology provides a key motivational source for the homosexual to seek couple relationships. Clearly homosexuality must be viewed against this backdrop of 'taken for granted' beliefs, since they serve as a constant reminder to homosexuals of how the world 'really is'. Homosexuals find themselves constantly, though perhaps dimly, reminded of the importance of love, marriage, family life, the proper roles of men and women and the importance of settling down with a mate. Such beliefs simultaneously shape their daily experiences. (Of course the context of homosexuality should not be seen simply as stable, consensual, clear and uniformly opposed to homosexuals and in favour of couples, sex negativism and sexism. Many changing, contradictory and often ambiguous responses to homosexuality exist, and what people are supposed to believe is not always mirrored by their actual beliefs, statements or behaviour.[22])

In brief, the indirect elements instil in homosexuals a strong desire for couple relationships: the direct homophobic elements restrict their ability to meet these socially induced desires.

The stages through which people go in their search for a homosexual mate illustrate this point. These stages may be divided into: (i) the motivation for a couple relationship; (ii) the initiation of a homosexual relationship; (iii) the establishment of the right type (that is, couple) relationship; and (iv) the maintenance of the relationship. Each of these stages involves fewer people. I will discuss each in turn.

OBSTRUCTING GAY COUPLES

(i) *Motivation:* As I have said, the problem of forming couples has its roots for homosexuals in the wider structure of society. A great deal of childhood play is concerned with preparing children for adult roles as husband and wife, father and mother. The educational system and the media reinforce these notions. It can be taken for granted that by adolescence any 'normal' male will wish to 'act like a man', 'find himself a girl', 'settle down' and ultimately 'have children'. Such is the *leitmotif* of most male members of the western world.

Again I am oversimplifying and do not wish to suggest total consensus. In a pluralistic society ambiguities surround many values and some individuals gain access to groups championing different norms and others reject values earlier supported. If homosexuals gain access to such beliefs many problems do not exist for them, and most recently such beliefs have been forcefully, if not originally, put by the Gay Liberation Front. As one respondent said to Westwood in 1959:

> The idea of romantic homosexual marriage is nonsense. The great advantage of homosexuality is the freedom it gives. To translate this into terms of marriage and fidelity is vulgar and bourgeois.[23]

Indeed, in a survey in which I took part in 1970, a quarter of some 2,000 male homosexuals interviewed were not sure they wanted homosexual love relationships lasting more than six months, and about 10 per cent said they did not want such a relationship at all. Such findings emphasize that the problem is not a universal one, and that couple formation is not universally subscribed to.

Nevertheless most homosexuals as well as heterosexuals probably do seek couple relationships. This motivation may be so strong that some homosexuals marry heterosexually; but others are committed to finding a homosexual mate. The problem of finding a mate is a central problem in the lives of many.[24]

The homosexual motivated to find a stable relationship soon finds the world running in reverse. The heterosexual is facilitated, almost dragooned, into such a relationship, the homosexual is typically thwarted. The settings in which he has to meet other homosexuals, start relationships and maintain them are not the conventional ones.

(ii) Initiation: Heterosexuals find access to potential partners almost anywhere. For homosexuals the search for lovers is made difficult by the need for secrecy and anonymity created by the perception of a hostile society. If a homosexual were to make advances to any man who interested him he would have to learn to cope well with ridicule, rebuttal, rage or risk of life. Only the foolhardy, the stupid or the troublesome would take such actions. To find a partner becomes an arduous task, for he must either gain access to a pool of potential partners or to a repertoire of skills which allow him to 'sound out' people within the general population.

The existence of a gay subculture may provide him with potential partners and skills. But while the subculture is widespread, all homosexuals do not have instant or easy access to it. Many are not even aware of its existence, and others who are have difficulty locating it, particularly those men who live in rural areas where the subculture is less systematically organized. Many homosexuals thus spend their lives without effective interaction with other homosexuals and consequently with little chance of establishing a homosexual relationship. As one respondent wrote:

I know that I could give so much to homosexual marriage with the correct partner, yet I am denied simply because I don't know where to begin. I am not ashamed of what I am, but desperate, unhappy and very lonely because the social system prevents me from finding a young man in similar circumstances as myself ...

Even access to the subculture by no means guarantees a permanent partner. Within the subculture courting rules may be ambiguous. For heterosexuals the tacit assumption is generally that the man will pursue the woman, while the woman will make symbolic gestures of encouragement. A novice in the gay world may not know who should make the first move, each participant leaving the opening move to the other. Once involved, tacit rules do operate and they have much in common with those of heterosexuals – the older usually approaches the younger, the less attractive approaches the more attractive. The novice may not know these rules and his early failures may lead him to withdraw from the subculture. Another difficulty with parallels in the heterosexual world is the fear of rejection.

I think ... the only aspect of their self which male homosexuals are able to adequately present in a bar situation is their physical appearance. If they are restricted in making a conversational opening, this is interpreted (probably correctly) to mean a rejection of that crucial part of themselves, namely their desirability as a sexual partner. Hence their self-esteem is very much at stake, and they have a great deal to lose by being rejected ... in the Gay World the only criterion of value is physical attractiveness; consequently a rejection by a desired partner is a rejection of the only valued part of one's identity in that world. When we understand this, I think we understand why the fear of rejection is so prevalent among homosexual men.[25]

I think Hoffman in this passage makes the sense of rejection too narrow, for some homosexuals feel generally rejected by society and suffer from a trauma of inadequacy as a result of seeing their entire lives defined as illegitimate. Homosexuals who believe themselves to be inadequate and rejected may be unable to believe that others could find them attractive or pleasant. They may make no approaches because they believe others would not respond. These beliefs may result in self-fulfilling prophecies: dull, nervous, shy, they may not be able to elicit responses, so confirming their own suspicions. A spiral which is hard to break may be set in motion, especially since success in gay bars and clubs is defined largely in terms of extrovert behaviour – camp humour, drinking, dancing. In this sense, such people are objective failures in the gay world, where shyness and insecurity progressively weaken the chances of initiating relationships.

That other factors inhibit relationships even when homosexuals do have access to the subculture should not be overstated, for once the norms are familiar less risk is attached to making advances and the problems recede with success. Lack of success does, however, mean that many homosexuals leave the homosexual world disillusioned with its ability to provide a partner.

(*iii*) *Establishing a Relationship:* For heterosexuals, most boy–girl meetings are seen as bases from which couple relationships could develop; for homosexuals most relationships are seen as transient unless there are good grounds for believing otherwise. At least two factors contribute to these transient relationships. Firstly, the way in which the gay world is structured so that people meet each other primarily as sex objects, and secondly, the norms generated in the gay world partly as a defence against threats from the 'straight' world and partly as a positive response to a new situation.

First, then, people in the gay world often have virtually nothing in common but their homosexuality and their role as sexual outcasts. Heterosexual lovers may meet in many places, places associated with many interests other than sexual ones. The college boy is likely to find a college girl, the religious devotee another religious devotee, the ballroom champion another ballroom champion. The gay world does not provide this diversity – many classes, age groups, races, occupations, nationalities and interest groups gather together in homosexual bars and meeting places, with little in common except their homosexuality and their oppression. Relationships embarked upon will probably be between partners who differ greatly in social background and will function on the basis of limited traits such as youth and beauty, traits not typically leading to permanent relationships when not associated with reciprocal interests.

Of course, for homosexuals to meet others with similar inter-

ests is possible, but in homosexual bars the basis of most
relationships is sex. Were homosexuality more acceptable and
homosexual groups based on non-sexual criteria, the chances of
meeting partners on other than purely sexual grounds would, of
course, be increased. Over recent years a range of specific
interest groups within the homosexual world have emerged. The
Gay Liberation Movement brings together many with common
links in the universities, third world movements, and so forth,
while more specific groups such as the Gay Marxist Study
Group, The Gay Christian Movement, the Jewish Homophile
Group and the Gay Librarians group have already started to
bring together many common interests.

Secondly, the existing norms of the gay world encourage
transient relationships. The assumption is that a relationship embarked upon with a stranger will quickly result in sex and an
anonymous departure.[26] These norms may be explained firstly as
a *defence strategy*, highlighting some of the areas most at risk for
homosexuals in their relationship with the wider society.

A homosexual's masculinity is made an issue for him by
society. In this culture to be sexual is valued if one is a man; to
be emotional is devalued if one is a *real* man. Thus, by accentuating the sexual side of his life and divorcing it from the
emotional, a homosexual can protect himself from the loss of his
masculine identity and from self-conception as deviant. As
Horowitz remarks, 'Men regard sexual acts as less deviant than
a male–male tenderness.'[27]

A homosexual also has his total identity put at risk by society.
He may choose to avoid being seen by others as a homosexual
and thinking of himself in this way. He may give accounts of
himself which suggest that he is not really a homosexual.
However, embarking on a love affair and living with another
homosexual means a daily confrontation with evidence of his
homosexuality. Engaging in casual relationships renders the risk
to self-conception less. The norms again serve to protect him.

Norms, however, are not only reactions and defences. They
are also the consequence of *constructive activities* by the gay
world where a release from dominant norms of society is seized

upon as an opportunity for building up alternative ones. No universal linkage exists between sex, love and marriage; such linkages are socially constructed. The relationships among these three institutions may be highly functional for the smooth flow of this society, but the benefits may not acrue to all groups. The procreation and rearing of children may make the linkage a highly functional one, but when children are not an issue the linkage may be dysfunctional, in as much as it may limit the potential for loving outside of sexual relationships and limit the range of sexual experience. Homosexuals, divorced from routine sexual meanings, are in a position to actively explore and create alternatives.

(iv) *Maintaining a Relationship:* Even when homosexuals establish couple relationships many factors work to break them up, a fact equally true of heterosexual relationships. Sociologists studying the family have produced long lists of factors which correlate with family/marital breakdown.[28] But while dissimilar backgrounds, non-religious homes, incongruent attitudes, premarital petting and even lack of a church wedding may be associated with the demise of both heterosexual and homosexual couples, homosexuals may more readily part company than heterosexuals. As Altman notes, 'A bad "homosexual marriage" is likely to be dissolved far more easily than a bad "straight" one.'[29]

Homosexual affairs probably dissolve speedily firstly because the relationship is given little validation or recognition by the outside (heterosexual world) and, secondly, because the gay world itself poses threats.

Heterosexual marriage involves formal institutions, the gay couple does not. The law does not protect it, nor does the church give it its blessing 'till death do us part'. Family, community and society, if not outrightly hostile, refuse to recognize the couple as a unit. The break-up of a couple after many years together may be seen by outsiders simply as a decision to move flats; the tax man grants no relief; hospitals do not recognize partners as 'next-of-kin' in emergencies; observers look mockingly or violently upon homosexuals kissing each other goodbye; hotel keepers refuse to give a double bed to two men; heterosexual colleagues and friends ignore the existence of a partner in a way that would be offensive to heterosexual couples.

The scarcity of homosexual couples and the taken-for-granted norms of transient relationships mean that the common assumption is that all homosexuals are available for sex unless proven otherwise. A homosexual in a bar who does not show obvious signs of 'being with someone' is assumed 'open' and 'available' to all. In contrast, among heterosexuals over a certain age, individuals are often assumed unavailable unless proven otherwise. If contact is maintained with the homosexual world, this risk to the couple is constantly present. Should homosexuals detach themselves from the reified, abstract meaning of coupling, a meaning which suggests that for couple relationships to survive 'promiscuous' sexual relationships should be avoided, they could experience both casual sexual relationships in the gay world and stable couple relationships outside it. But as long as they believe that casual sex precludes stability *and* that sexuality must be associated with exclusivity, they are faced with the dilemma of being unable to enjoy transient sex because it is unstable and being unable to enjoy stable sex because of unfaithfulness. The inability of many homosexuals to divorce themselves from the constraints of the heterosexual culture places many relationships under severe strain.

A further threat to stable relationships is posed by the very fact that homosexuals can afford to be more idealistic in their pursuit of a mate than heterosexuals.[30] Homosexuals do not have to 'settle down by their mid-twenties' and 'make the most of it' when they do. A homosexual may find a lover and settle down for a few months, only to discover that his mate is not ideal and depart to find another. Stable lovers are desperately sought, only to be dropped through unlimited aspirations.

NINE GAY COUPLES: GETTING ROUND PROBLEMS

Some homosexuals do, of course, circumvent the problems I have outlined;[31] some homosexuals do meet outside the gay world and do develop stable relationships. The following discussion centres primarily on nine couples I interviewed between 1969 and 1970.[32] The couples all lived in London and had been together for at least three years. Two couples had spent over twenty years together.[33] Both partners in eight of the couples had full-time occupations and only one of these occupations could be termed unskilled. Among the occupations were lawyer, doctor, professional musician, social worker, clergyman, lecturer, journalist. In age, they varied from early twenties to mid-sixties and with the exception of one couple with an age difference of twenty years partners were of similar age. Some had been active in the homosexual world from an early age; others had their first significant homosexual experience with their partner and revealed an almost total ignorance of the sub-culture. Clearly such a small sample allows no valid generalizations to be made, though I have tried to draw some limited conclusions from these examples.

Initiation: The men met under a variety of circumstances. Only three couples met during involvements with the homosexual world, another three met at work, one at a 'straight' party, another through a pen-pal column in *Woman's Own*, and another was a priest who met his future partner while parish visiting. Most met in routine heterosexual situations and the relationship was not immediately seen as a homosexual one.

Establishing a Couple: Since they mostly met in routine situations outside of the gay world they did not encounter the expectation of a transient relationship. Instead, many had been strongly influenced by the 'romantic love' ideology of the dominant culture.

I saw this rather dishy creature. He was playing in the first orchestra, and I was playing in the second. I thought, that's nice, but obviously straight. I avoided looking at him at first, because I thought he'd beat me over the head. Then during the performance I noticed he was staring at me madly, so I sort of stared back, and by half way through the performance we were falling about laughing. Absolutely hopeless. In the evening I had to tear off, so I threw my pay packet at him with my name and address, and lo and behold he rang me the following day. I never doubted from that moment on that this was it – I know it sounds silly ... (23-year-old with a 3-year relationship)

The first two months were rather like poetry books, all hearts and flowers. We didn't know any other people. (37-year-old with a 9-year relationship)

We were both cruising around (Pub) ... and looked at each other. We were both infatuated – we were ideal for each other. He was everything I sort of cared about, still is for that matter ... (23-year-old with a 3-year relationship)

In this last case the encounter did take place in a homosexual bar, though both participants were new to the homosexual world (the first and second time respectively that they had been to a bar) and they were naïve about 'gay life' and had not had time to encounter the norms of transiency.

Some were slow to define their relationships as permanent. One couple met at work during their teens but did not acknowledge each other's homosexuality for fifteen years and did not settle down together till five years after that. At the time of the interview they had been together for about ten years and were convinced that a 'soul mate' is never found by looking, 'he just comes along'. Another couple took six months to discover and interpret the nature of their relationship, as did a further couple who met in a public convenience. The report on the interview with them reads:

They met in the gent's lavatory at Marylebone station, where both were 'cottaging' in adjacent cubicles. There was the usual 'hole-in-the-wall' and exchange of notes. They began in a very casual fashion. Peter wasn't looking consciously for an affair, but there was a distinct hope that it might happen one day. They began living together after six months of casual meetings ... The initial feeling on Peter's part was that they could both benefit from a settled affair. Peter was from the first 'inordinately fond of his partner', and now, after seven years of intimacy, 'can't bear to think of life without him'.

A number of couples commented that they were not actively seeking love partners when they met. One man in his late twenties, who had never previously had a homosexual relationship and had not defined himself as a homosexual, commented on his meeting with his partner:

I didn't plan it at all. Although I think I knew at this time [that I was a homosexual], I hated queers. I didn't go for his sort of thing at all.

Another remarked that finding a partner was the reverse of his expectations – 'It was against everything that I'd planned. I had wanted a father figure, but found a son.' On the other hand, one man said he had found his partner – with whom he had been living for twenty years – after a period of chronic depression and during a phase in his life when he was actively searching for a man to love and to share his life.

Seven of the couples had sex within a matter of weeks of meeting, the others at the first meeting. Most settled down to live together within six months, many within a few days.

Maintaining a Relationship: These couples had evolved two strategies to cope with threats from the homosexual world. Firstly, having non-exclusive relationships – most had developed rules which allowed partners to have sexual relationships with other men – and, secondly, withdrawal from the gay world. I will look at each in turn.

Only two couples professed fidelity. The others had experienced a range of sexual relationships, varying from long-term emotional commitments to other men through to more casual and impersonal sexual relationships. One couple, together for ten years, described how they had evolved long-standing love affairs with other men which did not threaten their relationship:

FRANK: The first two months were rather like poetry books, all hearts and flowers. We didn't know any other people. In 1962 we went to Canada and had an agreement not to be jealous. But I was jealous. He had an affair but got bored ... Later, when we returned to London I picked up a chap in Piccadilly and I stopped feeling jealous ... We have sex occasionally now. For the physical side I have a West Indian friend from Brixton who is married with six kids. John [the partner] also has an affair but neither threatens our relationship. I get an occasional spark of jealousy ...

JOHN: On Monday evening Frank had his lover boy in – who I think is an adorable bloke, I think he's wonderful, the most darling man, top of the pops in anybody's book. Well, he comes here and we all get on like a house on fire ...

This couple had accepted a non-exclusive relationship, feeling this was possible only because they were completely honest and open with each other.

For us honesty is the be all and end all ... and not just about sex – about everything. If we hadn't been honest it would have broken up ages ago ...

The first time one of them had a sexual relationship with somebody else had led to a serious crisis, but their ability to withstand this and to evolve a strategy for coping with further ones seemed to have strengthened their relationship.

Another couple, with twenty years' difference in their ages, had accommodated additional sexual relationships almost from the beginning. (Most couples seem to have a short period of absolute fidelity.) When they met, one was in his early twenties and the other in his forties. That the younger would find other partners nearer his own age seemed likely, and this was, indeed, the case. The older partner described how the younger often came home to cry on his shoulder about some of his short-term affairs with men of his own age. But during the twenty years of their relationship neither partner had doubted its permanence. Recently sexual activity with others had declined in frequency and the older partner wanted his friend to find another permanent partner so that all three could settle down together. Such an arrangement was desired because of their age difference and possible because of the nature of their relationship: not a threat, a third party would ensure a less lonely old age for the younger man when his older partner died.

Not all additional relationships were so permanent as these. One couple allowed each other sexual activity with strangers, providing it was kept out of their home. Nor did they tell each other of their activities, which should be not only out of sight but limited to a 'one night stand'. Yet another partner had several friends with whom he had sexual relationships from time to time. During my field work several more limited contacts also commented on how they remained emotionally faithful to their lovers but could have sexual relationships with others providing no affection was displayed. For example, they would not kiss other men, nor go to bed with them, and did not even want to know their names. Intimacies of this kind were reserved for the lover.

The two couples who had developed rules about fidelity and appeared to abide by them were uninvolved in the homosexual world. As I suggested earlier, the second main strategy for protecting stable relationships is withdrawal from the gay subculture. My own observations on this point corroborate those of a field worker in America, Sonnenschein, who wrote:

It was constantly observed in the subject community that as soon as any two individuals entered into a sexual or socio-sexual relationship that was hoped to last for any period of time, these individuals rapidly withdrew from the activity of the community and decreased their participation in group affairs regardless of how active or popular they were before: the institutions that were more conducive to sexual interaction were particularly avoided.[34]

The couples may still go to 'gay places' but become less involved than formerly. None of the nine couples had any great involvement in the bar scene in London, though two did go occasionally. Most did have contact with other homosexuals (often other couples), and sometimes this contact had increased since they settled down. But knowing a network of other homosexuals is not the same as regularly frequenting bars and clubs, and none of the respondents did this. Most commented that they found such places 'fickle' and 'pseudo'.

If homosexual couples have to work hard to protect themselves from the gay world, they have to work harder to counterbalance the lack of support that heterosexual couples would receive. Heterosexual married couples may have difficulty finding homes, but they can apply to local councils and may be able to raise a mortgage together. Homosexuals, in common with other unmarried couples, have the same problems of finding a home, but greater difficulty in applying to councils or getting joint mortgages. (One respondent gave an elaborate account of the refusals of various building societies to give him and his partner a joint mortgage.)

Roles allotted to men and women in marriage often have a clear demarcation, but for gay couples the problem of who cooks, shops, does the housework, and pays the bills, has to be carefully worked out. Most of the nine couples merged such tasks rather than adopting conventional role divisions. Ownership rights presented further difficulties. If a home is furnished jointly, whose property is it in law? One couple had made a list of their respective purchases so that they would know who owned what, should they part company. If one partner dies without leaving a will, his property would by right go to the nearest kin, which could never be the lover. One couple felt strongly about this:

If somebody dies, the family would come along to see what they could get. And we didn't want either to be left in the position of having to cope with families saying 'Well, he was our brother' or 'We should legally get it'. We'd say 'balls': the family means less to us than our relationship. I mean, after all, we're man and wife.

Families could also cause problems in other ways. A simple act like sending a wreath signed by both partners to the funeral of a deceased mother caused uproar around the grave and a great deal of ill-feeling. The couples were unable to talk over problems with their families, colleagues or friends, nor even ask their neighbours for help if the partner was ill. The author of a homosexual novel portrays these difficulties when he writes about saying goodbye to his lover on board a ship:

As you turn away, you feel his hand squeeze your arm. But you mustn't stop; if you do, you won't be able to help yourself from suddenly blubbing like a big kid. And that won't do ... Everybody else that's normal, they can blub away and fall over each other as much as they like. But you – you've just got to stand there and make yourself look as though it's only a business acquaintance or someone who's going away. *You* can't show anything; people would only sneer if you did, sneer and jeer their little pinched souls out, laughing at you. That's why you've got to get away ... you [must] fight back those bloody tears in your eyes. Maybe if anyone does see you, they'll just think you're losing a wife or a sweetheart or someone. Maybe it'll never occur to them that a man can love another man – yes, sexually and all – because they're taught and told it's something you can't do. The hell you can't. So they'd never guess that for you it's just like the end of the world.[35]

Such problems prove stumbling blocks in the way of stable relationships, though paradoxically, they may also strengthen some. For many heterosexuals liaisons may be routine, not rapture, but homosexuals who are challenged at every point must often give a fuller consideration to what they are doing. They have to think about their relationships with the community, to work out a relationship with their families, to consider carefully the roles they will play. None of these can be taken for granted, the meanings and rules which govern their relationships must be consciously constructed.

The presence of children is often thought to be a central stabilizing influence in marriage. While childless couples (about 10 per cent of married couples) tend to score more highly on marital adjustment scales than couples without children, they are represented in the divorcing population about two to three times more frequently than in the married population generally.[36] Childless couples may expend the time and emotions otherwise occupied by children on other things. At present, male homosexual couples cannot have children, but the couples I interviewed had strong, time-consuming interests in common – similar occupations, music, the local church – which may have partially compensated for the lack of children.

No real contradiction exists between the difficulties of couple formation I have outlined and the existence of such relationships, for, once under way, nothing succeeds like success. Commitments are built up by which it becomes increasingly easy to stay together and increasingly costly to part. Obstacles mastered together add strength and stability; two separate lives develop a mutual reality of common history, common friends, a common home, making return to individual roles increasingly difficult. Or, as one man more basically put it:

Another bloke couldn't break us up because I'm much too lazy to go and start all over again.

Whether it be through love, laziness or simply a desire to remain a couple in a society where the single are devalued, many relationships are viewed as permanent:

I can't bear to think of life without him.

I need it. I need someone solid, otherwise I just get ever so lost without someone firm, someone to lean on ...

It would have been difficult after a few years to split up. The world would have crashed around us.

There has never really been a danger of us breaking up. We need each other as emotional props. We are not like two persons, we are one person ...

I couldn't see our love fading now. We have a mature love and although the initial sexual attraction has continued, our love no longer depends on sex to feed it ...

I'm not the same person I was. I don't have to go out trolling to get sex ... I don't have to waste time doing all that ... I've got a settled permanent base, I've got somebody to talk to. There's nothing else I need. Whereas before I had nothing ...

THE FUTURE OF GAY COUPLES

Given the changes occurring in this society two things seem probable: first, gay couples may become more frequent, more accepted and more institutionalized; and second, gay couples will take on a wider range of forms.

An Increase in Couples?: I have suggested that the pervasiveness of couples and of marriage instils in homosexuals a strong need to seek couple relationships, while the widespread hostility towards homosexuals serves to inhibit the development of such relationships. Recent changes in these areas could have important consequences. Marriage and diversified forms of couple relationships are increasingly popular among heterosexuals, and attitudes towards homosexuals seem to be becoming less harsh.[37] Given these changes, stable homosexual relationships should become more frequent and more recognized, since the motivation for them is strengthened while the obstacle of hostility is decreased.

There is some evidence that these changes are already occurring. Recently there has been much discussion within the homosexual community about the possibility of homosexual marriage – the feasibility of legal contracts, religious ceremonies and even the adoption of children. As I have already said, ceremonies of 'marriage' have been held in America, Canada and England. Now computer dating, introduction agencies and 'marriage' counselling services for homosexuals have been introduced. Such issues are not only being raised within the gay community, but discussion of homosexual couples now has a legitimate part in more academic discussions of marriage and couples. Popular bestsellers, like Alvin Toffler's *Future Shock*, suggests that 'homosexual family units' are one of the future paths the family will take. As Toffler writes:

As homosexuality becomes more socially acceptable, we may even begin to find families based on homosexual marriages with the partners adopting children.[38]

Since social science knowledge can never exist apart from the social world of which it is a part, these very discussions may actually add to the legitimacy of the processes they describe.

More Forms for Gay Couples?: The meanings attached to couples and to marriage among heterosexuals are themselves becoming increasingly diversified, ambiguous and changing – a simple consensual portrait of men and women acting out gender roles in the romantic love context of a 'till death do us part' family is insufficient. Studies of alternatives to orthodox families have recently occupied many social scientists. Many of these writers, in claiming that orthodox families are a thing of the past and in predicting new forms for the future, themselves create a context where change becomes plausible even if not yet with us. As Gagnon and Simon have commented:

Significant social change does not come about only when there have been changes in overt behaviour patterns. The moment of change may simply be the point at which new forms of behaviour appear plausible.[39]

Some changes have already occurred. The increasing possibility of divorce has tacitly rendered precarious the meanings of marriage as 'life-long', 'natural' or 'inevitable'. Marriage is now a contract which may be more easily broken if required. Large numbers of 'parents without partners' – divorced, separated, deserted, widowed and never married people with children – demonstrate that in America, for example, quite substantial numbers of the population are already living something different from 'orthodox family lives'.[40] More polemically, a range of alternative life-styles are being suggested by a wide range of people. So we read of the importance of childless families; the growth of 'two stage marriage' – one stage without children, one with; the increase of 'mate swapping' as a mechanism for sustaining the family while bringing change into it; the erosion of gender roles and the arrival of the 'radical feminist' and the 'manipulated man'; the role played by youth in creating the new families of the future through a 'new humanism' in which communes of great diversity and tolerance are established; post-retirement child-rearing and geriatric group marriages.[41]

Homosexuals are embedded in this pluralistic and changing context and their experiences must obviously be affected by it. While some may pursue more conventional closed 'marriages', others will experiment with and embrace new life styles. Arguably, homosexuals, released from the responsibilities of children, are in a position to facilitate experimentation and exploration of new life styles: homosexuals may be acting out today what society may routinely script tomorrow. However, any claim that they are leading the way in this respect is, I think, wishful thinking on the part of some homosexuals, for their desire for concealment and anonymity has also concealed their innovative styles. Only recently have homosexuals been willing to be publicly recognized and to make their own life styles available for analysis.[42] Rather than leading the development of new styles, homosexuals have been led by them – the discussion of alternatives, life in communes and so forth have created preconditions for gay people to 'come out' and consequently provided them with rhetorics which they now often adopt as their own. But although they may not have instigated the changes, they are now amongst the most articulate spokesmen for them.

Of these spokesmen, the Gay Liberation Front in its diverse groupings has been the most sophisticated, and one quick to condemn the emulation by gay people of heterosexual marriage. As one American liberationist wrote:

Homosexual marriage submitting to the guidelines of so-called conventional rites must be classed as reactionary. The gay lib movement does not need these kinds of tactics. We're involved in rational warfare, not irrational. Now, don't you agree it isn't relevant to gay liberation when we start imitating meaningless, bad habits of our oppressors and begin instituting them? That *isn't* the freedom we want. That isn't *our* liberation. That *isn't* the equality we want. And that *ain't* revolutionary . . .[43]

Perhaps the London Gay Liberation Front Manifesto Group, writing in 1971, put the simplest yet most coherent view of what conventional couple formation means and some of the alternatives to it. It is a provocative place on which to end this article – and one which captures my personal beliefs. They wrote:

We do not deny that it is as possible for gay couples as for some straight couples to live happily and constructively together. We question however as an ideal, the finding and settling down eternally with one 'right' partner. This is a blueprint of the straight world which gay people have taken over. It is inevitably a parody, since they haven't even the justification of straight couples – the need to provide a stable environment for their children (though in any case we believe that the suffocating small family unit is by no means the best atmosphere for bringing up children).

Monogamy is usually based on ownership – the woman sells her services to the man in return for security for herself and her children – and is entirely bound up in the man's idea of property; furthermore in our society the monogamous couple, with or without children, is an isolated shut-in, up-tight unit, suspicious of and hostile to outsiders. And though we don't lay down rules or tell gay people how they should behave in bed or in their relationships, we do want them to question society's blueprint for the couple. The blueprint says 'we two against the world' and that can be protective and comforting. But it can also be suffocating, leading to neurotic dependence and underlying hostility, the emotional dishonesty of staying in the comfy safety of the home and garden, the security and narrowness of life built for two, with the secret guilt of fancying someone else while remaining in thrall to the idea that true love lasts a lifetime – as though there were a ration of relationships, and to want more than one were greedy. Not that sexual fidelity is necessarily wrong; what is wrong is the unturned *emotional* exclusiveness of the couple which stunts the partners so they can no longer operate at all as independent beings in society. People need a variety of relationships in order to develop and grow, and to learn about other human beings.

It is especially important for gay people to stop copying straight – we are the ones who have the best opportunities to create a new life-style and if we don't, no one else will. Also, we need one another more than straight people do, because we are equals suffering under an insidious oppression from a society too primitive to come to terms with the freedom we represent. Singly, or isolated in couples, we are weak – the way society wants us to be. Society cannot put us down so easily if we fuse together. We have to get together, understand one another, live together.[44]

9. Couples, Constraints and Choices

Individuals involved in different kinds of sexual relationships find them acceptable or satisfying to different degrees.[1] More personal relations are not necessarily more comfortable; personal experience is as likely to be divisive as to be cohesive, to produce conflict as to produce harmony. Joint activities and decisions, the sharing of household tasks, may attest to the closeness of some relations, but for some wives their husband's involvement in domestic chores and decisions results only in a feeling that they have no area of life which they control, no field of expertise they can call their own. Husbands and wives who see little of each other may decry the fact or appreciate the freedom it allows for each to ignore the other; married couples surrounded by friends and relatives may find these as much a source of irritation and interference as of aid and companionship; those without may feel cut off and deprived or enjoy the relative privacy of their marital life.

Gay liberation and women's liberation movements attest to a growing feeling, however, that individuals should be free from constraints imposed by social attitudes to gender. Both movements want to ensure that the positions people achieve and the social relations they develop are not determined by these attitudes. They also want to liberate sexual behaviour itself from ideas about propriety and perversion, leaving people free to pursue their sexual interests and inclinations as they choose.

In general, liberation has been aimed mainly at impersonal structures, perhaps because we think of social constraints primarily in terms of rules, morals, norms, more or less explicit ideas about what should or should not be done, all of which are impersonal. In the case of sexual liberation considerable emphasis has, therefore, been placed on either changing the marriage contract to make it less restricting and more egalitarian, or banishing it entirely. Some people have taken the notion of sexual liberation further, to an attack on couples as such.

Changes of these kinds pose major problems about the organization of domestic activities, the composition of households, child-rearing, and so on. Some of the people who have attempted to realize a more or less completely egalitarian society in which sexual differences are abolished have tried to solve these problems by some form of communal organization. These communes typically involve numbers of people in common residence, the pooling of resources and labour, a relative independence of the world outside, and the collective rearing of children.[2] In many such communes the ideal of equality, harmony and commitment prevail; each individual contributes to the commune, the commune provides for the needs of all. The ideals of equality and freedom must often, however, coexist with rules which ensure the day-to-day functioning of the commune and its continuation over time. However, by rotating tasks and responsibilities through the commune membership the link between social positions and the individuals who fill them is broken; by making birth or residence in the commune the important criterion for establishing rights and obligations, and by rearing children collectively, continuity over time is made independent of particular connections between adults and children. As a result, there is little reason for marriage as something concerned with the social identities of children and the placement of succeeding generations in a system of kinship classification, and many communes have dispensed with it. In addition, the sexual division of labour may be eliminated or reduced: men and women therefore no longer depend on each other either individually or collectively, and are supposed to deal with each other primarily as co-members of the commune.[3]

However, in some communes couples very clearly remain. Perhaps the best known examples are the agricultural *kibbutzim* of Israel. In these communes men and women are not supposed to marry, though they may apply to share a room (otherwise each individual has a separate room and eating and leisure facilities are shared by all).[4] Simply to have a sexual relation may not be sufficient grounds for room sharing, and permission may rest on acknowledgement of a special kind of relation:

... in addition to the physical intimacy of sex, the union also provides a psychological intimacy that may be expressed by notions such as comradeship, dependence, succorance, etc. And it is this psychological intimacy primarily that distinguishes couples from lovers. The criterion of the couple relationship, then, that which distinguishes it from a relationship between adults of the same sex who enjoy psychological intimacy, or from that of adults who enjoy physical intimacy, is love. A couple comes into being when these two kinds of intimacy are united in one relationship.[5]

The man and woman become a couple (*zug*); they think of themselves in this way and are recognized as such by others.

But such relatively exclusive and special relations between the sexes present problems for many communards. These problems exist at three levels. Firstly, communards may wish not to differentiate among social relations, stressing that all are equivalent. Secondly, relations implying a special commitment between two people may be seen as a threat to commitment to the community as a whole – the unit of concern is the commune and conceptual boundaries should not exist within it. Thirdly, some people are concerned as much with attacking personal structures as more impersonal ones, sensing that personal experience, the knowledge people have of each other as individuals, and the expectation that the relation will continue, limit and bind as much as notions of status.

Simply to allow individuals to develop sexual relationships as they wish within a commune permits the expression of individual preferences but leaves the way open for jealousy, to which sexual relationships seem to be particularly susceptible – one person feeling that a partner's involvement with another is a threat to his/her own relationship. Such jealousies may lead to conflict and resentment. Communards have adopted a number of different solutions to this problem, with varying degrees of success.

An obvious, if rather ascetic answer, and one adopted by

many nineteenth-century American communes during at least some periods of their existence, is to ban sex entirely. In eliminating any form of sexual relation, celibacy not only overcomes the problems of couples in communes but underlines the equivalence of all social relations irrespective of the gender of those involved. If communes are to reproduce themselves all their members cannot, of course, practise celibacy at all times, but those who do may be considered more worthy members. The only truly successful celibate communes are convents and monasteries, which, in addition to banning sex, confine their membership to either men or women and accept a continuing dependence on the sexual world outside for new members.

A second solution is a system of 'free' love. In principle such a system insists that all men and women should be sexually available to each other; in practice it may impose restrictions and develop mechanisms for controlling who sleeps with whom. In smaller communes decisions about sexual arrangements may be taken by an arbiter, or a rota system may be established. In larger groups the controls may be even more formal, committees processing applications for access to particular individuals and taking steps to disrupt relations which show excesses of special affection or exclusivity. The relations of offending couples might, for example, be broken up by insisting that each partner mate with someone else, as was sometimes the case in the famous Oneida community founded by John Humphrey Noyes in New York State in 1848.[6]

A less extreme solution, which is also, perhaps, more of a compromise, is sometimes adopted. The tension between egalitarian community and exclusive couples is resolved by the claim that sexual relationships are different but not to be valued above others.[7] This kind of approach is illustrated by the attitudes of young members of a small modern commune in Philadelphia in which a number of the founding couples are legally married but insist that 'marriage' is a feeling, a particular kind of personal experience.

I think all the relationships we establish here are just as important as the husband wife relationship. I don't think any one replaces the other or should.

Love isn't on a vertical scale, my love for Nancy is different from my love for Laura, but it's the difference between a love for a wife and a love for a sister. That's why sex is in its place here ... sex isn't really important when you consider we're already sharing our deeply felt emotions with each other, the many aspects of our really private individual selves.

I don't think I can ever be married to one person again. I don't want to possess anyone and I don't want anyone to possess me. Marriage is a beautiful thing, not just something sexual. It's the beauty of a special relationship, of sharing and working together and that's what we have here. I feel married to everyone in this house, both the men and the women.[8]

But measures to prevent the formation of couples may be found no less constraining than the constraints they attack. Personal relations, though sometimes comfortable, reassuring and undemanding, may be repetitive, boring and stifling. Some communards have tried to achieve a life totally free of constraints and structures. Their concern is less with a functional collective life than with a more mystical and personal sharing with others – a sense of oneness, of communion.

Thus, they prefer candid, total, effusive, and unrestrained expression of feeling – joy and sensuality, as well as anger and hostility – to the careful, guarded, modulated balances and instrumental (or manipulative) modes of personal relatedness; 'upfrontness' is for them a term of high praise ... They affirm the present, the immediate, the *now* over careful future planning and anticipated future gratification ... Their sensibility is given to impulse and spontaneity rather than to calculation and structure ... They prefer the primitive to the sophisticated, transcendent ecstasy to order and security ... Their impulse is to share as much of their lives as they can with the community of their brothers and sisters, sometimes even beyond the point where it threatens those areas of privacy and reserve to which many communards are still at least partially attached. They want to share a mutually dependent communal fate without the obligatory restraints of social bonds; indeed, they depend upon the affirmation of their brothers and sisters of the value of personal expressiveness to enable each of them to exercise an unbounded freedom to do his thing; to engage, above all, in a spiritual search for personal meaning, for health and happiness, for self and selflessness, for transcendence and godhood.[9]

All of these are attempts to realize very real human aspirations, have a very long history and are likely to persist. But in any kind of society, simple or complex, their success is limited. In small-scale societies personal relations predominate, but where such societies are stable and long-lasting they seem always to develop well-defined notions of status and have to contend with ongoing jealousies and competition. Periodically, and usually by ritual means, people in these societies experience the sense of oneness, the levelling of status, referred to above.[10] But these experiences are always of limited duration and people in these societies do not expect them to be anything other than intermittent. As one social anthropologist who has made a special study of these sorts of societies and experiences has commented:

> But the spontaneity and immediacy of communitas – as opposed to the jural-political character of structure – can seldom be maintained for very long. Communitas itself soon develops a structure, in which free relationships between individuals become converted into norm-governed relationships between social personae.[11]

He goes on to say:

> Wisdom is always to find the appropriate relationship between structure and communitas under the *given* circumstances of time and place, to accept each modality when it is paramount without rejecting the other, and not to cling to one when its present impetus is spent.[12]

I very much doubt that these experiences in our own society can be more than limited and temporary. Practical problems of living may be submerged but cannot be eliminated, a fact which does not permit the aspiration to total liberty to become fully realized for all people in our society at all times.

The growth of sexual liberation movements and the proliferation of experiments in communal living, when taken together with general changes in household composition, in divorce rates, in the importance of kin relationships in the wider society, contribute to a feeling, a sense, that the traditional institutions of marriage and the family in our society are no longer adequate and are rapidly being undermined. We are constantly informed that 'the nuclear family' is declining, is degenerating, is losing its functions, is, in brief, in crisis. But any analysis engendered by this sense of crisis must be treated with caution.

At least part of the difficulty is that '*the* family' is an extremely unsatisfactory analytic notion. Arguments about '*the* family' mix a concern for household composition with concerns for activities within households, with child-rearing, with kinship, with couples and with a highly variable collection of dyadic relations. But any thorough-going analysis of these phenomena and any assessment of their current state and future possibilities must carefully distinguish among them.[13]

In any event, prediction is a hazardous enterprise and not one in which I engage with any sense of confidence, except to say that sexual relations will undoubtedly continue, are likely to be highly personal and to involve couples. Our capacity to act on the basis of personal experience and our peculiarly human capacity to structure our interaction in terms of concepts is unlikely to decline. The future of marriage, in the sense in which I have used the term, is far less certain. As I have implied throughout, my guess is that marriage must decline in importance as kinship and the social 'work' required of kinship diminish. Firstly, taking kinship in its strictest sense, to the extent that restrictions on sex and marriage in terms of relatedness disappear, so should marriage. Once anyone can marry anyone else, there is no reason to marry at all.[14] Secondly, the link made in our culture between marriage and family is becoming increasingly superfluous.

The observation that a wider range of kinsmen may be of relatively little relevance in complex societies is commonplace; the 'familiar' aspects of kinship dominate western culture. In other words, unlike people in many other societies, we tend to associate marriage and kinship primarily with the creation of a social unit of parents and the children for whom they have responsibility and who, in turn, have claims upon the persons and property of the parents. But we also accept that families can and do exist without marriage – an acceptance reflected in such labels as 'one-parent families'. Increasingly we see families as units created by the facts of biology and co-residence and, as I have suggested earlier (pp. 155–6), any legislation which attempts to establish that all children have the same rights to subsistence, property and status, irrespective of the circum-stances of their birth, reinforces these notions. In theory at least, legislation of this kind implies that rights involved in parent/child relations result from the fact of birth and not of contract. If no distinction exists between contract and absence of con-tract, the contract is redundant.

However, a declaration of equality of rights for children does not necessarily ensure that claims and obligations can be en-forced equally. The difficulties of establishing paternity are well known. Our present cultural viewpoint accentuates the problem of women when men deny responsibility for children they father. But in the absence of contracts, a man wishing to bring up children of his own may equally be faced with the woman's denial of his claims, putting for men a greater premium on marriage than for women. Should paternity be mutually ack-nowledged or agreed, however, the problems of enforcing rights and obligations are no greater or no less than for those estab-lished by marriage.

I think people will probably continue to get married for some time to come but also that 'marriage' will gradually imply something quite different. Having no major implications for affinal relations, for descent, for future marriages, for the trans-mission of social identity from one generation to another, it will be primarily a public legitimation and fortification of the fact that two people are a couple. Though not marriage in a kinship sense, it will by no means be meaningless. The state may continue to use it as a legal contract to regulate the claims of one spouse to the property of the other and to decide the priorities of other claimants, including children. At a less legal level, it will be a public affirmation of the couple's identity, of relevance mainly to the members of the same community or social network.

Of course, more people may decide to live their domestic and sexual lives with a number of others simultaneously, either reducing the importance of couples or eliminating them altogether. Sometimes some of these arrangements have been called 'group marriage'.[15] Marriage in this context is a meaningful term only in as much as here, too, it designates people who wish to mark themselves off from others, to be, like a couple, an identifiable unit in which sex plays an integral part.

In saying we should not approach these topics with a sense of crisis I do not wish to ignore the obvious distress and dissatisfaction of many people with their sexual relationships, however structured. My point is simply that there is no 'peculiar state of crisis' in these relations; everywhere social relations, whatever their structure, present problems for those engaged in them. If we detect a crisis this may not reflect a peculiar state of our social relations; it may simply be an artefact of our capacity for self-analysis. Human beings are unique in that they can use concepts as well as instinct and individual experience to structure their social relations. If our society is peculiar it is in the extent to which it has developed an 'academic culture' (used in the widest possible sense) which elaborates this use of concepts in a seemingly unending discussion and analysis of human experience, to which we often add a concern to manipulate, to improve the quality of individual lives. In using concepts analytically we often reify and rigidify, misrepresent the past and misconstrue the future. Our delight in talking about our experiences, in making them explicit, in encapsulating them in concepts, often leads to a certainty about them, a sense of mastery over them which may not only be misplaced but may also demean the experiences.

This book is a typical product of such a culture and I am very much aware of the inherent tendencies I mention. But even though the writings of social scientists, journalists and so forth are part of social reality and impinge upon the lives of at least some people, I, as an anthropologist, believe that man is truly *homo sapiens* and not *homo academicus*. Our attempts to capture the essence of human interaction and experience always lag behind the reality. People continue to combine and recombine different kinds of structures. Happily, they also attempt to transcend the structures they create.

Notes

1. Introduction

1. The study of marriage and personal relations in complex societies has tended to be lumped together under the rubric of 'sociology of the family', a branch of the discipline often considered its 'poor relation'. As Michael Anderson summarizes in his introduction to *Sociology of the Family* (Penguin Books, 1971, p. 8):
'... the reputation of the sociology of the family among professional sociologists is still rather low. Many see it as an academic dead-end which contributes little or nothing of importance to the discipline as a whole; as concentrating on trivial and value-laden problems of more concern to journalism and social work than "hard" sociology; as methodologically naïve and conceptually underdeveloped.'
Many discussions focusing on 'declining morality', how to achieve a 'happy' marriage, attacks and defences of the family, justify these criticisms. But at least part of the problem stems from the difficulties I have outlined and the complexities of the relations themselves. Whether the study of such relations is relevant to 'hard' sociology is another question – but an understanding of the kinds of social relations so central to the lives of many people can scarcely be considered irrelevant to an understanding of social behaviour and social life in general.

2. These ideas may be idiosyncratic or those more generally held in the society.

3. Indeed the ethos of many such relations is that personal experience should be discounted in this way, an ethos epitomized by the dealings of bureaucrats with members of the public. The bureaucrat is expected to treat each person only in terms of the formal rules of the bureaucracy, irrespective of any personal experience of them.

4. Although it is analytically possible to separate their social relation into distinct elements – doctor/patient on the one hand, golf-

partners on the other – they remain two people involved in a single social relation.

5. To make this statement at a theoretical level is, of course, much easier than to demonstrate for any particular relation how such a mix and balance occurs. Also, though this limited discussion gives some indication of the factors involved in the structuring of social relations, it is by no means a complete account either of the reality or of the arguments I would wish to advance about the ways in which social relations are structured.

6. In many small-scale societies most social relations are of this kind. People may be connected to each other by a variety of statuses, but what they do in one capacity is influenced by the totality. Ritual is often used not only as a means of stating in which capacity the individuals are acting at a particular point in time but also as a way of focusing on the statuses to the exclusion of all else – moving the interaction from the personal to the impersonal. For a discussion of ritual and social relations see M. Gluckman (ed.), *Essays on the Ritual of Social Relations*, Manchester University Press, 1962. In complex societies people are less likely to be connected by a number of statuses, and if they are, these tend to be separated by place and time.

7. This sense of identity involved in couples has been interestingly dealt with by P. Berger and H. Kellner in 'Marriage and the Construction of Reality', which originally appeared in *Diogenes*, 46, 1964, pp. 1–25. In 1970 it was reprinted in *Recent Sociology*, No. 2, edited by Hans Peter Dreitzel, and on p. 58 the authors point out in relation to marriage: 'As of the marriage, most of each partner's actions must now be projected in conjunction with those of the other. Each partner's definitions of reality must be continually correlated with the definitions of the other. The other is present in nearly all horizons of everyday conduct. Furthermore the identity of each now takes on a new character, having to be constantly matched with that of the other, indeed being typically perceived by people at large as being symbolically conjoined with the identity of the other.'

8. Arguments about how marriage should be defined are complex and sophisticated and this is not the place to pursue either them or the reasoning behind my own assertions, except to say that I regard marriage and kinship as inseparable concepts and that a concern with both is basically a concern with classification rather than with social relations. For discussions of the meaning of marriage see, for example, E. R. Leach, 'Polyandry, Inheritance and the Definition of Marriage', *Man*, 54, 1955, pp. 182–6; R. Needham, *Rethinking Kin-*

ship and Marriage, Tavistock, 1971; K. Gough, 'The Nayars and the Definition of Marriage', *Journal of the Royal Anthropological Institute*, 89, 1959, pp. 23–34.

I think it is legitimate to say that marriage always involves a man and a woman. Among the Nuer of East Africa (see E. E. Evans-Pritchard, *Kinship and Marriage among the Nuer*, Oxford University Press, 1951), a man who dies without heirs to continue his male line may be married to a living woman, any children she bears by another designated male being classified and treated as children of the dead man. The fact that the husband is a 'ghost' is largely irrelevant. A male line that is about to die out because there are only women left may be continued by another kind of fiction, 'woman-to-woman marriage'. One of the women of the line that would otherwise be without heirs takes a bride. The children this bride has by a designated man are the children of the female husband. To all intents and purposes the woman who is the husband becomes an honorary man.

Although I have said 'a man and a woman', each man or woman may have a number of marriages simultaneously – though the classificatory problems presented by one woman marrying a number of men are rather greater than those where one man marries a number of women.

9. 'Ghost marriages', referred to above (note 8), are one kind of example of marriage that does not involve ongoing social interaction between one of the married people and the spouse and children. But for the Nuer such marriages are the exception rather than the rule. The Nayars, a warrior caste of the Malabar Coast, S. India, were perhaps the best example of a system of marriage which did not involve ongoing interaction between those married or between men and the children of the woman whom they have married. Nayar girls went through a ritual with men of another kin group linked to their own, after which they were free to accept lovers, any of whom could father their children. No further contact between the woman and the man with whom she underwent the ritual was necessary, and when she became pregnant any of her lovers could acknowledge paternity by paying the midwife's fees. Neither he nor the original man involved in the ritual was socially responsible to the child nor need continue the association with the mother, nor be under any obligation to her. For a discussion of Nayar marriage see K. Gough, op. cit.

10. Robin Fox, *Kinship and Marriage*, Penguin Books, 1967, p. 54.

11. The control of a wife's sexuality is not always related to concerns for physical paternity of the children she bears – in some societies this may be of little relevance and in others the connection

between sex and procreation is not an accepted part of the culture. The control may involve exclusive rights for the husband himself, permitting him to take retributive steps against any who infringe them, or may allow him to determine who else has sexual access to his wife. He may, for example, lend her to other men, as among some groups of North American Indians. Wives less frequently have control over their husband's sexuality as a *right* of marriage.

12. In Western societies people often think of sexual intercourse as something men in particular seek whenever they have the opportunity, which is desirable in and for itself. But in many societies sex is a threatening activitiy – contacts with females may be believed to weaken male strength, for example – and sometimes men fear sexual activity because of its polluting nature to such an extent that they may shun it beyond that necessary from procreation. See M. Douglas, *Purity and Danger*, Routledge & Kegan Paul, 1969, pp. 140–58, for a discussion of notions of purity and pollution surrounding sexual behaviour.

13. See E. Friedl, *Vasilika, a Village in Modern Greece*, Holt, Rinehart & Winston, New York, 1962.

14. The following observations about rural southern Spain are based on my field work as an anthropologist in a large and socially heterogeneous town in the province of Malaga where I lived for almost two years. The generalizations I make apply much less to the wealthy landowners of the town than to the majority of the population, who are engaged either in agricultural wage labour or in service industries, construction work, or technical and clerical jobs in the town. An account of courtship practices and ideas about men and women for a much smaller and more homogeneous town in the same region is given by J. Pitt-Rivers, *People of the Sierra*, University of Chicago Press, Chicago and London, 1961.

15. Parents make discreet inquiries about the family of the boy or girl in whom their own child is showing interest if the family is not already known to them. Often parents of the boy and girl are fairly familiar with each other anyway as many groups are associated with specific neighbourhoods. In general, people prefer families they already know about rather than those they have to find out about, and often the difficulty of finding out about the family of a boy who comes from another town means that associations between such boys and local girls are discouraged. The greater ease of social interaction among families who are kin to each other, and the lesser constraints put on the relations of unmarried boys and girls who are related to each other through kinship, also tend to en-

courage matches between cousins and the siblings of a man and woman who have married. The wealthy are not restricted in the same way as the poorer people, knowing more people outside their own towns and being able to find out about others with greater ease. In one instance a man's parents, for example, hired private detectives to investigate the family of the British girl their son wished to marry – the family still lived in Britain.

16. At present divorce is not possible in Spain, though legal separations may be granted. The difficulties of such separations, however, and the fact that people cannot re-marry, tend to mean that married people stay together.

17. A very nice account of the sexual division of labour in a different region of Spain is given by C. Lison-Tolosana, *Belmonte de Los Caballeros*, Oxford University Press, 1966.

18. B. Malinowski, *The Sexual Life of Savages in North Western Melanesia*, Routledge & Kegan Paul, 1932.

19. ibid., p. 64.

20. ibid., p. 75.

21. ibid., p. 95.

22. ibid., p. 15.

23. ibid., p. 33.

24. ibid., p. 97.

25. Obviously, the legal obligations of marriage are the same for everyone. But usually these obligations only become important in the event of a dispute, divorce or in dealing with government agencies, for example, in applications for welfare benefits and social security. Often husbands and wives may be unaware of their legal obligations and commitments.

26. This kind of arrangement has been seen as a possible new trend for families. See, for example, R. Rapoport and R. Rapoport, *Dual Career Families*, Penguin Books, 1971.

27. E. Bott, *Family and Social Network*, Tavistock Publications, 1971 (first edition 1957).

28. ibid., p. 53.

29. ibid., pp. 53–4.

30. See E. Slater and M. Woodside, *Patterns of Marriage*, Cassell & Company, 1951, pp. 165–9, 174.

31. E. Bott, op. cit., p. 73. The idea that sex is somehow threatening reflects some of the attitudes found in much simpler societies. See note 12 above.

32. Other than simply the connectedness of social networks, the ages of people in the networks and whether or not they are kin may,

for example, be important. Possibly, too, the separate networks of husband and wife need to be examined rather than dealing with their network as a whole. See, for example, C. Turner, 'Conjugal Roles and Social Networks; A Re-examination of an Hypothesis', *Human Relations*, Vol. 20, 1967, pp. 12–30. The second edition of Bott's book, to which I refer, incorporates a consideration of later works and criticisms. Obviously the problem of how one measures both connectedness of network and the degree of segregation of conjugal relations cannot be ignored. Perhaps too, the questions of the domestic division of labour and of the way in which husbands and wives spend their leisure time need to be examined separately, especially given changing leisure pursuits.

33. C. Harris, *The Family*, Allen & Unwin, 1969, p. 175.

34. E. Bott, op. cit., p. 92.

35. Some of the best-known examples include: M. Kerr, *The People of Ship Street*, Routledge & Kegan Paul, 1958; N. Dennis, F. Henriques and C. Slaughter, *Coal is our Life*, Eyre & Spottiswoode, 1956; Michael Young and Peter Willmott, *Family and Kinship in East London*, Routledge & Kegan Paul, 1957.

36. See, for example, Michael Young and Peter Willmott, op. cit.

37. Bott, for example, comments that couples with close-knit networks found answering questions about how husbands and wives should ideally behave easier than did those with loose-knit networks.

38. M. Kerr, op. cit., p. 40.

2. Couples in Communities

1. People who spend a good deal of their time away from the public gaze of a community – shepherds for example – are sometimes therefore automatically considered less moral and respectable than others. Women who work in the fields may similarly be considered less reputable than others if their behaviour cannot be watched, as in some parts of Italy. See, for example, J. Davis, *Land and Family in Pisticci*, Athlone Press, 1973.

2. Wealthy husbands and wives in the town do go out together and meet other couples in bars and restaurants and hold parties of various kinds for their friends. These are the only people who can afford such entertainments and their freedom to act as couples in this way is heightened by the fact that they have servants living in the house to take care of children. In the kinds of bars frequented by working men the presence of a woman is sufficient to bring all conversation to a halt until she leaves under the pressure of their dis-

approval; in those bars frequented by the wealthy, men and women are frequently to be found drinking and smoking together.

South Italian Couples

1. The proportions engaged in these sectors are increasing, as agriculture declines in importance (though what remains is more profitable). While unemployment is not a great problem for agricultural labourers in the town it is becoming one for qualified school-leavers. As in many other developing areas, investment and growth in education has outstripped growth in job opportunities, and emigration for a few years is a common solution to this problem. About 1,000 people are absent from Quercio in any one year, most commonly going to the North, Luxembourg or Germany.

2. In 1951 in Quercio, of the 60 per cent of all the women who worked, 94 per cent were in agriculture. By 1961 these figures had fallen to 50 per cent and 89 per cent respectively.

3. Investment in homes has always been a close second to investment in land in this area.

4. This account applies to all people in Quercio. There are only minor variations between classes in terms of circles they mix in, money they can spend on presents and outings, and strictness of chaperoning, but these do not really affect the basic picture drawn.

5. These are brokers, licensed by the local council, who deal mainly with crops, and sometimes property.

6. Just before Lent.

7. The amount of land and wealth a girl receives as her dowry is deducted from what she may expect to receive as her inheritance when her father dies.

8. In contrast to many other Italian towns.

9. *Il corredo* must be at least *panni sei* (six sets of linen) and bedroom furniture worth a quarter of a million *lire* (approximately £170). The bridegroom is expected to furnish the kitchen. Other relatives, especially maternal uncles, if they are able, provide furniture for *il salotto* (the sitting room). A girl who is *diplomata* (a qualified school-leaver), however, should bring *panni quindici* (fifteen sets of linen) and bedroom furniture worth 800,000 *lire* (£530) – in the words of one informant, 'to live up to my diploma'.

10. Until quite recently *il corredo* would be displayed in the bride's house for a few days about a week before the wedding. Neighbours and relatives would be invited to view it and such a display was a very public claim to status on the part of the bride's mother.

She, rather than her husband, is responsible for the sewing and the purchase, though he may occasionally help with small sums of money. Nowadays most of *il corredo* is bought ready-made. One travelling salesman specializes in suitable articles and his visits (or lack of visits) are carefully noted. Girls who bring hand-stitched sheets and petticoats trimmed with hand-made lace are still, however, much admired. I was invited to see what most people said was probably the last of these public displays. The bride, Anna, was a teacher marrying a well-to-do Air Force Officer. Her widowed mother was a dressmaker, and had been preparing *il corredo* since Anna was a small child. It consisted of fifteen sets of sheets, table-cloths, nightdresses, underwear and babies' nappies, nearly all hand-made, intricately embroidered and trimmed with lace made by the mother. Anna told me she would never have chosen such things herself; some were twelve years old and their style dated. Also, with such a supply, she would probably never have the chance to choose pretty new things for herself. Some women in their fifties told me they still had sheets they had never used and some had mothers who died without ever needing to open some of their *corredo*. Anna agreed to the display because her mother was proud of her handi-work, her life's work and investment. *Il corredo*, as well as being practical, is also one of the most traditional forms of conspicuous consumption.

11. Sydel Silverman also notes this, writing of Central Italy, in 'The Life Crisis as a Clue to Social Functions', *Anthropological Quarterly*, July, 1967.

12. Most couples have too few working years to have saved enough money to live independently, and hire purchase is un-common, so they must depend on their parents. As education con-tinues later and later and marriage occurs younger, the dowry main-tains its importance and implies the interest kin groups maintain in the process of courtship and marriage.

13. These families are not productive units as they are in more definitely peasant societies, but all wages go into the common coffers for the benefit of all, though now some young people are allowed to keep some of their earnings for themselves. But if the household is in difficulties because of illness or poor harvest, for a particularly suc-cessful member to keep back his savings would be unthinkable.

14. If there are no brothers, sisters' husbands become publicly responsible.

15. A similar distancing occurs in relationships with his brothers, who will be his rivals for the family's patrimony on the death of

their father. At marriage daughters, and sometimes sons, receive parts of their inheritance, as property and/or money, and this is then deducted from their shares (males and females having equal ones) when the final division is made. Since the division of the patrimony occurs over a long period, and since the patrimony itself may increase, if more property is acquired after the marriage of the first child, there is plenty of scope for quarrels about what do constitute equal shares.

16. It was calculated by Silverman (op. cit.) that in the area studied by her in Central Italy many brides were pregnant and only a minority were virgins, but there is no evidence to show that this is the case in this part of the South. Sexual honour is still important, if a girl wants to marry well, and few are willing, or able, to risk the shame of being deserted by a fiancé after sleeping with him. Young boys say that, given the chance, they will – proclaiming honourable intentions – try to seduce a girl. If she refuses, they say they are sorry, but they are too young to marry, anyway. If she gives in, they then use this as an excuse for leaving her. The attitude is rather like that of Groucho Marx towards certain posh clubs – they wouldn't want to have any girl who could be had by them.

17. Accusations of unchastity are commonly levelled at such women, and though in the majority of cases they are quite blameless, they are considered fair game by rogue males, and a few do succumb.

18. John Davis, 'Honour and Politics', *Proceedings of the Royal Anthropological Institute*, June, 1970.

19. If he has more than two children, this means actually increasing his property, since a person expects the property he inherits to be equalled by that of his spouse.

20. I talk here of respectability rather than honour, since this latter term implies something more exotic in English (typified by the attitude of Chimène in *Le Cid*) than the Quercesi imply when they talk of *reputazione*.

21. Other South Italians use *honore*.

22. They are not members of distinctive groups such as tribes or castes which regulate their lives. One of the points which Elizabeth Bott makes in relation to urban families is that social control is dispersed among several agencies, so that each family has a relatively large measure of freedom and privacy to regulate its own affairs. Clearly the degree of individuation and social isolation of most of the twenty London families Bott studied was greater than that of the majority of Quercesi families, but in that there are no organized

groups controlling their lives, some comparisons are valid. Elizabeth Bott, *Family and Social Network*, Tavistock, 1957.

23. For an excellent description of such a community of expatriate Sicilians in Australia, see Constance Cronin, *The Sting of Change*, University of Chicago Press, 1970.

24. It is possible, also, that the presence in Quercio of a strange English couple, with rather different habits, might have had an influence. Anthropologists have always had to face the problem that they might well be contaminating the field they are observing, and can only try to be aware of what this influence may be. One of the times when my husband and I were particularly conscious (in retrospect) of our influence was when we invited three married couples, minus their children, to come to the local cinema to see *The Spy Who Came in from the Cold*. Such a visit was almost without precedence in Quercio, and the audience of men and boys spent most of the evening watching us, not the film. In this case the influence was marginal, since we had all been too embarrassed to want to repeat the outing.

25. Few Quercesi now demonstrate any great attachment to the land, and may never have done so.

3. Getting Married

1. C. Lévi-Strauss, *The Elementary Structures of Kinship*, Social Science Paperbacks, Tavistock Publications, 1970, p. 39.

2. The husband received a great deal in the way of harvest gifts from his wife's relatives.

3. Divorce was also most frequently sought by women – the men had much more to lose – and husbands usually attempted to get their wives to return to them.

4. Raymond Firth, in discussing attitudes to marriage in his study of another Pacific society, Tikopia, comments on how the restraints of marriage for a woman are balanced by the 'emancipation' of now being mistress of her own household and controlling a great part of her own life, despite the fact the Tikopian girls 'in song sometimes assert their intention of scorning marriage'. Tikopian men see marriage mostly in terms of restraints on sexual freedom (though in theory they still retain this) and the assumptions of obligations and economic responsibilities contrasting with the minimum of economic effort demanded of them as bachelors. The resulting difference in attitudes between the sexes sounds very much like that often attributed to men and women in Western cultures: 'This sacrifice of

freedom is the greatest drawback to marriage in the eyes of the Tikopian youth, just as the security of a house of her own is the greatest inducement to it for a girl. The natives recognize a clear difference of attitude between the sexes in this respect. The girls desire marriage, the young men try to evade it. This leads to a conflict of interests, some recriminations, serious as well as feigned, and certain ingenious devices on the part of young women to accomplish their desires.' See Raymond Firth, *We, the Tikopia*, Beacon Press, Boston, 1963, p. 434.

5. Some evidence suggests that in some places divorce rates are higher for couples where the bride was pregnant before marriage. (See, for example, H. T. Christensen and H. H. Meissner, 'Studies in Child Spacing: III Premarital Pregnancy as a Factor in Divorce', *American Sociological Review*, 18, 1953, pp. 641–4.) Undoubtedly many factors are involved, but the fact that people are supposed to 'marry for love' may lead some continually to seek reassurance that they are wanted or to look for things which confirm that they are not, putting greater strain on the relation.

6. Like most friends, spouses are usually of similar age, educational level, social class, ethnic group, share similar values and have personality 'needs' which complement each other – those who like to be dominated, for example, tending to associate with those who like to dominate. A great deal of such 'compatibility' results from the normal patterns of social interaction in complex societies – the fact that people of similar age, race, social class are more likely to meet, share leisure activities, etc., than those of different ones, and the relations of unmarried couples are perhaps just as likely to be characterized by these features as those of the married. For discussion of some of these points, see A. C. Kerchoff, 'Patterns of Homogamy and the Field of Eligibles', *Social Forces*, 42, 1963–4, pp. 289–97; R. F. Winch, 'Another Look at the Theory of Complementary Needs in Male Selection', *Journal of Marriage and Family*, 29, 1967, pp. 756–62; Martha Baum, 'Love, Marriage, and the Division of Labour', in Hans Peter Dreitzel (ed.), *Family, Marriage and the Struggle of the Sexes*, Macmillan, New York, 1972; R. Rapoport, 'The Transition from Engagement to Marriage', *Acta Sociologica*, 8, pp. 36–55.

7. For a discussion of how at least some people accept from the outset a more limited relationship when they live together, see E. Macklin, 'Heterosexual Cohabitation Among Unmarried College Students', *The Family Coordinator*, 1972, pp. 463–71. However, the fact that so many studies of spouse selection, courtship and cohabita-

tion have been conducted on college students perhaps in itself places a disproportionate emphasis on the 'working out' of relationships and the less instrumental reasons for marriage. It is perhaps worth noting that passion and love are in a sense taboo topics in the social sciences, unlike adjustment and manipulation. E. Walster points to these kinds of difficulties in an article entitled 'Passionate Love', in B. I. Murstein (ed.), *Theories of Attraction and Love*, Springer Publishing Company, New York, 1971.

8. For a complete discussion of rites of passage see M. Gluckman (ed.), *Essays on the Ritual of Social Relations*, Manchester University Press, 1962; E. R. Leach, 'Time and False Noses', in E. R. Leach, *Rethinking Anthropology*, Athlone Press, 1961; V. W. Turner, *The Ritual Process*, Routledge & Kegan Paul, 1969. For a discussion of social boundaries and the problems associated with crossing them, see M. Douglas, *Purity and Danger*, Routledge & Kegan Paul, 1966.

A Proper Wedding

1. Mary Stott, 'Getting Uptight About White', *Guardian*, Thursday 26 August 1971, p. 11.

2. See, for example, Bryan Wilson, *Religion in Secular Society*, Penguin Books, 1969, and W. S. F. Pickering, 'The Persistence of Rites of Passage: Towards an Explanation', *British Journal of Sociology*, 1974, pp. 63–78.

3. See Mary Douglas, 'The Contempt of Ritual', *New Society*, 31 March 1966, pp. 23–4, and Mary Douglas, *Natural Symbols*, Penguin Books, 1973, pp. 19ff.

4. See Colin Bell, 'Marital Status', in Paul Barker (ed.), *A Sociological Portrait*, Penguin Books, 1972, pp. 64–75; Joan Busfield, 'Ideologies and Reproduction', in M. Richards (ed.) *The Integration of a Child into the Social World*, Cambridge University Press, 1974; Robert Chester and Jane Streather, 'Demarriage: Some Sex Differences and Paradoxes', British Sociological Association conference paper, mimeo, 1974.

5. See Diana Barker, 'Young People and Their Homes: Spoiling and "Keeping Close" in a South Wales Town', *Sociological Review*, November, 1972.

6. Statistics to support these assertions can be found in *Social Trends*, 1974; *Registrar General's Statistical Reviews for England and Wales*, annually, Vols. II and III; and P. R. Cox, 'Changes in Ages at Marriage, Childbearing and Death', Appendix 4 in M. Young

and P. Willmott, *The Symmetrical Family*, Routledge & Kegan Paul, 1973.

7. See Diana Barker and Paul Thompson, 'The Comparative Study of Courtship and Marriage in Twentieth Century Britain: A Methodological Discussion', paper presented to the Thirteenth International Seminar of the International Sociological Association, mimeo, 1973.

8. See E. Bott, *Family and Social Network*, Tavistock, 1957, p. 68.

9. See *The Marriage Act* (1949), and *Law Commission* (1973). There are certain exemptions for Jews and Quakers, dating from the mid-eighteenth century when the first modern legislation was passed.

10. The desire of some people in the U.S.A. to make the ceremony more 'personal' leads to some bizarre choices of locale. See Marcia Seligman, *The Eternal Bliss Machine: The American Way of Wedding*, Hutchinson, 1974.

11. There are more civil weddings in conurbations (Tyneside, W. Yorks, W. Midlands and S. Wales), and in S.E. England they reach a peak in Greater London (42 per cent in 1967, 53 per cent in 1972); and least in rural areas and small towns (N.W. 26 per cent in 1967; N. and Central Wales 37·2 per cent in 1972). Figures from *Registrar General's Statistical Review of England and Wales*, 1971, Vol. II, Appendix C2, pp. 206–7; and *Registrar General's Statistical Review of England and Wales*, 1974, Vol. II, Appendix D2, p. 220. There used to be even more regional variation than exists today; see O. Anderson, 'The Incidence of Civil Marriage in Victorian England and Wales', *Past and Present*, No. 69, November 1975.

12. The national figures on mode of solemnization of marriage are published every five years in an appendix to the *Registrar General's Statistical Review of England and Wales*, Vol. II for 1967 and 1972. Figures supplied to me by the Registrar General for January–March 1968 show that Swansea has a very slightly above average proportion of civil weddings.

| | England and Wales | | Swansea |
	1967	1972	1968 (first quarter)
Religious	65·9	54·5	63
Civil	34·1	45·5	37

Swansea has a rather higher than average proportion of Nonconformist weddings – not perhaps a surprising finding in South Wales.

	England and Wales		*Swansea*
	1967	1972	1968 (first quarter)
Anglican	68·1	67·0	61
Roman Catholic	17	17·1	16
Nonconformist	12·8	13·2	20
Other Christian	1·5	1·9	3
Jewish	0·6	0·7	—

13. In his quinquennial statistics on the mode of solemnization of marriage the Registrar General follows the same distinction in differentiating 'religious' and 'civil' wedding ceremonies, although historically and in terms of legal formalities the distinction is between the Anglican church and the rest.

14. In every one of the forty church weddings in my sample, the bride wore a long white dress.

15. The outline of the ceremonial will be familiar to all British readers. In every case the bride wears a long white dress with a veil and carries a bouquet. She is accompanied by several bridesmaids. She travels from her home to the church in one of several hired limousines, the front of which is decorated with white ribbon streamers. All the guests, invited by specially printed invitations – silver on white – are assembled in the church before the bride arrives. The ushers (young male relatives and friends) sit the bride's guests on the left of the church and the groom's on the right, with the closer relatives sitting towards the front. The bride makes an entrance on the arm of her father while the organ plays 'Here Comes the Bride', and she walks to the chancel steps where the groom and his 'best man' are waiting – wearing dark suits or hired morning suits. There are several hymns, chosen for their familiar tunes and because they feature the word 'Love' prominently. The vicar, priest or minister officiates, and, in the case of the Anglican service in particular, the words are familiar.

After the ceremony and the signing of the register in the vestry, the couple and their parents and attendants proceed from the church – the bride's mother on the arm of the groom's father, etc. Outside the church porch, dozens of photographs are taken by a professional hired photographer, and relatives and friends take snapshots and cine-films. Small children – even dogs – are used to carry 'good luck' tokens (silver cardboard horseshoes, small silver plastic boots or shoes, wooden spoons painted with a red L, all with white heather) to the bride. Then the bride and groom, dodging over-enthusiastic confetti throwers and thrusters, proceed in the hired car to a reception, held either in a hotel or a club-cum-restaurant which specializes in wedding receptions, social and sports club outings. The rest of the 40 to 140 guests travel in various cars, or a coach may be provided so that everyone will be able to drink as much as they want to. The reception involves a 'sit-down' three-course meal. (In other parts of Britain buffet meals are more common and cheaper; in Wales they are more expensive than 'sit-down'/set meals. In Wales weddings are usually in the morning, so the reception is the midday meal. In S.E. England weddings are often in the afternoon.) A drink is provided to toast the bride at the end, when speeches are made. The bride and groom cut (and are photographed cutting) an elaborate multi-tiered cake, decorated with doves, silver slippers or boots, white heather, pink hearts and/or horseshoes. (Pieces of the cake are eaten at the wedding and some are sent to relatives and friends who could not come and to neighbours who were not invited.) The couple usually leave to go on honeymoon, being given a riotous and bawdy send-off in a decorated car or railway carriage, though if they have a home of their own to go to, they may opt to save money and just take a couple of weeks off work. (See Diana Barker, 'The Confetti Ritual', *New Society*, 22 June 1972, pp. 514–17.) The guests who are left behind usually have a 'quiet cup of tea' at the homes of the families who live in the town, and they may meet up again in the evening to go out for a meal, or to a pub or club, or at one of the couple's parents' homes for a party. (Evening parties are more common among the working class.) This is, by Swansea standards, 'a proper wedding'.

Bridal magazines describe register office weddings as 'minimum fuss', 'simple', 'weddings which are part of everyday life'; as distinct from 'grand', 'traditional' and 'romantic' church weddings. See *Brides*, 1969, 'Your Kind of Wedding', Autumn Preview, and *Brides*, 1973, 'Take Three Girls', Autumn Preview.

A very small proportion of the weddings in Roman Catholic and Anglican churches are the second weddings of widows or widowers. These are usually very quiet, with only a handful of guests and the bride in a normal 'Sunday best' attire – certainly if it is her second wedding, but probably even if it is her first if she is of mature years (though one informant of mine was over forty when she first married and she had a full white wedding). See Marcia Seligman, op. cit., for comparison with the U.S.A.

16. Marriage by licence is both quick and secret as, while notices of forthcoming marriages by certificate are displayed in the register office, marriages by licence are merely recorded in the superintendent registrar's book. 46 per cent (50 per cent) of civil marriages are by licence – suggesting that speed and/or secrecy are frequently of importance. Only 6 per cent (5 per cent) of Anglican weddings and 12 per cent (13 per cent) of other religious weddings are by licence. *Registrar General's Annual Statistical Review*, Vol. II, for 1967 and 1972. Percentages given first are for 1967; those in brackets are for 1972.

17. In a very few cases the bride may wear a long white dress. I never saw such a thing, but the register office staff assured me that it occurred – though they thought it very odd and commented: 'Why not get married in church if you're going to go to all that trouble?'

18. Two couples in my sample of twenty had, in fact, booked a date with the vicar and subsequently changed their minds.

19. Previous researches have shown that register office weddings are common among young brides, pregnant brides, and where one partner – especially when this is the bride – has been married before. For example, Rowntree, in a National Survey of England and Wales in 1959–60 (Griselda Rowntree, 'New Facts on Teenage Marriage', *New Society*, 4 October 1962), found that:

   (i) teenage brides had more civil weddings than those in their twenties (30 per cent against 18 per cent);
  (ii) fewer teenage brides wore white (43 per cent against 69 per cent), or had receptions (86 per cent against 95 per cent);
 (iii) teenage brides who were pregnant were more likely to marry in the register office (48 per cent against 22 per cent non-pregnant), or to wear white (17 per cent against 54 per cent), but more had receptions (91 per cent against 83 per cent).

August B. Hollingshead, in 'Marital Status and Wedding Behaviour', *Marriage and Family Living*, 1952, pp. 308–11, reports from New Haven, U.S.A., that the greatest ceremonial in weddings occurs where it is the first marriage for both, markedly less where it is the second marriage for the woman, least where it is the second marriage for both.

20. The Superintendent Registrar's view of his job varies considerably from this; he sees himself as having definite legal and pastoral responsibilities towards the couples he marries, and he may

well talk to the couple at length and try to persuade them to pause and reconsider.

21. Other impediments concern one or other parties being unbaptized (in the Church of England) or non-members (many of the smaller sects and the Roman Catholic Church), living outside the parish boundaries (Church of England), or the couple being within the prohibited degrees of kindred and affinity of the church – though not of the state (Church of England, Roman Catholic Church). These are of minor importance in terms of numbers of couples affected and will be ignored here.

22. A point which Goffman says is commonly true of people with 'spoiled identities'. See Erving Goffman, *Stigma*, Penguin Books, 1968.

23. Especially noteworthy given that young men are the group most likely to be hostile to the church. See Geoffrey Gorer, *Exploring English Character*, Cresset Press, 1955, and David Martin, *A Sociology of English Religion*, Heinemann, 1967. Also, for comparison, Alasdair MacIntyre, *Secularization and Moral Change*, Oxford University Press, 1967, and Peter G. Forster, 'Secularization in the English Context: Some Conceptual and Empirical Problems', *Sociological Review*, 1972, p. 153.

24. Susan Budd points out that secularists are also predominantly found in large towns and cities. Over half of the members of the National Secular Society had moved long distances to towns. Some had moved *because* they were atheists and radicals, others moved and thus came into contact with atheists and radicals. Others simply escaped the pressures to conformity. See Susan Budd, 'The Loss of Faith in England; 1850–1950', *Past and Present*, April, 1967.

25. See Audrey Richards, *Chisungu: A Girl's Initiation Ceremony Among the Bemba of Northern Rhodesia*, Faber, 1956.

26. However, there are anxious minutes for vergers, trying to chase away one wedding party, on their fiftieth photo, before the next wedding guests arrive.

27. The register office may be many miles away – for example, people living on Gower or in Neath have to come to the Swansea register office.

28. See, for example, C. C. Harris, 'Church, Chapel and the Welsh', *New Society*, 1963, and Colin Rosser and Christopher Harris, *The Family and Social Change*, Routledge & Kegan Paul, 1965. See also David Martin, op. cit.

29. The dress is also the chief object of attack in Mary Stott's article, quoted at the beginning of the chapter.

30. I recognize that the number of hired and second-hand dresses must have been considerably under-reported to me. For example, a friend's daughter bought a second-hand dress and swore her mother to secrecy (not very efficiently, since her mother told me; but I don't think that to this day her daughter knows that I know). The shame and the shared values about 'second-hand dresses' are what are of interest and concern here, however.

31. See Diana Barker, 'The Confetti Ritual', op. cit.

32. See Michael Schofield, *The Sexual Behaviour of Young Adults*, Allen Lane, 1973.

33. See C. W. Cunnington, *English Women's Clothing in the Present Century*, 1952.

34. White is also the colour of rejoicing in the church (though here the colour for mourning is purple). Thus the flowers, vestments and altar hangings at weddings are white (if they are changed for the service).

35. See Leonore Davidoff, Jean L'Esperance and Howard Newby, 'Landscape with Figures', in A. Oakley and J. Mitchell (eds.), *The Rights and Wrongs of Women*, Penguin Books, 1976.

36. I only learned of the pregnancy when I called back two months after the wedding. It was kept quiet during our initial talk. (These are 1969 prices.)

37. The minister of the church she went to is a well-known local character. He is a Christian Socialist and uses his crypt as a refuge for alcoholics, tramps and discharged prisoners. He is known for his tolerance and willingness to marry divorcees and girls who are pregnant if he feels convinced of their 'sincerity'.

38. Van Gennep compares rituals associated with passage from one status to another in many different cultures and suggests that life-cycle passage rites typically involve a symbolic 'death' in the old status, a transitional period 'outside' the society, and a symbolic 're-birth' in the new status – separation, transition and reincorporation. It is interesting in this connection to note that children in our culture are quite often a little alarmed at the sight of a bride, thinking she is a ghost (i.e. someone dead, yet not dead). Arnold van Gennep, *The Rites of Passage*, trans. M. B. Vizedom and G. L. Caffee, Routledge & Kegan Paul, 1960 (first published 1909).

39. Some women keep dresses for lack of any clear idea of what to do with them; some to make a christening gown for their first child. Certainly, many do keep them for years and a few were even able to show me their mothers' dresses.

40. In addition, where a 'proper wedding' can take place will be

related to the facilities provided by the local authority. If register offices had the characteristics of churches one might expect white weddings in them. The Superintendent Registrar is responsible to the Registrar General in London, but the local register office is provided and maintained by the local government authority. Hence, if local councillors share the dichotomous view of 'proper' and 'other' weddings outlined in this chapter, they will be unlikely to devote money from the rates to improve the register office facilities.

41. See Pickering, op. cit.

42. Business people, of course, also introduce new 'customs' to sell more products.

43. John Beattie, 'Ritual and Social Change', *Man*, 1, 1966, pp. 60–74.

44. See P. M. Bromley, *Family Law*, Butterworths, London, 1966 edn.

45. The concern with getting all the details of a ritual 'right' is very commonly seen in ceremonies in other cultures, and it has often been suggested that one function this serves is catharsis and succour – it gives the actors in a stressful situation help in purging their emotions and also something to do which they believe will bring about their desired ends. And, of course, because they devote so much time and thought and act jointly to achieve an end, it is arguable that the ritual makes them more likely to achieve the result anyway. See, for example, B. Malinowski, *Coral Gardens and Their Magic*, Vols. I and II, 1935.

46. The verbal part of the 'giving away' of the bride by her father is now (1976) omitted from the revised Church in Wales marriage service.

47. Gluckman has argued, on the basis of research in Africa, that rituals emphasizing structural distinctions in society are *more* necessary when there is a danger of differences being muddled. Therefore, in terms of the material presented here, the more young adult men and women dress and behave alike, and the more they live together or have sexual intercourse without being married, the more important will weddings become in stressing the differential roles of husband and wife, and the distinctions between the unmarried and the married state. Max Gluckman, *Custom and Conflict in Africa*, Blackwell, 1965.

48. Mary Stott, for example.

49. See A. Whitehead, 'Sex Antagonisms in Herefordshire', in Diana Leonard Barker and Sheila Allen, *Dependence and*

Exploitation in Work and Marriage, Longmans, 1976.

50. See Geoffrey Gorer, *Sex and Marriage in England Today*, Nelson, 1971, and Schofield, op. cit.

51. See for example discussions in:

Christine Delphy, 'Continuities and Discontinuities in Marriage and Divorce', and Yves Dezalay, 'French Judicial Ideology and Working Class Divorce', in Diana Leonard Barker and Sheila Allen, *Sexual Divisions and Society: Process and Change*, Tavistock, 1976.

Jessie Bernard, *The Future of Marriage; His and Hers*, Souvenir Press, 1972.

Colin Bell and Howard Newby, 'Husbands and Wives. The Dynamics of the Deferential Dialectic', in Diana Leonard Barker and Sheila Allen, *Dependence and Exploitation in Work and Marriage*, Longmans, 1976.

52. Abner Cohen, *Two-Dimensional Man*, Routledge & Kegan Paul, 1974, p. 132.

4. Marriage and Sex

1. Even in societies where the sexes are kept strictly apart and marriages are arranged, notions of 'romantic love' and great passions may abound in the literature and folk tales – such restrictions on them do not deny their existence. Romantic love, however, is not associated with anything as mundane as marriage, and while the consummation of such emotions may be seen as a great personal satisfaction and their thwarting and betrayal as agony, consummation is often associated with tragedy. The idea that the existence of social barriers themselves serve as the impetus for 'romantic love' was claimed by Freud, who said: 'Some obstacle is necessary to swell the tide of libido to its height; and at all periods of history whenever natural barriers in the way of satisfaction have not sufficed, mankind has erected conventional ones in order to enjoy love.' S. Freud, 'The Most Prevalent Form of Degradation in Erotic Life', in E. Jones (ed.), *Collected Papers*, 4, Hogarth, 1925.

2. From A. Hayes, *Sexual Physiology of Women*, Peabody Medical Institute, Boston, 1869.

3. In traditional Japan, for example, unwanted daughters were sold off in this way. See T. Fukutake, *Japanese Rural Society*, Oxford University Press, 1967.

4. Little systematic information exists on this kind of behaviour and on mate-swapping generally in Britain. However, J. F. Cüber and P. B. Harroff mention it in their discussion of marital relation-

ships in the U.S.A., 'Five Kinds of Relationships', in *Sex and the Significant Americans*, Penguin, Baltimore, 1965. They also describe how some couples believe that they should not recount their experiences to each other, while others gain vicarious pleasure by doing so.

5. Carolyn Symonds, in her master's thesis, 'Pilot Study of the Peripheral Behaviour of Sexual Mate Swappers', University of California, Riverside, 1968, distinguishes between two types of 'swinger' – the recreational and the Utopian. I am here primarily referring to the 'recreational' swingers – the Utopian tend also to wish to share other aspects of their life with others in community living. See also C. Symonds, 'Sexual Mate-Swapping; Violation of Norms and Reconciliation of Guilt', in J. Hanslin (ed.), *Studies in the Sociology of Sex*, Appleton, Century, Crofts, 1971.

6. D. Danfield and M. Gordon, 'Mate Swapping: The Family that Swings Together Clings Together', p. 440 in M. E. Lasswell and T. E. Lasswell, *Love Marriage Family, A Developmental Approach*, Scott, Foresman & Co., Illinois, 1973, pp. 432–40.

7. Available literature on 'swinging' and 'mate-swapping' in general often indicates more about the practices of swinging and the social characteristics of those who swing (Symonds's study for example suggesting that most are middle-class couples who adhere to a liberal political philosophy) than it does about the relationships which exist between husbands and wives who 'swing'.

8. M. Mead comments: 'In parts of old Japan, the four-year-old male, because he was a male, could terrorize his mother and the other females of the household. His maleness overrode any difference in size that would have made it possible for any of the females to have given him a sound thrashing.' *Male and Female*, Penguin Books, 1962, p. 87.

9. For accounts of traditional Japanese rural life and the significance of household, see Fukutake, op. cit., and C. Nakane, *Kinship and Economic Organisation in Rural Japan*, Athlone Press, 1967.

10. For a discussion of some of these changing attitudes see Takashi Koyama, *The Changing Social Position of Women in Japan*, UNESCO, Paris, 1961 (reprinted in W. J. Goode (ed.), *Readings on the Family and Society*, Prentice–Hall, New Jersey, 1964). Ezra Vogel, for example, argues that the go-between in arranging Japanese marriages took on a special importance during the period of most rapid industrialization. E. Vogel, 'The Go-Between in a Developing Society: The Case of the Japanese Marriage Arranger', *Human Organisation*, 20, pp. 112–20 (also reprinted in W. J. Goode, op. cit.).

Aspects of Japanese Marriage

1. With grateful acknowledgement to Professor Hiroshi Wagatsuma, Department of Anthropology, U.C.L.A., for his valuable comments.

2. The anthropologist Befu translates the Japanese concept *ie* as 'stem family', and defines it as consisting of '... all those who commonly reside together and share social and economic life. It is primarily composed of close kin as its core, but may include distant kin and non-kin, e.g. employees, insofar as they reside with the core kinship group and participate in its social and economic life. It is, in addition, a corporate group, that is to say, it perpetuates itself from generation to generation beyond the life span of any single member of the group ... This contrasts with the nuclear family of the United States, which starts when a couple sets up co-residence and, after the birth, maturation, and departure of children, dissolves when one or both of the couple dies.' H. Befu, *Japan – An Anthropological Introduction*, Chandler, San Francisco, 1971, p. 38.

3. According to Blood, this stress on continuity of the *ie* put a biological emphasis on mate-selection. See R. O. Blood, *Love Match and Arranged Marriage – A Tokyo–Detroit Comparison*, Free Press, New York, 1967.

4. Outcastes are described in detail by G. A. De Vos and H. Wagatsuma, *Japan's Invisible Race: Caste in Culture and Personality*, University of California Press, Berkeley, 1966.

5. See R. K. Beardsley, J. W. Hall and R. E. Ward, *Village Japan*, University of Chicago Press, Chicago, 1959.

6. A detailed description of the go-between's role is given by E. Vogel in 'The Go-Between in a Developing Society: The Case of the Japanese Marriage Arranger', *Human Organization*, 20, 1961, pp. 112–20.

7. See W. Caudill and H. Weinstein, 'Maternal Care and Infant Behaviour in Japan and America', *Psychiatry*, 32, 1969, pp. 12–43.

8. R. Frager, 'Jewish Mothering in Japan', *Sociological Inquiry*, 42, 1972, pp. 11–17.

9. See W. Caudill and D. W. Plath, 'Who Sleeps by Whom? Parent-Child Involvement in Urban Japanese Families', *Psychiatry*, 29, 1966, pp. 344–66.

10. L. T. Doi, *The Anatomy of Dependence*, Kodansha, Tokyo, 1973.

11. The Thematic Apperception Test consists of several cards. Each one shows a different drawing (usually of two or more persons),

sufficiently vague so that respondents can tell imaginative stories in response. It is hypothesized that story contents frequently reflect conscious and/or unconscious problems experienced by the respondents.

12. H. Wagatsuma and G. A. De Vos, 'Attitudes toward Arranged Marriage in Rural Japan', *Human Organization*, 21, 1961, 187–200, p. 188.

13. Dore has shown that in a sample of 244 respondents the percentage of 'love marriages' increased from 11 per cent (those who married before 1921) to 46 per cent (those who married between 1946 and 1951). But even here no more than 4·5 per cent of the total had had a love marriage *not* formalized by relatives or a go-between. See R. Dore, *City Life in Japan: A Study of a Tokyo Ward*, University of California Press, Berkeley, 1967.

14. R. O. Blood, op. cit., p. 95.

15. ibid., p. 19.

16. See Chie Nakane, *Kinship and Economic Organization in Rural Japan*, Athlone Press, 1967, p. 153.

17. ibid., p. 154.

18. ibid., p. 29.

19. See M. Joya, *Things Japanese*, Tokyo News Service, Tokyo, 1958.

20. See Beardsley, Hall and Ward, op. cit., p. 330.

21. J. W. Hall and R. K. Beardsley, *Twelve Doors to Japan*, McGraw-Hill, New York, 1965, p. 380.

22. H. Wagatsuma, personal communication.

23. H. Wagatsuma, personal communication.

24. R. Dore, op. cit., pp. 96–7.

25. Chie Nakane, *Japanese Society*, Weidenfeld & Nicolson, 1970, p. 11.

26. R. Dore, op. cit.

27. Beardsley, Hall and Ward, op. cit., p. 330.

28. ibid., p. 533.

29. R. Dore, op. cit., p. 444.

30. Chie Nakane, *Japanese Society*, op. cit.

31. ibid., pp. 120–24.

32. R. Dore, op. cit., p. 110.

33. See Hayashiya et al., 'Nihonjin no chie', translated by A. J. Turney in *Japan Interpreter*, 7, 1971, pp. 67–70.

34. ibid., p. 69.

35. G. A. De Vos and H. Wagatsuma, *Heritage of Endurance*, typescript, to be published.

36. Quoted by R. O. Blood, op. cit., p. 7.

37. ibid., pp. 6–7.

38. Hall and Beardsley, *op. cit.*, p. 376.

39. M. Huerlimann and F. King, *Japan*, Viking Press, New York 1970, p. 15.

40. Strong ambivalent feelings could be deduced from the numerous cartoons, etc. in men's magazines, where women are shown a aggressive, fearsome, and dangerous. There is furthermore a stron streak of overt sadism in these publications, as well as in the 'blu films' called 'eroductions' (portmanteau-terms for 'erotic produc tions'). Here females are mercilessly beaten up or stabbed by th male hero, especially before rape scenes. The actress, after reachin a state of near-collapse, invariably starts enjoying the procedure an suddenly responds enthusiastically to the hero's sexual advances while the film, normally in black and white, turns to glorious colou The obvious interpretation is that of male sadism and femal masochism: the male's 'right' and the female's submission. Here too, however, things are more complex than they appear at firs Donald Richie, probably the best authority on Japanese films, men tions in his 'Notes on the Japanese Eroduction' (1973) that th underlying theme of these films is the denigration of women. Wome are maltreated most cruelly by man and finally submit to him, but b this time the 'hero' is impotent. However, this is never his fault it is the woman's. In the final scene the woman repents, or is kille by the man as revenge for making him impotent – obviously th worst humiliation the 'hero' in such a film can experience. Sometime man and woman just part – all this ecstasy wasn't worth it. Th motto is, according to Richie: 'To be completely denigrated.' Th is quite different from the run-of-the-mill pornographic films of othe countries where sadism is not the norm. In Japanese 'eroduction women are shown as vicious, since, due to their 'animal instincts they no longer possess their virginity. 'Since they are no longer pu they must be made completely impure. It is thus that women wh naturally, humanly, warmly acknowledge their emotional needs a regarded as vicious. Men who so acknowledge their needs are, course, not.'

Another aspect depicted, often unintentionally, is the man's im maturity as regards women. To Richie, the excessive preoccupatio with breast-fondling is a sign that the male re-enacts the mothe child relationship where the mother is seen as powerful and evil. Th sadism he shows towards his victim really exposes his inadequac especially since he is often made impotent. Sadism is, however, a cording to Richie, inverted masochism: the all-male audience is suffering by what it sees, and this stimulates them sexually.

'That woman is an enemy is a sensation that all men have experienced, but it is not one we usually or necessarily believe ... with a truly compulsive insistence, it [the 'eroduction'] monomanically maintains that the nursery vision is the only one, that women are evil, that men are their prey, and that sex is their instrument ... Prolonged viewing indicates that the tortures almost invariably result from fear felt by men. They are doing in the women, before the women have a chance to do them in. That this is an extremely primitive view of the male–female relationship is obvious, but it is as basic as it is barbaric.

... In Japan the eroduction seems to be a habit, like smoking, drinking, biting the nails. Its gratifications are instant, meaningless and necessary.' See D. Richie, 'Notes on the Japanese Eroduction', *Film Comment*, 1973.

41. Chie Nakane, *Japanese Society*, op. cit.

42. R. Dore, op. cit., p. 119.

43. ibid., p. 178.

44. H. Wagatsuma, personal communication.

45. Wagatsuma remarks that he has counselled many such mothers in Japan.

46. H. Morsbach and Chie Okaki, 'A Cross-cultural Study of Future Expectations and Aspirations among Adolescent Girls', Min-zokugaku Kenkyū (*The Japanese Journal of Ethnology*). Proceedings of the VIIIth International Congress of Anthropological and Ethnological Sciences, Tokyo, 1969, pp. 381–5.

47. E. Vogel, *Japan's New Middle Class*, University of California Press, Berkeley, 1963, pp. 112–13.

5. Marital Harmony and Conflict

1. Legal separation is sometimes allowed where divorce is not permitted and remarriage therefore prohibited. The conditions under which separation is allowed may be similar to those for divorce in other countries. Because the circumstances under which divorce is allowed are so variable, because divorce rates must be looked at in the context of demographic factors, because the continuation of a marriage does not necessarily mean the continuation of a 'normal' marital relation, and because interests of others in the marriage and what marriage itself entails also affect the rates at which people divorce, comparison of divorce rates in different societies or in one

society over time is no immediate indicator of relative discontent with marital relations.

2. Not fulfilling obligations may range from being barren to failing to treat in-laws with due respect. Where marriage is primarily concerned with the rights of men over women, the man as the only party with rights may be the only one allowed to sue for divorce.

3. Prior to this, divorce was granted on the basis of a marital offence, the 'innocent' party being the only one who could instigate proceedings. A woman whose husband had left her for another could therefore prevent his remarriage by refusing to seek a divorce, and a husband and wife who simply did not get along had to concoct some kind of 'offence'. The new laws incorporate the old offences but make it much more difficult to preserve a marriage in the minimal legal sense and allow a divorce by consent. The claims of a new personal relation on a married individual may in this sense take precedence over the obligations of marriage. See, for example, M Puxton, *Family Law*, Penguin Books, 1971, pp. 125–45. This change goes a long way towards recognizing marriage primarily as a legitimate couple relation and moves towards making the end of the relation the end of the marriage. (However, we have not yet reached the sophistication of the Trobriand Islanders in this respect, among whom to simply pack up, leave home and refuse to return constitute divorce!)

4. As might be supposed in a society of this kind I had more opportunity to learn about the women's opinions than the men's.

5. An 'injured' party could seek separation on the basis of a marital offence, but such separations, like many divorces, were not easy to obtain and could never result in a marriage to someone else during the lifetime of the spouse.

6. M. Kerr, *The People of Ship Street*, Routledge & Kegan Paul 1958, p. 40.

7. The interviews to which I refer were conducted as part of the research for the book *Managers and Their Wives* by J. M. & R. E Pahl, Allen Lane, 1971. The following quotations are taken from these interviews. My account of the interviewing and how the couple responded is given as an appendix to the book.

8. For a general discussion of the kinds of contacts wives at home do or do not have, see H. Gavron, *The Captive Wife*, Routledge & Kegan Paul, 1966.

9. Some of the men interviewed during this research felt that their wives should be home in the evenings to keep them company an

that their wife's job was to make the home a comfortable place for them to retreat to from the 'outside' world. Some wives, too, felt that this was their contribution to the husband's 'success', and many husbands believed that their pursuit of success was something they did for their families – even if it resulted in ignoring them.

10. I am not suggesting that these kinds of marriages are more or less unhappy than others, but simply pointing out that they are subject to different kinds of stresses. Obviously straightforward economic factors, for example, place a great deal of strain on many marriages, and almost certainly a combination of financial constraints and 'isolation' would be particularly problematic.

11. In addition, marital relations may be more focused on obligation and duty when there are children, and being a couple may be less important during this time. Bott, for example, suggests that conjugal relations tend to become more segregated with the birth of children. E. Bott, *Family and Social Network*, Tavistock Publications, 1971.

12. J. F. Cüber and P. B. Harroff, 'Five Kinds of Relationships', in *Sex and the Significant Americans*, Penguin, Baltimore, 1965. An insightful study attempting to distinguish among kinds of personal marital relations.

Marital Breakdown as a Personal Crisis

1. This chapter draws substantially upon material reported in *When Marriage Ends – A Study in Status Passage*, Tavistock, 1976.

The term divorce is used here as a status category to refer to individuals whose marriages have broken down, i.e. divorced and separated men and women.

2. The christening ceremony is one example of a *rite-de-passage*. By means of this ritual, the child is named and his moral and religious education as a social being provided for.

3. 89 per cent of women and 85 per cent of men between the ages of 30 and 39 are married. Census of population, H.M.S.O., 1966.

4. R. Chester, 'Contemporary Trends in the Stability of English Marriage', *Journal of Biosocial Science*, 3, 1971, p. 389.

5. By the end of the sixties, the percentage of marriages terminated by divorce was probably somewhere in the region of 12–15 per cent. The figure of 20 per cent is a prediction based upon a rigorous analysis of recent trends and it includes other forms of marital breakdown besides divorce. The exact magnitude of marital break-

down in Britain is impossible to calculate. Not all separated couple
seek a legal resolution for their parting; even the recorded figures o
those that do carry many difficulties of interpretation (F. Chester, op
cit.).

6. The Divorce Reform Act, 1969, became effective on 1 January
1971. It removed the concept of matrimonial offence from the statut
book and made the irretrievable breakdown of marriage the sol
ground for divorce; after two years of living apart and five year
separation a divorce may be granted with the consent of only on
spouse.

7. The author spent twenty months in the late 1960s studying th
club and its members.

8. Reciprocal obligations between two spouses are not completel
dismantled by the legal process. A couple may be united by economi
links long after the law has recognized the demise of the union.

9. Bohannen suggests that there are 'six stations of divorce'. Thes
six overlapping experiences are:
'(1) The emotional divorce, centred around the problem of a de
teriorating marriage; (2) Legal divorce, based on grounds; (3
Economic divorce, which involves money and property; (4) Th
co-parental divorce which deals with custody, single parent home
visitation; (5) Community divorce, surrounding the changes c
friends and community that every divorcee experiences; (6) Th
problem of regaining individual autonomy.' See P. Bohannen
Divorce and After, Doubleday, New York, 1970, pp. 33–4.

10. W. Waller and R. Hill, *The Family: A Dynamic Interpreta
tion*, 1938; revised edition 1951, Holt, Rinehart, Winston, Nev
York.

11. For a discussion of the trauma of separation and divorce i
America, see W. Goode, *After Divorce*, Free Press, New York, 195
(reprinted as *Women in Divorce*) 1965.

12. Marris, in a study of widows, described the difficulties of ad
justing to the end of a conjugal relationship. See P. Marris, *Widou
and Their Families*, Routledge & Kegan Paul, 1958.

13. See E. Goffmann, *Stigma*, Penguin Books, 1968.

14. In retrospect, some may have come to agree with these sent
ments. In reply to the question, 'Do you have any regrets?' severa
said that an unhappy marriage was better than being separated.

15. W. Goode, op. cit.

16. Most divorced people (66–75 per cent) remarry, and for th
men the probability is higher than for women. The remarriage pro
pects of club members were probably diminished by their age, the

experience of a fairly long married life, their low level of income, and the fact that many had custody of dependent children.

17. One example of the kind of institutionalized support which is extended to the newly widowed is the resettlement allowance which the state grants to widows during the six months following the death of the husband. This sum is paid irrespective of any superannuation or insurance policies which may provide for the widow's livelihood, and when the six months are up the widow may receive a pension from the state for the rest of her life. No similar provision is made for the divorcee.

18. W. Goode, op. cit.

6. After Divorce

1. J. C. Westman and D. W. Cline, 'Divorce is a Family Affair', *Family Law Quarterly*, 5, 1, 1971.

2. Westman and Cline (op. cit.) give, for example, these accounts of the ways in which relations and conflict may be prolonged and the importance of their children in the relation of divorced people: 'As an extreme example, the parents of a 12-year-old girl continually quarrelled over her management. Although custody had been awarded to the mother who had full-time employment, the father continued regular visits and found fault with his former wife's housekeeping, cooking and control of their daughter.'

Or:

'For example, a 9-year-old boy visited his father on weekends and told him stories about the harsh treatment he was receiving from his mother. When he returned to his mother, he told her about the idyllic existence of his father, leading her to believe that her son was being over-indulged by his father. The parents developed exaggerated pictures of what went on in their respective homes. When they were brought together and had an opportunity to obtain a more realistic picture of their son's role in exaggerating their concerns, they dropped their complaints and established regular contact to discuss plans for their son. They previously had decided to avoid direct conversation. In effect, their son was trying to bring them together in the only way available to him.'

3. The rise of marriage bureaux and escort agencies attests to the difficulties many people have in establishing relations with members of the opposite sex. In *The World of the Formerly Married* (McGraw-Hill, 1966), Morton Hunt discusses some of the difficulties people who have been married once may have in finding partners,

their preferences often being for people who have had a similar experience, and the ineffectiveness of the 'matchmaking' attempts of married friends.

4. W. J. Goode, who has written extensively about marriage, divorce and remarriage. Quoted in B. Rollin, 'The American Way of Marriage: Remarriage', *Look*, 21 September 1971.

Couple Relationships

1. Work on this study was supported by a grant from the Department of Health, Education and Welfare, Social Rehabilitation Service, C–R–D 294(2) 7–245 and from the National Institute of Mental Health, 5–RO–1–MH–15428.

2. The last study has been reported in R. Weiss, 'The Contributions of an Organization of Single Parents to the Well-being of its Members', *Family Coordinator*, July 1973, pp. 321–6. See also R. Weiss, *Loneliness*, M.I.T. Press, 1973.

3. My comments on the form are based on a quite small number of instances in our data, though supported by descriptions of living together arrangements which appear in the literature on lower-class life. The economic stress in the lower-class stratum makes all partnerships difficult, marriage as well as living together. This may there give special importance to the theme of considerateness or exploitiveness.

4. Such suspicions are reported by J. Blake in her study of sexual relationships in Jamaica. See J. Blake, *Family Structure in Jamaica*, Free Press, New York, 1961.

5. It is sometimes proposed that marriage is the enemy of love. See, for example, P. Slater, in R. Coser (ed.), *The Family*, St Martins Press, New York, 1965. This seems not to be true; emotional attachment, at least, is evident in most marriages. On the other hand, marriage may be an enemy to considerateness.

6. Prince Peter has suggested as a definition of marriage which has cross-societal validity that it is the relationship which causes men to become husbands, and women to become wives. See Peter, Prince of Greece and Denmark, 'For a New Definition of Marriage', *Man*, 1956, p. 48.

7. There is some evidence in a study currently under way at the Laboratory that widows of suicides do not observe mourning rituals or moratoria on dating in the same way as other widows. At least some of them feel they were abandoned, and that their marital obligations were therefore ended.

7. The Choice Not to Marry

1. Obviously the inheritance of wealth still affects the individual's life chances, as may the nature of the social relations he has with parents and kin, as many studies of educational achievement have shown.

2. I mean 'father' in a kinship sense and not simply the recognition of biological paternity.

3. For a discussion of some of these issues of legitimacy see B. Farber, *Family and Kinship in Modern Society*, Scott, Foresman and Company, Illinois, 1973. In 1967 a subcommission of the Commission on Human Rights of the United Nations demanded that 'every person once his filiation has been established, shall have the same legal rights as a person born in wedlock'.

Married and Unmarried Cohabitation in Sweden

1. Eilert Sundt, *Om Giftermaal i Norge*, Oslo, 1967 (first published in 1866).

2. From the 1930s until 1966 there was a very slow increase in the rate of marriage in Sweden, if we use 'mariage rate' to mean the number of marriages in relation to the number of non-married 20–49-year-old males and non-married 15–44-year-old females. We thus make, as Sundt did, a correction for the number of children born some time earlier or, more exactly, the population from which the marriages are recruited, but this slight increase can well be explained in the Sundt manner by saying that the demographic measure used is a rough one (which in fact, it is). For data and a discussion of this period, see Jan Trost, 'Marriage-Rates in Sweden', in Frijling (ed.), *Social Change in Europe*, E. J. Brill, Leyden, 1973.

3. In fact this tradition has remained as a fairly common tradition in Iceland. See Bjorn Bjornsson, *The Lutheran Doctrine of Marriage in Modern Icelandic Society*, Oslo, 1971.

4. Erik Manniche and Kaare Svalastoga, 'The Family in Scandinavia', Kobenhavn, mimeo, 1968.

5. See Jan Trost, 'En undersöking av allmänhetens inställning i några familjeekonomiska frågor', in S.O.U., 1975, 24, Tre sociologiska rapporter, Stockholm.

6. See Pal Locsei, 'Syndyasmos in Contemporary Budapest', Budapest, mimeo, 1970.

7. See A. Nasholm, 'Sammanboende gifta och sammanboende ogifta', in S.O.U., 1972, 34, Familjelag I, Stockholm.

8. See J. Trost, 'Marriage Rates in Sweden', op. cit.

9. The old law was in action from 1920 until 1 January 1974. In 1969 a governmental committee was created with the aim of suggesting a new family law. The committee published a book in June 1972, containing suggestions for a new law mainly concerning marriages and divorcees, and in 1977 another volume was published, the latter suggesting changes in the internal family economy. Most of the suggestions presented by the committee in 1972 were accepted as laws by the parliament in 1973.

10. The last available figures.

11. See Manniche and Svalastoga, op. cit.

8. Homosexual Couples

1. For a general discussion of lesbianism see C. Wolff, *Love Between Women*, Gerald Duckworth, 1971, in which the author discusses the particular emotional dispositions involved in lesbianism as well as the sexual ones.

2. With the exception of 'cousins' we systematically distinguish among kin in terms of sex. Although we do use (usually in reference rather than in address) 'collective' terms such as 'parent', 'child', 'sibling', this does not negate the fact that we usually distinguish between mother and father, son and daughter, and brother and sister, and that these are the terms usually used when we wish to imply kinship rather than to evoke biological connections. The following example illustrates the problem and the adaptation necessary. The person married to my father's brother (my uncle) is my aunt. If this person were male, one would have the oddity of a male aunt, unless he were to be reclassified as an uncle, which we would, perhaps, regard as less odd. In other words, we would have to say that persons married to parents *siblings* are uncles if male, aunts if female.

Men in Love: Observations on Male Homosexual Couples

1. I have ignored both broader anthropological studies and studies of lesbian couples, which from all counts are more frequent.

2. This article was written in 1971 and remains substantially unaltered. Helpful criticisms were made by Michael Schofield, Peter Urbach and John Gray. Some of the material has been outdated, but there remains no major research in this area except for that of Blumstein and Schwartz at the University of Washington, which is currently being conducted.

3. M. Leznoff and W. Westley, 'The Homosexual Community', in J. Gagnon and W. Simon, *Sexual Deviance*, Harper & Row, 1967; and see also C. Warren, *Identity and Community in the Gay World*, Wiley, 1974.

4. C. Warren, op. cit.

5. Some homosexuals have told me that this kind of relationship is common, but my own observations suggest it is not.

6. See D. Sonnenschein, 'The Ethnography of Male Homosexual Relationships', *Journal of Sex Research*, 1968, pp. 69–83.

7. See, for example, *The Advocate*, 12 April 1972, and *Gay News* No. 8, No. 34.

8. For the documentation of such legal battles see D. Teal, *The Gay Militants*, Stein & Day, 1971, p. 282.

9. C.f. A. Kinsey, *Sexual Behaviour in the Human Male*, W. B. Saunders, 1948, p. 633.

10. Some key empirical studies are G. Westwood, *A Minority*, Longmans, 1960; M. Schofield, *Sociological Aspects of Homosexuality*, Longmans, 1965; J. Gagnon and W. Simon, *Sexual Conduct*, Aldine, 1973; *Social Needs Survey*, Albany Trust, 1970; and C. Williams and M. Weinberg, *Male Homosexuals*, Oxford University Press, 1974.

11. M. Schofield, op. cit.

12. E. Bergler, *Homosexuality: Disease or Way of Life*, Hill & Wary, 1957.

13. C. W. Socarides, 'Homosexuality', *International Journal of Psychiatry*, 10, 1972, pp. 118–25.

14. B. S. Robbins, 'Psychological Implications of the Male Homosexual Marriage', *Psycho-analytic Review*, 30, 1943, pp. 428–37.

15. Bieber, *Homosexuality*, Basic Books, New York, 1962, p. 253.

16. M. Freedman, *Homosexuality and Psychological Functioning*, Brooks/Cole, 1971, p. 87.

17. Clinical explanations may apply in some cases, of course, but such explanations may also be invoked for the instability of many heterosexual relationships.

18. M. Hoffman, *The Gay World*, Basic Books, New York, 1968, p. 176.

19. K. Plummer, *Sexual Stigma*, Routledge & Kegan Paul, 1975.

20. R. Turner, *Family Interaction*, Wiley, 1970, p. 51.

21. R. May, *Love and Will*, Fontana, 1972.

22. See K. Plummer, op. cit., pp. 46–56.

23. G. Westwood, op. cit., p. 115.

24. M. Hoffman, op. cit., p. 58.

25 ibid.

26. C.f. E. Hooker, 'The Homosexual Community', in J. Gagnon and W. Simon, *Sexual Deviance*, op. cit., p. 176; L. Humphreys, *Tea-Room Trade*, Duckworth, 1970, p. 47.

27. M. J. Horowitz, 'The Homosexual's Image of Himself', *Mental Hygiene*, 48, 1964, pp. 197–201.

28. See, for example, R. C. Williamson, *Marriage and Family Relationships*, Wiley, 1966, ch. 13.

29. D. Altman, *Homosexual: Liberation or Oppression?*, Outerbridge & Lazard, 1971, p. 221.

30. See J. Ackerley, *My Father and Myself*, Penguin Books, 1971.

31. Cf. B. Dank, 'Coming Out in the Gay World', *Psychiatry*, 34, 1971, pp. 180–97.

32. The couples were located through different sources and all were 'pre Gay Liberation Front'. On this part of the article, I am very grateful for much help from Anthony Gray, Malcolm Johnson, Michael Butler, Fabian Couper and Tony Cross.

33. I have heard of couples who have been together for over forty years but have not interviewed any.

34. D. Sonnenschein, op. cit., p. 82.

35. N. Jackson, *No End to the Way*, Barrie & Rockliff, 1965, p. 116.

36. E. Burgess and P. Wallis, *Engagement and Marriage*, Lippincott, 1953; J. Dominain, *Marital Breakdown*, Penguin Books, 1968.

37. E.g. C. Bell, 'Marital Status', in P. Barker, *A Sociological Portrait*, Penguin Books, 1972; and K. Plummer, op cit., ch. 6.

38. A. Toffler, *Future Shock*, Bodley Head, 1970.

39. J. Gagnon and W. Simon (eds.), *The Sexual Scene*, Transaction Aldine, 1970.

40. In the United States in the 1960s approximately one child out of every nine was a stepchild; approximately 600,000 families had only a father and 4–5 million only a mother.

41. For a sample of such writings, consider: N. O'Neill and G. O'Neill, *Open Marriage: A New Life Style for Couples*, Addison-Wesley, 1973; A. S. and J. S. Skolnick, *Family in Transition*. Little-Brown, 1971; S. Firestone, *The Dialectic of Sex*, Cope, 1971; R. Kanter, *Communes*, Harper & Row, 1974; J. R. and L. G. Smith, *Beyond Monogamy*, Hopkins, 1974; P. J. Stein, *Single*, Spectrum Books, 1976.

42. Why this should have happened at this time is a question beyond my brief here.

43. R. Hall, 'The Church, the State and Homosexuality', *Gay Power*, No. 14.

44. *Gay Liberation Front Manifesto*, London, 1971, pp. 13–14.

9. Couples, Constraints and Choices

1. Some researchers have attempted to measure people's 'satisfaction' with their marriages and other relations by asking such questions as whether or not the individual has ever thought of leaving his/her spouse and, if so, how frequently. They have also asked people to rank their marriages as very, moderately, or not at all satisfying and correlated the results with all kinds of attributes of the individuals. Many of these attempts do, I believe, display the characteristics of triviality, social work concern and methodological naïveté that have brought the sociology of the family into disrepute.

2. The term commune has been used to refer to collectivities of this kind, from those with only half a dozen people or so to those with several hundred. Sometimes very small 'communes' are made up of people who share a home, labour and resources as well as their sex lives but have little sense of identity of themselves as a unit. For an excellent comprehensive discussion of past and present communes see Rosabeth Moss Kanter, *Commitment and Community, Communes and Utopias in Sociological Perspective*, Harvard University Press, 1972. Kanter's edited collection, *Communes: Creating and Managing the Collective Life*, Harper & Row, New York, 1973, is also useful.

3. Sometimes this equality has worked less well in practice when heavy jobs have had to remain men's work and domestic jobs consequently women's. Each sex works collectively rather than individually for the other.

4. Couples often do marry, however, to ensure the legitimacy of their children in the world outside the *kibbutz*.

5. From M. Spiro, 'Is The Family Universal – The Israeli Case?', *American Anthropologist*, 56, 5, 1954, pp. 839–46.

6. See Kanter, *Commitment and Community*, op. cit., for further discussion of these points. 'Free' love is more characteristic of modern communes than is celibacy, though neither has really been more than temporarily successful with limited numbers of people.

7. This kind of arrangement is almost the reverse of that practised by 'recreational' swingers. For these communards, unlike the swingers, loyalty and commitment are extended to people beyond the

couple. The boundaries of the couple are defined primarily by sexual exclusivity.

8. From 'The New Arrangement' by Gaeton Fongi. The article originally appeared in *Philadelphia Magazine*, 1970, 98–104, 126–35, but is reprinted in M. Gordon (ed.), *The Nuclear Family in Crisis*, Harper & Row, New York, 1972. These comments may be found on p. 193 of this edition.

9. B. M. Berger, B. M. Hackett and R. M. Miller, 'Child-Rearing Practices in the Communal Family', in A. Skolnick and J. H. Skolnick, *Intimacy, Family and Society*, Little, Brown & Co., Boston, 1974.

10. Obviously a connection exists between this experience and experience of the sacred referred to earlier (p. 54), but this is not the place to pursue the connection.

11. V. W. Turner, *The Ritual Process*, Routledge & Kegan Paul, 1969, p. 132.

12. ibid., p. 139.

13. I hope to be able to make these distinctions in a future publication. I think the arguments involved are too technical and complex to pursue in this context.

14. This assertion reflects my belief that the essence of kinship lies in the transmission of categories of marriageability from one generation to generation, but this, too, is a more technical argument which need not detain us here.

15. 'Group marriage' is a term encountered with increasing frequency, but it is seldom dealt with in an analytic manner and has been used to refer to a wide range of sexual arrangements. L. L. and J. M. Constantine demonstrate this 'modern' approach to marriage in the following statement, attempting to distinguish between 'group marriages' and 'communities': 'The individual in a community either makes no commitment or commits himself to the community, its purpose, or its philosophy. Marriage is a fairly long-term commitment to other *individuals*. We have found it adequate to accept the individual's perception as an operational criterion. If he says he is married to all the others, we can assume he is. We also require a group to have confronted and creatively dealt with sexual sharing to be included. A 'joint family' consisting of several monogamous couples, though an interesting alternate family structure, is simply not a group *marriage*.' L. L. and J. M. Constantine, 'The Group Marriage', in M. Gordon (ed.), *The Nuclear Family in Crisis*, Harper & Row, New York, 1972, p. 211. I do not find this a particularly useful way of looking at marriage.

Notes on Contributors

DIANA LEONARD BARKER is at present a lecturer at the Institute of Education in London. She studied natural science, archaeology and anthropology at Cambridge University and conducted research on courtship and marriage at the University of Swansea. With Sheila Allen, she is editor of the books *Sexual Divisions and Society: Process and Change* (Tavistock, 1976) and *Dependence and Exploitation in Work and Marriage* (Longmans, 1976).

NICKY HART is now a lecturer in sociology at the University of Essex. She took her first degree at the University of London and her Ph.D. at the University of East Anglia. Her research on divorce is published in her book *When Marriage Ends* (Tavistock, 1976). Between 1973 and 1976 she was a lecturer in sociology at the University of Salford.

BARBARA LITTLEWOOD took a B.A. in philosophy at Sussex University and later a diploma in social anthropology at the University of Edinburgh. As a postgraduate at the University of Kent at Canterbury, she conducted fourteen months' anthropological field research into marriage and kinship in southern Italy. Since 1970 she has been a lecturer in sociology at the University of Glasgow.

HELMUT MORSBACH was trained in natural sciences, psychology and sociology and took his Ph.D. in social psychology at the University of Cape Town. He is at present a senior lecturer in social psychology at the University of Glasgow. He is particularly interested in anthropological approaches to psychology, and his interest in Japan stems from his appointment as an assistant professor of psychology at the International Christian University of Tokyo between 1967 and 1969. He returned to this position for a term in 1972 and for further research in Kyoto during the summer of 1976.

KEN PLUMMER studied for both his B.Sc. and his Ph.D. at the

University of London. His research on homosexuals was also conducted in London and is published under the title *Sexual Stigma: an Interactionist Account* (Routledge & Kegan Paul, 1975). He is at present a lecturer in sociology at the University of Essex.

JAN TROST is a *universitetlektor* at Uppsala University, Sweden. He was trained at the same university, where he also took his Ph.D. in sociology. He has conducted research on marriage, divorce and mate selection in Sweden, and has been visiting professor at the University of Minnesota and at the Catholic University of Louvain in Belgium.

ROBERT WEISS is professor of sociology at the University of Massachusetts in Boston and lecturer in sociology at Harvard Medical School's Laboratory of Community Psychiatry. He is the author of *Marital Separation* (Basic Books, New York, 1975) and *Loneliness* (M.I.T. Press, Cambridge, Mass., 1974).

MARIE CORBIN took a B.A. in anthropology at the University of London. Her Ph.D. in social anthropology from the University of Kent at Canterbury was based on eighteen months' field research on marriage and kinship in southern Spain. Since 1971 she has been a lecturer in the School of Social Studies at the University of East Anglia.

Some other books published by Penguin
are described on the following pages.

Gordon Rattray Taylor

RETHINK
Radical Proposals to Save a Disintegrating World

Rethink looks at how society changes, at the growing disillusionment with our present way of living, and at what we must do to create a less frustrating, more rewarding environment. Considering both economic and political institutions, Gordon Rattray Taylor declares that politicians and economists, preoccupied with technology and with material wealth, simply never ask themselves what human happiness really is and how we can all work toward it. In the light of this failure, *Rethink* proposes 'a paraprimitive solution' – a solution that takes account not only of man's new technological skills but also of his primitive, age-old needs.

J. L. Mackie

ETHICS
Inventing Right and Wrong

In this complete (and controversial) account of moral theory the author argues that there are no objective values, that morality cannot be discovered but must be made. He refers to recent discussion as well as to the work of Plato, Aristotle, Thomas Hobbes, David Hume, Immanuel Kant, and others. This is a thought-provoking book, written for a wide readership.

Michael Young and Peter Willmott

THE SYMMETRICAL FAMILY

Here, by the authors of *Family and Kinship in East London*, is a provocative look at the changing patterns of family life today. Based upon a survey of nearly two thousand people in London, this book shows that 'the family has re-established a new kind of primacy, not as the unit of production so much as the unit of consumption'. With television replacing the local pub, men as consumers have grown more 'home centred'. Women, on the other hand, purchasing gadgets that offer freedom from domestic enslavement, now take outside jobs. The result of these changes is that the roles of husband and wife have become more equal, more 'symmetrical', and that today's couples are partners in a greater leisure founded on increased consumption. This new, more leisurely family life is, however, balanced by a corresponding decline in public and communal activity. 'A brilliant book', said *The New York Times*, while *Library Journal* called *The Symmetrical Family* 'a major contribution' to research on the family in the Technological Age.

H. J. Eysenck

PSYCHOLOGY IS ABOUT PEOPLE

In this dazzling defense of behavioural psychology Professor H. J. Eysenck believes that the claims of humanity and sympathy are compatible with the rigors of scientific investigation – and he proves it in these witty essays on education, politics, society, pornography, and the interrelation of sex and personality.

I. M. Lewis

SOCIAL ANTHROPOLOGY IN PERSPECTIVE

This introductory volume surveys the principles and subject matter of social anthropology against backgrounds ranging from desert and jungle to ice pack and broad steppe. Professor I. M. Lewis begins by reviewing the ideas that tribal societies hold about themselves, as expressed in religion and myth. He then discusses the relationship of such societies to the natural world, the importance they attach to gifts and exchange, and their kinship systems, politics, and laws. Throughout, explicit parallels with Western civilization add 'perspective' to the exposition. I. M. Lewis's *Ecstatic Religion: An Anthropological Study of Spirit Possession and Shamanism* is also published by Penguin.

Jim Orford

THE SOCIAL PSYCHOLOGY OF
MENTAL DISORDER

Here is a lucid review of the social aspects of mental disorder. Among the questions considered are: What is the link between certain features of family life, like birth order, and later patterns of behaviour? How are the various types of personality related to mental illness? Can 'mental health' be defined simply as socially desirable behaviour? Is deviance 'amplified' or even created by the labeling process? What sort of relations between therapist and patient are most effective in restoring normality, and what does this tell us about other relationships?

Peter Gould and Rodney White

MENTAL MAPS

Two geographers explore the images of geographic space that people carry in their minds. Such 'mental maps' are vitally important, say the authors, for it is through them that people evaluate physical and social space and its residential desirability. In considering how information about places far and near is absorbed, *Mental Maps* also points out misperceptions about the future of various environments – for example, a Californian's calm attitude towards the virtual certainty of a major earthquake in the near future. Recognizing that this 'geography of perception' plays a key role in human behaviour, Peter Gould and Rodney White offer provocative findings with important ramifications for informed future planning.

Jonathan Glover

CAUSING DEATH AND SAVING LIVES

What are the moral issues involved in taking and in saving lives? Jonathan Glover here probes some of the most explosive topics of our time: medical questions about abortion, infanticide, euthanasia, and allocation of scarce life-saving resources; as well as more general problems in regard to the morality of war, revolution, assassination, and capital punishment. One of his aims is to encourage readers to work out systematically their own views, for only then can discussion go beyond the mere exchange of intuitive prejudices.

Charles Mercer

LIVING IN CITIES
Psychology and the Urban Environment

What has environmental psychology contributed in dealing with the problems created by modern cities? In what ways are people influenced by the buildings and towns they live in? Is overcrowding damaging in itself, or are other factors at work? How do different environments foster or hinder community? To what extent are children socially shaped by working-class or middle-class environments? Examining questions like these, Charles Mercer relates them to studies carried out in laboratories and in cities and builds a composite picture of how men and women react to the pressures of city life.

Gerald Foley with Charlotte Nassim

THE ENERGY QUESTION

Here is a review of the world's energy resources and of their potential for development in the light of today's quadrupled oil prices. The authors show how energy consumption and the advance of industrial civilization are inextricably joined. The living standard and social progress of any country, they say, depend upon the input of energy; even food supplies are contingent on farmers' ability to turn fossil fuels into comestibles. Since it is now clear that if some of our goals are to be met, others must be abandoned, this book explains the facts on which such choices will be based. It is neither optimistic nor pessimistic and enables the reader to form his own conclusions.

Arthur Blumberg and Robert T. Golembiewski

LEARNING AND CHANGE IN GROUPS

This is a lively review of the nature and evolution of sensitivity training, T-groups, and encounter groups – and of what happens to the people in them. Professors Arthur Blumberg and Robert T. Golembiewski explain the reasons behind the rapid growth of such groups and analyze their potential as agents for learning and change. A key chapter looks at the crucial role of the trainer, and, in conclusion, group learning is put in the context of the 'back home' situation. This is not simply 'another book about T-groups', nor is it an attempt to promote such groups. Rather, the authors have provided an up-to-date account of experiential learning groups – and of their strengths and weaknesses in regard to the development of both individuals and organizations.

J. A. Trevithick

INFLATION
A Guide to the Crisis in Economics

This volume explains the Phillips curve, trade-union power, 'helicopter money', floating currencies, incomes policy, and indexation as it shows how inflation can be controlled (though no one measure is enough, says J. A. Trevithick). A combination of treatments is required, based on a full understanding of the nature of the disease.

Alice Heim

INTELLIGENCE AND PERSONALITY
Their Assessment and Relationship

In this angry look at intelligence, creativity, and personality tests, the author maintains that psychological phenomena (including dreams, introspection, and feeling) are well worth studying and that, because of the oneness of human nature, intelligence and personality are inseparable and cannot be assessed in compartments. She attaches much of the blame for present dichotomies in psychology to the cold and sometimes sadistic attitudes of behaviourists, with their revolting experiments on rats, cats, and monkeys. This is an indignant book that clearly outlines the specialized field of testing in all its aspects.

Carleton S. Coon

THE HUNTING PEOPLES

One of the greatest of contemporary anthropologists surveys the quarter-million people still living in the Old Stone Age: Eskimos and pygmies, bushmen and Australian aborigines, scattered tribes in Asia and America. 'The greatest fun! It is anthropology without the jargon' – Naomi Mitchison. 'A rich feast' – *New Statesman*.